REVISITING

THE USE OF SELF

REVISITING

THE USE OF SELF

QUESTIONING PROFESSIONAL IDENTITIES

EDITED BY

DEENA MANDELL

Canadian Scholars' Press Inc.
Toronto

Revisiting the Use of Self: Questioning Professional Identities
Edited by Deena Mandell

First published in 2007 by
Canadian Scholars' Press Inc.
180 Bloor Street West, Suite 801
Toronto, Ontario
M5S 2V6

www.cspi.org

Canadian Scholars' Press Inc. gratefully acknowledges financial support for our publishing activities from the Government of Canada through the Book Publishing Industry Development Program (BPIDP).

Library and Archives Canada Cataloguing in Publication

Revisiting the use of self : questioning professional identities / edited by Deena Mandell.

Includes bibliographical references and index.
ISBN 978-1-55130-334-5

1. Social workers—Professional relationships. 2. Social service—Psychological aspects. 3. Self-perception. 4. Self. I. Mandell, Deena, 1950–

HV40.35.R49 2007   361.3'2   C2007-904359-3

Cover design: John Kicksee/KIX BY DESIGN
Interior design and composition: Brad Horning

Printed and bound in Canada

Canadä

MIX
Paper from
responsible sources
FSC
www.fsc.org   FSC® C004071

TABLE OF CONTENTS

ACKNOWLEDGEMENTS

When I began this project, I was warned that editing a collection of new work can be gruelling, inordinately time-consuming, and frustrating. I heard numerous tales of unco-operative authors, prima donna personalities, and the pain of watching deadlines come and go while one waits for chapters to be submitted. None of this came to pass in the course of bringing this project to light. The authors of this volume have been, to a person, wonderfully responsive and thoughtful, and respectful of timelines and purpose. Working with them has been enormously gratifying. Each one of them struggled to some degree with the challenge of writing about self, though not all for the same reasons. They dug deep, some finding it painful, others enjoying the departure from more traditional academic forms. I feel blessed to have been able to work with such an outstanding group of colleagues, and I am grateful to each of them for saying "yes" when I asked them to participate in creating this book.

Amy Rossiter, my colleague, mentor, and cherished friend, prodded me (as she is wont to do) to produce a book quite different from the one I first imagined, and for that I am especially grateful to her. As a result of input from Barbara Heron, Yuk Lin Renita Wong, Narda Razack, and Harjeet Badwall I was able to come to a deeper understanding of the critique of "use of self" and the politics of presenting the painful stories of others. This understanding informed the project as it went forward. Jill Grant offered crucial feedback on the first draft of my chapter, which enabled me to write a better one. Comments on the collective manuscript at pre-publication stage from Akua Benjamin, Adrienne Chambon, and Atalia Mosek were greatly appreciated and very helpful. Susan Silva-Wayne, our editor at Canadian Scholars Press Inc., offered unwavering support from start to finish, and her faith in the project was sustaining. Working with her has been the kind of gratifying experience that academics do not often report when speaking of their publishers.

My late mother often used to quote a Hebrew saying, "Mi-kol melamdai hiskalti," which means, "From all my teachers have I gained wisdom" or, more prosaically, "Everyone has something to teach me." This means that learning is to be found everywhere, in all our experiences and relationships, and I have certainly found this to be true. This seems like a good place to acknowledge that my most important learning about teaching has come from my students, and my most important learning about social work—indeed, about life—has come from the service users whom I have encountered in my role as social worker.

Finally, I would like to express profound appreciation for my two wonderful children, Alex and Jonah Hundert, whose pride in their mother's accomplishments is my most meaningful reward.

INTRODUCTION

Deena Mandell

The objective of this book is to expand the concept of "use of self" in social work practice in order to establish its relevance to critical social work practice in a variety of fields of service. Specifically, it aims to explore the adequacy of the concept of use of self for critical social work; to provide grounded accounts of practitioners' use of self in critical practice approaches; to broaden the scope of the concept of critical use of self to fields of service where it is undertheorized (e.g., community work, corrections, "ethnic matching" of worker and client, community mental health, child welfare, and so on).

It therefore places anti-oppressive and critical practice within a transformed framework for the concept of use of self. In the wake of critiques concerning the way the social work profession has drawn on "use of self" discourses in order to remain unaware of its inevitable complicity in dynamics of power, an approach that can integrate power and subjectivity with use of self is needed. The marrying of theory and practice in this book's objectives should make it appealing to both academics and practitioners at all levels of education and experience.

Our collective work began with dialogue among a number of us about our respective understandings of what "use of self" means; we found this much more challenging than anticipated. It was, in fact, in a series of dialogues with Amy Rossiter that I was able to arrive at a tentative concept of "use of self" that made possible a starting point for myself and the contributors to the book. In some cases it served as a point of departure rather than agreement, but that, too, was productive. This starting point was the conceptualization of use of self as the dimension of the *personal* through which theoretical knowledge is mediated in the context of a social work relationship. (By *social work relationship*, I mean one that has a formal purpose of offering support, solidarity, and collaborative efforts toward desired change.) Thus, the priority for the use of self is reflection on the elements of subjectivity that one brings to this relationship. What emerges from these writings is the important idea that critical reflection on the use of self is the link that mediates theory and practice in social work practice. In other words, *who we are* as human beings is not merely a few threads in the fabric of our work, but part of the frame on which the work of weaving is done. In some cases this view is explicitly formulated; in others it is implied. Reading this book is a bit like looking at a painting: From each chapter you get a very different perspective on the whole. Some chapters function like the "details" of paintings often found in art books. They make it possible to grasp the nature of the whole from close examination of a small part. The authors were asked not to provide extensive literature reviews or remain in an abstract realm. Except for Amy Rossiter, who plunged bravely into theorizing what we had initially found conceptually elusive, all have complied. The result is one wonderful theoretical chapter and 10 wonderful chapters that use practice or research examples to illuminate how reflecting critically on use of self actually "looks" and operates to shape and inform practice.

In some social work programs, use of self per se has been eliminated as a course or focus of study, particularly in those programs that have adopted an anti-oppression or critical approach. At Wilfrid Laurier University in Canada (where I teach), the Faculty of Social Work maintains separate fields of concentration: one for Individuals, Families, and Groups (IFG) and one for Community, Policy Planning, and Organizations (CPPO). A new Integrated stream was introduced several years ago. The course on Use of Self is mandatory for IFG students and for Integrated students with a major in IFG; it is not offered to CPPO students and is optional for Integrated students with a CPPO major.

Very recently, a new course was developed by one of the contributors to this book, a CPPO faculty member (Ginette Lafrenière), called "Reflective Group Practice," which intentionally highlights the personhood of the worker in community practice.

Students who choose to do an international field placement—whether IFG or CPPO—are required to take a preparatory course on "Self, Identity, and Diversity." A number of years ago, I was privileged to teach this course while the colleague who ran the International Placement program was on sabbatical. I was unable to wrap my head around a course of this nature that did not include some of the excellent literature on intrapersonal awareness and snuck a few of these articles into the syllabus. Thereafter, I could no longer return to teaching the Use of Self course without content on identity theory, diversity, and power. My journey toward integration had begun and plods slowly but steadily onward.

Another impetus toward producing a book of this kind was realizing how difficult it is for many students and practitioners to grasp how one "does" use of self critically and how to talk and write about this process. Although the unique collection of papers you hold in your hands was initially intended to reflect my own vision in seeking a text for my purposes as a teacher, I am happy to say that in the process of generating the book, that vision has been powerfully influenced by the work of each of the contributing authors. A number of them have also indicated that in doing the work for this collection—which has been different from anything most had done previously in an academic context—their own ideas and understandings were shifted in important ways.

The contributors are individuals with diverse practice expertise and a well-developed critical perspective on the use of self. Most are academics and a few are MSW practitioners; they bring extensive backgrounds in a wide range of practice modes and settings, research, and education. The group also comprises considerable diversity with respect to personal and practice backgrounds. Each was asked to write about use of self from a critical perspective and each has undertaken to do this in his or her own unique way, offering a fascinating range of analyses and insights across fields of practice. In some of these accounts the authors share personal moments of politically fraught crisis that are deeply moving; in others, we have illuminating analyses done from some emotional distance while maintaining self awareness. I am extremely appreciative of the spirit of adventure in which these chapters were undertaken by everyone involved; all have written *through* use of self, not just *about* use of self. I hope readers will enjoy this dimension of the book.

INTRODUCING
THE CONTRIBUTORS

Gerald de Montigny is associate professor at Carleton University's School of Social Work, Ottawa, Ontario. He is a middle-aged White man who fears, after 28 years with a MSW and 20 years of teaching social work, that his identification with "the working class" has become more nostalgia than reality. Although his academic work is organized by a desire to improve child protection and service to children and their families by building face-to-face dialogic relations, he believes that people do not live by talk alone. He thinks that people need their bodies to talk and the social relations of daily life in order to have anything worth saying. As a dad of three young adults, he suspects that his kids survived their childhoods because he and his spouse of three decades cooked meals, cleaned messes, played, and cared for them.

Jeff D'Hondt is a community-based practitioner with over a decade of experience in the Aboriginal community, gained at penitentiaries, hospitals, homeless shelters, youth programs, and rehabilitation services. He is a member of the Lenape Nation and hopes one day to write a self-reflective piece in his Aboriginal language as an effort to revitalize a language nearly made extinct by colonialism.

Jill Grant is assistant professor in the School of Social Work at the University of Windsor. She draws on her experiences as a service user and service provider in her teaching and research in the areas of mental health, housing, and collaborative research.

Martha Kuwee Kumsa is associate professor at Wilfrid Laurier University in the Faculty of Social Work, Waterloo, Ontario. She is a former refugee from Ethiopia. She is interested in critical and reflexive methodologies of research and practice and so her interest in the use of self comes out of a deep-seated desire to transform oppressive relationships in multiple forms and at multiple levels.

Ginette Lafrenière is associate professor in the Faculty of Social Work at Wilfrid Laurier University. She teaches in the area of diversity, oppression and marginalization, community interventions and research, and is the director of the Social Innovation Research Group, which values university-community collaboration. Her current research relates to community interventions with survivors of the residential school system and contexts of best practices for social service providers working with survivors of war, torture, and organized violence in Africa.

Deena Mandell is associate professor at Wilfrid Laurier University's Faculty of Social Work, Waterloo, Ontario. Her fascination (some would say, obsession) with and continually evolving understanding of the concepts of "use of self" and self-reflection tell the story of her development as practitioner, teacher, and learner in the field of social work, as well as in life.

Paul Morrel is a MSW community practitioner in Cambridge, Ontario. He has worked in the areas of child welfare and medical social work.

Shoshana Pollack is associate professor at Wilfrid Laurier University's Faculty of Social Work, Waterloo, Ontario. She teaches courses on Diversity Marginalization and Oppression, Use of Self, and Theory Construction. She also maintains a small private practice in Toronto. She continues to advocate with and on behalf of criminalized women.

Amy Rossiter is professor at York University's School of Social Work, Toronto, Ontario. She is interested in postmodern perspectives in social work theory, practice, pedagogy, and ethics. Her interest in ethics informs her thoughts about how social work might take up issues related to "use of self." Her persistent and lifelong question with regard to social work is: "Is social work worthwhile?" At the age of 57, she still has not answered this question, but perseveres in hopes of finding light at the end of the tunnel.

Jeanette Schmid holds a BA Soc Wk, a M.Ed (School Counselling) and a Diploma in Public Policy, Development and Administration all from the University of Witwatersrand, South Africa. Her 24 years of work and volunteer experience in South Africa, Switzerland, and Canada included the fields of child protection, trauma (political and criminal violence), restorative justice, mediation and conflict resolution, and refugee/settlement issues, among others. She was the Toronto Family Group Conferencing project coordinator prior to beginning her Ph.D in social work at Wilfrid Laurier University. Her dissertation will be focused on South African child welfare post-apartheid.

Eric Shragge is associate professor and director of the Graduate Diploma in Community Economic Development at the School of Community and Public Development, Montreal, Quebec. His areas of interest include community organizing and issues related to the rights of immigrant workers. He is active in several organizations in Montreal, including La Cooperative Maison Verte and the Immigrant Workers Centre.

Merlinda Weinberg is assistant professor at Dalhousie University's School of Social Work, Halifax, Nova Scotia. Her areas of interest are ethics, clinical practice from a critical perspective, mothering, and qualitative research. As seasoned practitioner, but a new scholar, writing this chapter pushed her thinking and, she hopes, closed a few of her synapses.

CHAPTER 1

USE OF SELF:

CONTEXTS AND DIMENSIONS

Deena Mandell

"Use of self" is considered a core concept in social work practice. It is an essential part of professional training and supervision. One author has argued that the professional use of self ought to be recognized as a "core component" in the very definition of social work as a crucial step toward reconceptualizing the field as a relationship-centred range of activities (Ramsay, 2003). The concept of use of self has its original roots in the clinical therapy literature, specifically the psychoanalytically derived literature on countertransference. Although some relatively current journal articles on use of self have been written by social workers, any collections I have been able to identify focus on a psychotherapeutic or family therapy frame.

When social workers have written about use of self, social work itself has typically not been problematized — that is, not critically examined — nor is there exploration of how awareness might make a difference to critical practice. The application of this literature to social work practice is limited due to its divergence from social work's distinct mission and values. Social work has increasingly distinguished its mission as based on human rights and social justice as a condition for ameliorating individual problems. Critical social work is premised on the notion that social arrangements, particularly with respect to maldistribution of resources and unjust recognition, are the root of personal troubles. The countertransference literature does not adequately support critical social work practice because it tends to split the individual and the social in ways that reduce social arrangements to manifestations of individual deficit or maladjustment. This literature continues to evolve, however, and in recent years has begun to attend to "the gap in the literature regarding the working alliance in cross-cultural treatment" (Shonfeld-Ringel, 2001).

Although a search of Web sites of North American schools of social work shows "use of self" frequently listed as a topic in a range of courses, no texts specific to social work can be found on related reading lists. Clearly, the centrality of the social work practitioner's own personhood is recognized as widely relevant, yet traditionally neglected in the literature outside conventional approaches to clinical practice. I am aware, in fact, of only one edited text focused on "use of self" in a sense broader than countertransference. Although prominent social workers are among the contributors, they focus on the context of therapy, and the perspective of critical theory is absent.

In previous decades, the concept of the social worker as someone seeking to resolve her or his own intrapsychic issues through practice (Rompf & Royse, 1994) is also framed as the "wounded healer" with both its positive and negative connotations (Miller & Baldwin, 1999). In recent years, several developments have stimulated new ways of thinking about the social worker's "self" (or "selves") in all aspects of practice. The focus on practice with diverse populations (including international social work), and the emphasis on anti-oppressive practice have highlighted elements of the social worker's relationship to her or his "clients." Specifically, this orientation concerns the worker's social location (power) and epistemological orientation (knowledge). Anti-oppressive approaches generally focus on the subjectivity of the practitioner as it is constructed in relations of domination. Thus, understanding privilege and power and understanding identity as constructed across interlocking oppressions are the basic goals of self-reflection. Such insight is meant to prepare the practitioner for practice that relates social work and social justice. In general, this aim conceptualizes the self within the frame of oppressor/oppressed identities.

The need for an expanded or otherwise revised conception of the use of self comes from a gap that is created when conventional (i.e., transference/countertransference) approaches to the use of self are trapped by their failure to address power, and anti-oppressive approaches are reductive to oppressor/oppressed relations and cannot draw on the concept of use of self because of the latter's historical association with the disregard of power.

It seems to me that a number of streams have co-existed in the practice literature:

- Use of self with a focus closely tied to concepts of countertransference and intersubjectivity, where the actual social identities of the counselor/therapist and the client were not of great interest. Gradually references began to appear in some of this literature to issues of power difference wherein their structural nature and inevitability were thought to be easily eliminated through the therapist's conscious use of self.

  These power differences were related to issues of diversity, increasingly acknowledged although in a tokenist manner, where "diversity" was seen as affecting the client, not the therapist. Postmodernist/post-structural ways of conceptualizing therapy have been particularly committed to the struggle to consciously "use oneself" to avoid reproducing the marginalization of those with whom we engage in practice. However, with some notable exceptions[1] the implicit assumption most often is that when speaking of diversity, culture, ethnicity, or disability, we are talking about clients, while the therapist/counsellor is assumed to be a member of the dominant culture. Even in theorizing, we maintain power hierarchies.

- Anti-oppression literature emphasizing the potential for social work practice to perpetuate power imbalances that keep some groups marginalized and disempowered. This literature has tended to be more helpful at identifying and critiquing ways in which social work is embedded in systems of social control than it has at offering us ways to establish ethical practices that promote social justice.

- Critical social work has embraced critical reflection as the method of choice in achieving ethical or socially just practice. While it focuses on the social positioning of the worker in relation to those with whom she or he is involved in order to identify and intentionally minimize power imbalances, it seems to eschew considerations of the worker's intrapersonal processes and is confined to aspects of subjectivity related to social location. This omission is not accidental; the emphasis on socially structured relations of power is a deliberate strategy meant to avoid individualized explanations for either the client's or the worker's positions and behaviours. The topic of "use of self" is often treated somewhat dismissively by community practitioners and educators who consider a focus on individual clients and workers a wrongheaded approach to social justice.

WHAT IS THIS THING CALLED USE OF SELF?

It is not easy to discern from the literature or from the discourses of social work practitioners what it is, exactly, that "use of self" means. People mean different things by it, depending on their theoretical orientation (acknowledged or not); their experience in education, practice, and supervision; and the focus or extent of their own personal awareness.

In the preface to her edited book called *Use of Self in Therapy* (1999a), social worker and family therapist Michele Baldwin writes about the "self of the therapist [as] the funnel through which theories and techniques become manifest" (p. xix). In order for "real therapy" to take place, the therapist must make "a real contact with the individual and/or the family members" (p. xx). She understands use of self to entail being "more fully human," which requires a foundation of congruence. Congruence is defined as "the ability to see and say things as they are, while respecting the Self, the Other and the Context," where context refers to the therapeutic modality of individual, couple, or family therapy (p. xxii). Baldwin decries the tendency for use of self to have been left out of early family therapy models. This deliberate omission meant that the therapeutic relationship was to be experienced by the family members with a distanced expert. In professional and academic writing about therapy, Baldwin notes the marginalization of use of self. She attributes this to predominance of models designed for brevity and shifting the emphasis away from the therapeutic relationship to a "focus ... on assessment, intervention and problem solving, thus keeping the attention primarily on client change" (p. xxi). Elsewhere in social work writing—specifically, in postmodern references to multiple realities and multiple voices—*context* has very different connotations. In these latter instances, it connotes localized meanings arising out of subjective experiences shaped by historical and cultural conditions.

Virginia Satir, well known—among other things—for bringing relationship and emotion into the discourse of family therapy, likened use of self to the use of an instrument by a musician; we are each, in effect, our own unique instrument (1999). The tonal qualities of our music are not produced by the notes in our heads or on a sheet of paper. This is a very helpful metaphor, as far as it goes. It helps us to understand that the music is mediated by the instrument and the technique with which it is played; it reminds us that technical production of sound is not all there is. This is where the "art" part enters into the old conundrum of whether social work is "art" or "science." This metaphor serves as a useful example of how focus on the therapist's own person obscures issues of the professional role and of social identities that structure the relations between client and worker before either has a chance to play their music at all. If we extend Satir's metaphor, we begin to think about the acoustical structure in which the music is played, whether the program has been constructed in a way that leaves the audience receptive to the particular piece, the focus toward which the program notes direct us, how receptive the listeners are to the kind of music being played, and so on.

Edward Hanna (1993) provides a helpful account of the development of the concept of countertransference over time, from its original reference to unconscious responses of the therapist arising from early experience to the contemporary conceptualization of therapy as "intersubjectivity," that is, as a two-person rather than a one-person psychology. This construction accounts for the conscious responses of therapist and client to one another arising from the dialogue and interaction in real time. While countertransference is regularly used in clinical social work articles, in settings (including social work programs) where the intended domain is broader than the unconscious, "use of self" is ubiquitous. Use of self is frequently mentioned in course syllabi and program statements; it is, however, rarely defined. It seems to be one of those taken-for-granted terms, requiring deconstruction in order to understand why it is *sine qua non* in one area of social work yet dismissed in others.

There are numerous basic social work textbooks that are atheoretical and have long served as trusted manuals of beginning practice for students. Although the term "use of self" is not always used in the texts and may not appear in the index, there is invariably clear emphasis on the personhood of the worker in one form or another. If we look across these texts, the range of elements subsumed under this umbrella covers (but is not necessarily limited to) the following: communication skills (listening, verbal and non-verbal expression—including tonality, body language and dress), insight, self-awareness, values and beliefs, biases, attitudes, openness, genuineness, warmth, and a non-judgmental stance. These are used in the service of setting and maintaining boundaries and confidentiality, conveying empathy and respect, building rapport and trust, and modelling constructive social behaviour.

A brief look at how three popular social work textbooks approach the issues related to the worker's personhood helps to clarify some of the different ways in which the construct of use of self is approached in the literature. Brill (1995) refers to the goal of self-awareness in order to achieve "clarity and honesty with ourselves and with others" to the greatest possible extent and "… [b]ecome sensitive to personal patterns of thinking, feeling and behaving that hamper our ability to work effectively with others" (p. 33). She stresses the importance of social workers recognizing the ways in which they "meet their own needs … ways of thinking, feeling and behaving" that may or may not be "conducive to the creation of effective open relationship with others" (p. 17). For Brill, optimal awareness and use of self are signalled by arriving at a state of freedom to use effectively our "innate capacity to relate," which requires self-acceptance joined with optimism about change. A figure in the text that shows a circle representing "the total individual" includes emotional, physical, spiritual, intellectual, and social, with the last defined as "relationship with other life forms" (p. 21). The therapeutic construct of transference is captured — though not named as such — through reference to "the assets and the liabilities that arise from personality and from prior experience" (p. 30); these, too, must be recognized and assessed for their impact on others. A worker's self includes her or his value system, needs (and how those needs are recognized and dealt with), relationships with small groups and with broader society. The worker must learn to relate equally effectively "to people who are higher on the scale … [or] lower" (p. 29). This is in the service of managing social pressures oneself, being able to tolerate "social disapproval" if necessary in order to gain "important objectives" (p. 29). Although social hierarchies are thus acknowledged, it is in a narrow context of being able to deal with one's own place in them in order to encourage clients to deal with theirs. The effects of structural relations of domination are not discernible in this formulation; appreciation of fundamental differences in what it might mean to incur "social disapproval" is not considered, nor is the ongoing experience of social disapproval by members of marginalized groups, whether client or worker.

A textbook by Hepworth, Rooney, and Larsen (1997), once quite popular in an undergraduate school of social work where I formerly taught, deals with use of self differently. In this text, the framework for considering the personhood of the social worker is a professionalized one. Principles are directly linked to the professional Code of Ethics and the values of the profession as a whole. The emphasis is thus on ethical practice as defined in the Code. This includes commitment to improving environmental conditions that contribute to human problems and respect/acceptance for "unique characteristics of diverse populations" (p. 10). At the micro level of practice, this translates into demonstrating "preferred behaviours" (p. 11), which are identified as warmth, caring, openness, responsibility, and protecting confidentiality. At the mezzo level, it means respecting the "characteristics of a strong community" (p. 11) and at the macro level to political issues. The focus here does not include the emotional, physical, and spiritual dimensions of the self that are an important part of Brill's (1995) "total individual"; rather, the perspective is one of professional and personal selves, corresponding roughly with the intellectual and social parts of Brill's individual and which may at times be in conflict.

A third (specifically graduate-level) text takes quite a different approach. In Mattaini, Lowery, and Meyer's 2002 edited volume, the discussion of the worker's personhood in Chapter 4 focuses on "diversity, ethnic competence and social justice." In order to develop "cultural understanding," social workers "must become lifelong learners, listeners, and participant observers" (Lowery, 2002, p. 76). This is fostered by "self-reflection and community feedback" (p. 76). They must be "authentic about their own discomfort in cross-cultural situations and examine their value base, biases, prejudices and racism ... be critical thinkers and recognize that there are multiple perspectives and interpretations of events and experiences ... [and] recognize that resources are not always formal, but informal as well" (p. 76). Ethnic competence demands that workers be open to learning from clients, recognizing the legitimacy of various forms of knowledge. Rather than "empowering" clients, workers are urged to help create space that allows others agency. In order to be attentive to issues of power, workers must acknowledge "privilege, conferred power, and the potential to abuse power on an individual, professional, group, and national level" (p. 77).

In recent years, the influence of feminist and postmodern/post-structural approaches to social work has emphasized elements of theoretical allegiance or ideological stance as a lens for observation and understanding; awareness of diversity in terms of values, beliefs, behaviours, and assumptions; developing a critical analysis of relations of power; the social worker's own embodied social location, and awareness of one's epistemological stance in the universe of competing discourses, as well as the location and ways of knowing of one's clients.

Methods of practice with individuals, families, and groups require that we loosen theoretical and practice models in order to be truly inclusive. Ways of doing this include adopting a stance of curiosity or "informed not-knowing" in order to avoid prejudgment or perpetuating dominant discourses (Anderson & Goolishian, 1992; Hare-Mustin, 1994; Rober, 2002) working with clients collaboratively rather than from a stance of expertise (Dyche & Zyas, 1995) and directly addressing issues of oppression and privilege (Laszloffy & Hardy, 2000). These contribute to the aim of creating spaces in which clients' subjugated discourses can be given voice. Rather than using our power, we facilitate the empowerment of others and avoid perpetuating clients' experience of social marginalization. What constitutes appropriate boundaries (especially around self-disclosure) and ethical behaviour may vary according to the context and one's theoretical framework.

Although personal integrity and relational ethics are clearly related, they have become more prominent in the literature of late. A critical perspective has extended the discussion of ethics in social work from the framework of professional codes and structured decision-making processes to the realm of relations of power and social justice, involving embodied identities of worker and client.

Occasionally, use of self still appears prominently and explicitly articulated. These days, this tends to occur when the author means to put a new "spin" on it or ties it to a particular concept. Weisman (2000), for example, understands *conscious use of self* as "questioning [one's] own behaviour, its motivation and its purpose" in order to develop a "new consciousness of self [to be] internalized and integrated" (p. 6). This emphasis on conscious awareness, although not new, explicitly calls for an iterative process through which use of self is made conscious through reflection, then internalized for the purpose of controlling personal reactions, which might or might not be unconscious. This is a pathway to "self-discipline" and "a more objective self" (p. 6). The idea of *consciously reflecting on use of self* brings us a step closer to the process captured in the chapters of this volume, though Weisman's objectives are rarely the ones focused on.

"DOING" USE OF SELF

How one accomplishes use of self is considered, in traditional practice wisdom, to consist primarily of self-awareness and self-monitoring, reflection done independently, with a supervisor or team, or through journalling. The degree to which one is expected to delve into personal history, emotions, and unconscious responses varies with the theoretical orientation, practice field, and setting. In some fields, such as child welfare, the literature consistently talks about the importance of regular case-related supervision for prevention of burnout and careful use of authority, and workers consistently talk about the importance of peer and supervisory support for effective practice and self-care. Nevertheless, there is often little time or attention devoted to these in a formalized way; in times of widespread funding constraints, the regular thoughtful agency supervisory sessions of decades ago, where use of self was carefully explored, have largely disappeared. Students who enter the MSW program with years of practice in the field already behind them often talk about the absence of opportunities in the field for reflection of any kind on their practice. Outside of social work educational settings, most practitioners have little access to truly useful guidance about what self-monitoring and reflection on use of self look like.

For the most part, "conscious use of self," or reflecting on use of self, involves a heuristic process of asking oneself (or being asked) questions. The answers themselves may then be questioned. The questions range from those in the countertransference tradition interrogating unconscious processes underlying impasses and inappropriate, intense or irrational responses to clients, to questions in a critical mode about where the power lies and how it operates, the privileged versus subjugated discourses in everything from policy to personal interchanges to record-keeping. In the countertransference tradition we might ask ourselves, for example, of whom the client reminds us in eliciting our emotional response, or which painful experiences of our own have been stirred by our work. What judgments are we making based on our own values? Were our self-revelations meant to meet the client's needs or our own? What were we hoping to accomplish by asking that question or making this comment at this time? Is that objective congruent with client goals and whatever principles inform our practice approach? If we could do it again, would we do it the same way or differently? And so on. This reflective process can be carried out through dialogue with another, internal dialogue, or dialogue with oneself through writing or audio-recording.

FAMILY THERAPY AND USE OF SELF

Family therapists have had to consciously struggle with the concept of use of self because the position of the therapist had to be worked out in relation to the family system as a whole, as well as to individual members within it. The departure of systemic approaches from psychodynamic therapy required new theory around how the therapist was to "use himself or herself." Different theories required different principles about use of self; for example, Aponte (1992) discusses differences between the necessary neutrality of the Italian systemic therapists and the "decidedly nonneutral" stance of structural family therapists (p. 273). Constructionist family therapists refer to themselves as collaboratively engaging with clients in co-constructing new preferred realities. One such therapist has written about the need to reconceptualize the "therapeutic use of self" in family therapy. Real (1990) writes about the "multiply engaged therapist ... positioned within, rather than as acting on, a system" (p. 1), bridging the earlier divides between extremes of "either pure interventionism or pure facilitation" reflected in earlier family therapy models (p. 1). Also taking a historical perspective more than a decade after Real, Flaskas (2004) reviews the vicissitudes in the family therapy literature regarding the therapist's use of self. The strong influence of postmodernism in this field has added to Real's snapshot the use of self through witnessing and listening, and the use of self as transparent within the therapeutic relationship. Erskine (2002) writes explicitly about anti-oppression family therapy that requires "a moral stance aimed at challenging inequalities, which organize and structure people's lives" (p. 295). She ties this to the therapist's use of self, but only in a cursory way, referring to "self-monitoring" and reflexive practice through team discussions (p. 294). The family therapy literature has embraced the challenge of trying to incorporate the goal of social justice in theorizing and practice (See Korin, 1994; McGoldrick, 1998).

DIVERSITY AND USE OF SELF

Attempts to address the extremely complex issues associated with cultural differences between worker and clients take various forms. They may critically analyze the applicability of developmental theories to a range of cultures or they may focus on ways to consider what Pérez Foster (1998, 1999) has called "cultural countertransference" as an integral element of the therapeutic relationship (Bula, 1999; Garcia & Bregoli, 2000; Greene, Jensen & Jones, 1996; Mishne, 2002; Shonfeld-Ringel, 2001). Other examples exploring countertransference issues in relation to marginalized populations include working with lesbian women (Horowitz, 2000), male prisoners (Sternbach, 2000), and disabled individuals (Esten & Wilmott, 1993). The resurgence of spirituality as an element to be recognized and worked with in therapy is also being addressed in explicit terms of use of self, for example, by Thayne (1998) and in distinctly postmodern terms, for example, by Moules (2000).

These have been transformative developments; however, there are shortcomings in this literature. First, there tends to be relatively little in the way of concrete practice examples that help us to understand what this kind of integration looks like. Second, we tend to be left with the vague impression that as individuals we have the capacity to overcome structural imbalances through self-awareness and goodwill. There is, I think, a degree of naïveté in this stance. When it is written by authors in dominant social locations, it risks being optimism born of privilege.

Anti-oppressive practice requires not only cultural sensitivity but an accompanying commitment to recognizing and addressing power imbalances arising from cultural differences (among other kinds of difference involved in power inequalities). Nash (1993) describes an experiential exercise in use of self as a way for workers to better understand the meaning of family to themselves and others. Self-reflection is the method and the goal is anti-oppressive practice. This draws on socially constructed racial and cultural identities, recognition of racism as located in social relations (rather than within the individual), and as psychologically damaging to those who are subjected to it (Erskine, 2002). Baker (1999) explicitly joins self-awareness with structural awareness in talking about the need for using "multiple lenses" to offset the potential colonizing effects of social agency intervention; cultural differences between worker and client that shape their respective values; and the effects of structural, historical, and economic inequities. Sakomoto and Pitner (2005) have attempted to apply anti-oppression principles to micro-level practice, an area they too identify as being generally neglected by anti-oppression practice.

POWER AND USE OF SELF

None of these authors deals with social workers' roles as agents of systems of control. The Canadian social work activist and academic who helped establish structural social work in Canada was Maurice Moreau (1979). Maurice was one of my professors in the first year of the MSW program I attended in the 1970s. He introduced us to his ideas of using ourselves as agents of change whether working with individuals or with communities. He talked and wrote about ways to use work with individuals to create communities of mutual support and activism, of the need to identify structures that maintain social inequalities, and of the need to be aware of our ways of moving through the world so as to remain alert to injustice. He worried about the ways people — including social workers — have of not registering pain and injustice around us even though we may be able to talk about it. Maurice began many of our classes with an exercise in "centring" ourselves—usually through rhythmic deep breathing—a striking statement of valuing individual self-awareness in the process of doing social work. Several decades later, Wong, who teaches critical social work, writes about using Buddhist principles of mindfulness to help her students deal with the "discomfort" they experience arising from their attitudes and experiences related to issues of diversity (2004).

Margolin's (1997) blistering critique of social work—particularly within the fields of welfare and child protection—identifies use of self (establishing rapport and trust, warmth, relationship building, etc.) as an insidious tool that professionals use to gain and then, by virtue of the worker's mandate, to abuse the trust of their clients. From Margolin's perspective, there is no possibility for redemption: Any positive use of self that can be taught or imagined is tainted by its service to the mandate of social control. Margolin renders impossible a naive view of the social worker's role and the idea that if we just do it sensitively, we can erase the contradictions inherent in our roles. Does this mean that social work as we know it reproduces social injustice? Although Margolin appears to have thought so, the contributors to this volume continue to struggle productively with this question.

CRITICAL SOCIAL WORK PERSPECTIVES

"[A] critical social work operates within the contingent fields of subjectivity and power," writes Stephen Webb (2001). Heron (2005) defines critical social work practice as "a refusal of/opposition to the interlocking relations of power that pervade social worker encounters with clients" (p. 341). Authors writing from a critical social work perspective share with Margolin an unflinching examination of power and subjectivity in social work relationships, drawing on the method of critical reflection. Amy Rossiter (2001) has described feeling that her "very identity is in jeopardy when I am called a professional within a state that uses the terms and definitions of professionals to hide its oppressive foundations; where the most innocent position we can take is chronic suspicion of who we are and what we are doing" (www.criticalsocialwork.com). She identifies the personal dilemma of many helping professionals when she says, "But I feel happy when I am helping. My identity is momentarily complete in the small moments of help," (www.criticalsocialwork.com), while acknowledging that the identities of helper and helped inevitably position us in relations of power.

Among four central dimensions defining critical practice, Healey (2001) includes "the adoption of a self-reflexive and critical stance to the often contradictory effects of social work practice and social policies," and Heron writes about "deconstructing the challenges and pitfalls of helping relationships across differences where power differentials between the 'helper' and 'helped' are foregrounded" (2005, p. 341). Miehls and Moffatt (2000) propose a social work identity "based on concepts of reflexive self rather than one based in ego psychology" (p. 340). Reflexivity is not meant to be about "managing anxiety" (p. 339) in relation to difference, which is how they understand countertransference, nor is reflection upon self an intrapsychic process that excludes "the other." Rather, "[t]he identity of the social worker is constructed in terms of intersubjectivity" (p. 342) and tensions aroused by difference are allowed rather than quelled. The objective of reflexivity is not simply the development of self-awareness but the contribution through subjectivity of "new social possibilities" (p. 343).

Napier and Fook's (2000a) collection of critical reflections by practitioners and educators makes an important contribution to our ability to imagine the ways in which "me, the practitioner" is not a "'fixed'... instrument of the theory" but a source of "knowledge from experience and the influences of value commitments," as well as the vicissitudes of personal courage, imagination, congruence, theoretical orientation, and clear thinking (Napier & Fook, 2000b, p. 5). Reflecting on one's own experiences with critical reflection in practice is intended to demonstrate the ways in which critical reflection can serve to get us "unstuck" when our theoretical lenses have rendered alternative possibilities invisible. Critical reflection is understood, in this context, as going beyond analysis to theorizing; its focus in the work of these authors is the context of structured relations of power in which social work unfolds. Rarely does a writer in Fook's book actually invoke the term "use of self" or its traditional referents. Sheila Sim (2000) is an exception, although she is not explicit about what meaning she attaches to it; not coincidentally, she is one of the few practitioners in that book focusing on practice with individuals.

Kondrat (1999) takes a critical perspective on self-reflection that recognizes the impossibility of separating the observing self from the experiencing self. Our own embeddedness in lived experience makes such objectivity unattainable. Kondrat offers a very helpful list of questions to help the social worker engage in critical reflectivity, or identifying one's implication as professional in relations of power with service users. Jill Grant writes about her application of this method to her own practice as a community mental health worker in Chapter 4 of this book.

COMMUNITY PRACTICE

Explicit talk about use of self is relatively rare in the literature on community practice. I was able to find only one such article in a recent search. Titled "Broadening the 'Use of Self': Steps toward 'Tactical Self-Awareness'" (Burghardt, 1983), it stands in opposition to the "Great Organizer Theory of Organizing" (p. 207) and calls for reflection on one's own personal attributes — strengths, weaknesses, interests — in order to be able to adapt and use them in varying situations just as one uses any other tactic. The goal is to "*actively* incorporate 'the self' into the socially and politically tumultuous world of organizing" (p. 205, italics mine). Like Weisman's (2000) "conscious use of self," intentional reflection is the method; among the aspects of self under consideration are sociability, co-operative/good nature, tidiness, responsibility, intellectuality, and more.

Critical social work authors have addressed the personhood of the community practitioner from the perspective of "insider" versus "outsider" identity based on social location. Lee, McGrath, Moffatt, and George (2002), for example, address the complexity of such identities (whether "achieved [or] ascribed"), their importance to the worker's effectiveness in a given community, the tensions that can arise for the worker, and challenges to traditional notions of professional boundaries.

RESEARCH

In positivist social science research, the goal is normally to conscientiously avoid use of self through methods designed to support objectivity. In contrast, the inevitable framing of observational and interpretive stances by theoretical orientations, disciplinary and social discourses has been problematized by qualitative researchers. The latter have acknowledged the problem of encroachment of the researcher's biases and knowledge on the process of systematic inquiry and have proposed numerous methodological ways to address this. As Janesick (1998) puts it: "[Q]ualitative researchers accept the fact that research is ideologically driven.... The qualitative researcher early on identifies his or her biases and articulates the ideology or conceptual frame for the study" (p. 41). Situating ourselves as researchers, bracketing our own knowledge and views, triangulation in the process of data gathering and analysis, and reflexivity are but some of the tools for monitoring and carefully channelling our use of self in research (see Cresswell, 1997; Denzin & Lincoln, 1998). What these processes look like in the various qualitative research methods, however, is not always clear. Novice researchers are urged to situate themselves and declare their biases, but other than forewarn the reader, they don't necessarily know what else to do with that acknowledgement. Feminist and action-based research methodologies not only permit but encourage value stances in the interest of pursuing social justice ends. They take into account the power issues involved in traditional relations between researcher as subject and participant as object and have developed strategies for establishing ethical research relationships.

MOVING FORWARD

Neither the traditional use of self literature nor the developing work on critical reflection seems to adequately capture a process of combining insight into one's own personhood—comprising individual developmental history and multiple social identities in the context of personal experience, education, socialization, and political milieus—with a critical analysis of one's role as a social worker in the relations of power that constitute our practice. In my view, this kind of multilayered process is what we should be aiming for. While a micro-level approach to practice that fails to fully integrate analyses of power relations and identity strikes me as highly problematic, it seems to me that the critical school has thrown out the baby with the bathwater. In its understandable attempts to direct and maintain our focus on not reproducing unjust relations of domination as we engage in our work with clients, it deliberately ignores the more idiosyncratic dimensions of who we are. These dimensions enter into all our work, and indeed into our every social interaction, and affect us and our clients at both conscious and unconscious levels. In addition, it is difficult for me to understand how what has come to be understood as just and ethical in one field of practice should be seen as irrelevant in another. What Amy Rossiter eloquently theorizes, and what all the contributors to this volume demonstrate, is an evolved conceptualization of use of self in the service of socially just practice.

NOTE

1. See, for example, Baker (1999), Jackson (1995), Pérez Foster (1998, 1999), and a number of authors in McGoldrick's *Revisioning Family Therapy* (1998), such as Ken Hardy and Elaine Pinderhughes.

REFERENCES

Anderson, H. & Goolishian, H. (1992). The client is the expert: A not-knowing approach to therapy. In S. McNamee & K.J. Gergen (Eds.), *Therapy as social construction* (pp. 25–39). London: Sage.

Aponte, H. (1992). Training the person of the therapist in structural family therapy. *Journal of Marital and Family Therapy, 18*(3), 269–281.

Baker, K.A. (1999). The importance of cultural sensitivity and therapist self-awareness when working with mandatory clients. *Family Process, 38,* 55–67.

Baldwin, M. (Ed.). (1999a). *The use of self in therapy* (2nd ed.). New York: Haworth.

Baldwin, M. (1999b). Introduction. In M. Baldwin (Ed.), *The use of self in therapy* (2nd ed.) (pp. 1–16). New York: Haworth.

Brill, N.I. (1995). *Working with people: The helping process* (5th ed.). White Plains: Longman.

Bula, J. (1999). Use of the multicultural self for effective practice. In M. Baldwin (Ed.), *The use of self in therapy* (2nd ed.) (pp. 167–182). New York: Haworth.

Burghardt, S. (1983). Broadening the "use of self" steps toward "tactical self-awareness." *Journal of Applied Social Sciences, 7*(2), 203–224.

Cresswell, J. (1997). *Qualitative inquiry and research design: Choosing among five traditions.* Thousand Oaks: Sage.

Denzin, N. & Lincoln, Y. (Eds.). (1998). *Strategies of qualitative inquiry.* Thousand Oaks: Sage.

Dyche, L. & Zayas, L.H. (1995). The value of curiosity and naivete for the cross-cultural psychotherapist. *Family Process, 34,* 389–399.

Erskine, R. (2002). Exploring racism, exploring race. *Journal of Family Therapy, 24*(3), 282–297.

Esten, G. & Wilmott, L. (1993). Double blind messages: The effects of attitude towards disability on therapy. In M.E. Willmuth & L. Holcomb (Eds.), *Women with disabilities: Found voices* (pp. 29–41). New York: Haworth. Also published in *Women & Therapy, 14*(3–4).

Flaskas, C. (2004). Thinking about the therapeutic relationship: Emerging themes in family therapy. *Australian and New Zealand Journal of Family Therapy, 25*(1), 13–20.

Garcia, B. & Bregoli, M. (2000). The use of literary sources in the preparation of clinicians for multicultural practice. *Journal of Teaching in Social Work, 2000, 20*(1), 77–102.

Greene, G., Jensen, C. & Jones, D. (1996). A constructivist perspective on clinical social work practice with ethnically diverse clients. *Social Work, 41*(2), 172–180.

Hanna, E. (1993). The implications of shifting perspectives in countertransference on the therapeutic action of clinical social work, Part II: The recent-totalist and instersubjective position. *Journal of Analytic Social Work, 1*(3), 53–79.

Hare-Mustin, R.T. (1994). Discourses in the mirrored room: A postmodern analysis of therapy. *Family Process, 33*(1), 19–35.

Healey, K. (2001). Reinventing critical social work practice: Challenges from practice, context, and postmodernism. *Critical Social Work, 2*(1). (E-journal)

Hepworth, D.H., Rooney, R.H. & Larsen, J.A. (1997). *Direct social work practice: Theory and skills* (5th ed.). Pacific Grove: Brooks/Cole.

Heron, B. (2005). Self-reflection in critical social work practice: Subjectivity and the possibilities of resistance. *Reflective Practice, 6*(3), 341–351.

Horowitz, L. (2000). Resisting amnesia in countertransference: A clinical strategy for working with lesbian patients. *Clinical Social Work Journal, 28*(1), 55–70.

Jackson, H.L. (1995). Treatment considerations when the therapist is the minority in the patient-therapist dyad. In J. Adleman & G.M. Enguidanos (Eds.), *Racism in the lives of women* (pp. 229–237). New York: Harrington Press.

Janesick, V. (1998). The dance of qualitative research design: Metaphor, methodolatry, and meaning. In N. Denzin & Y. Lincoln (Eds.), *Strategies of qualitative inquiry* (pp. 35–55). Thousand Oaks: Sage.

Kondrat, M.E. (1999). Who is the "self" in self-aware: Professional self-awareness from a critical theory perspective. *Social Service Review, 73*(4), 451–477.

Korin, E.C. (1994). Social inequalities and therapeutic relationships: Applying Freire's ideas to clinical practice. *Journal of Feminist Family Therapy, 5*(3/4), 75–98.

Laszloffy, T.A. & Hardy, K.V. (2000). Uncommon strategies for a common problem: Addressing racism in family therapy. *Family Process, 39*(1), 35–50.

Lee, B., McGrath, S., Moffatt, K. & George, U. (2002). Exploring the insider role in community practice within diverse communities. *Critical Social Work 3*(1). (E-journal).

Lowery, C. (2002). Diversity, ethnic competence, and social justice. In M.A. Mattaini, C. Lowery & C. Meyer (Eds.), *Foundations of social work practice: A graduate text* (3rd ed.) (pp. 73–94). Washington: NASW Press.

Margolin, L. (1997). *Under the cover of kindness: The invention of social work.* Charlottesville: The University Press of Virginia.

Mattaini, M., Lowery, T., & Meyer, C. (Eds.). (2002). *Foundations of social work practice: A graduate text* (3rd ed.). Washington: NASW Press.

McGoldrick, M. (Ed.). (1998). *Revisioning family therapy.* New York: Guilford Press.

Miehls, D. & Moffatt, K. (2000). Constructing social work identity based on the reflexive self. *British Journal of Social Work, 30,* 339–348.

Miller, G. & Baldwin, Jr., D. (1999). Implications of the wounded-healer paradigm for the use of self in therapy. In M. Baldwin (Ed.), *The use of self in therapy* (2nd ed.) (pp. 167–182). New York: Haworth.

Mishne, J. (2002). Multiculturalism and the therapeutic process. New York: Guilford.

Moreau, M. (1979). A structural approach to social work practice. *Canadian Journal of Social Work Education, 5*(1), 78–94.

Moules, N. (2000). Postmodernism and the sacred: Reclaiming connection in our greater-than-human worlds. *Journal of Marital and Family Therapy 26*(2), 229–240.

Napier, L. & Fook, J. (Eds.). (2000a). *Breakthroughs in practice: Theorising critical moments in social work.* London: Whiting & Birch.

Napier, L. & Fook, J. (2000b). Reflective practice in social work. In L. Napier & J. Fook (Eds.), *Breakthroughs in practice: Theorising critical moments in social work* (pp. 1–15). London: Whiting & Birch.

Nash, M. (1993). The use of self in experiential learning for cross-cultural awareness: An exercise linking the personal with the professional. *Journal of Social Work Practice, 7*(1), 55–61.

Pérez Foster, R.M. (1998). The clinician's cultural countertransference: The psychodynamics of culturally competent practice. *Clinical Social Work Journal 26*(3), 253–270.

Pérez Foster, R.M. (1999). An intersubjective approach to cross-cultural clinical work. *Smith College Studies in Social Work, 69*(2), 269–291.

Ramsay, R. (2003). Transforming the working definition of social work into the 21st century. *Research on Social Work Practice, 13*(3), 324–338.

Real, T. (1990). The therapeutic use of self in constructionist/systemic therapy. *Family Process, 29*(3), 255–272.

Robbins, S.P., Chatterjee, P. & Canda, E.R. (1998). *Contemporary human behavior theory.* Boston: Allyn & Bacon.

Rober, P. (2002). Constructive hypothesizing, dialogic understanding, and the therapist's inner conversation: Some ideas about knowing and not knowing in the family therapy session. *Journal of Marital and Family Therapy, 28*(4), 467–478.

Rompf, E. & Royse, D. (1994). Choice of social work as a career: Possible influences. *Journal of Social Work Education, 30*(2), 163–171.

Rossiter, A. (2001). Innocence lost and suspicion found: Do we educate for or against social work? *Critical Social Work, 2*(1). (E-journal).

Sakomoto, I. & Pitner, R. (2005). Use of critical consciousness in anti-oppressive social work practice: Disentangling power dynamics at personal and structural levels. *British Journal of Social Work, 35,* 435–452.

Satir, V. (1999). The therapist story. In M. Baldwin (Ed.), *The use of self in therapy* (2nd ed.) (pp. 17–28). New York: Haworth Press.

Shonfeld-Ringel, S. (2001). A re-conceptualization of the working alliance in cross-cultural practice with non-Western clients: Integrating relational perspectives and multicultural theories. *Clinical Social Work Journal, 29*(1), 53–63.

Sim, S. (2000). They took my baby. In L. Napier & J. Fook (Eds.), *Breakthroughs in practice: Theorising critical moments in social work* (pp. 16–37). London: Whiting & Birch.

Sternbach, J. (2000). Lessons learned about working with men: A prison memoir. *Social Work, 45*(5), 413–423.

Thayne, T. (1998). Opening space for clients' religious and spiritual values in therapy: A social constructionist perspective. In D. Becvar (Ed.), *The family, spirituality, and social work* (pp. 13–23). New York: Haworth Press.

Webb, S. (2001). The politics of social work: Power and subjectivity. *Critical Social Work 1*(2). (E-journal).

Weisman, C. (2000). A reminiscence: Group work principles withstanding time — from the settlement house to the United Nations. *Social Work with Groups, 23*(3), 5–18.

Wilson, M. (1996). Dilemmas and responses. In K. Cavanagh & V. Cree (Eds.), *Working with men: Feminism and social work* (pp. 36–44). London: Routledge.

Wong, Y.-L.R. (2004). Knowing through discomfort: A mindfulness-based critical social work pedagogy. *Critical Social Work, 5*(1). (E-journal).

CHAPTER 2

SELF AS SUBJECTIVITY: TOWARD A USE OF SELF AS RESPECTFUL RELATIONS OF RECOGNITION

Amy Rossiter

INTRODUCTION

As a proponent of critical reflexive social work, I have found myself eschewing terms like "use of self." It seemed to be a term that was hopelessly embedded in clinical discourses, with their attendant problems of social control through unexamined relations of power. Yet the challenge of this book—to conceptualize the importance of the practitioner's self in social work practice—demands that if we believe that the practitioner's self is crucial, we then need to examine the pitfalls of conventional conceptions of use of self. In this chapter, I will explore a case vignette that illuminates the problem of power in conventional applications of use of self. I then suggest how we might rethink the self within a framework that centralizes a conception of the self as constructed within relations of power, and enacted through patterns of domination and privilege. Such a frame will require a shift from the liberal humanist concept of self to a concept of subjectivity, which, I argue, better serves a justice-based ethics at the heart of critical reflexive practice.

My overarching interest in use of self issues is situating social work in social justice (Rossiter, 2000, 2005). Recent theoretical work on the theory of recognition by Axel Honneth (Fraser, 1995; Honneth, 1992; Honneth & Margalit, 2001) has great importance for social work because it explicitly ties human well-being to justice, and therefore makes justice fundamental to social work practice. I am interested in relating the concept of use of self to practice that is based on respectful relations of recognition as a requirement of justice. In defining recognition, Jessica Benjamin (Benjamin, 1988) says:

The balance within the self depends upon mutual recognition between self and other.... In Hegel's notion of recognition, the self requires the opportunity to act and have an effect on the other to affirm his existence. In order to exist for oneself, one has to exist for an other. (Benjamin, 1988, p. 53)

Honneth takes the position that human well-being or psychological health rests on the sense of integrity that can be gained only through intersubjective relations with others. The fact that we are dependent on others' recognition for our sense of self means that respectful recognition is a requirement of justice: We are obligated to engage in respectful relations of recognition as a matter of justice:

We owe our integrity ... to the receipt of approval or recognition from other persons. [Experiences of degradation or insult] are related to forms of disrespect, to the denial of recognition. Negative concepts of this kind are used to characterize a form of behaviour that does not represent an injustice solely because it constrains the subjects in their freedom for action or does them harm. Rather, such behaviour is injurious because it impairs these persons in their positive understanding of self — an understanding acquired by intersubjective means. (Honneth, 1992, pp. 188, 189)

I will argue in this chapter that respectful relations of recognition — as a matter of justice — are not adequately handled by conventional concepts of use of self. Instead, justice-based practice requires a concept of self that theorizes the self as constructed within the inevitable play of power relations. With the self understood as subjectivity, we then can question the effects of power on our professional capacity for respectful relations of recognition with our clients.

USE OF SELF AS COUNTERTRANSFERENCE: A CASE VIGNETTE

The concept of use of self has been limited to clinical social work, with its conventional focus on individual adjustment, change, healing, empowerment, etc. As a clinical social work concept, it has been paired consistently with psychoanalytic ideas about countertransference. Countertransference holds that a therapist's reactions to patients may be based on the therapist's own personal issues, which need to be resolved in order to relate effectively to the patient. But because of its development through possessive individualism and related historical developments of capitalist state power, clinical social work has been linked with, but relatively blind to, its entrapment in practices of social control. The case vignette I examine demonstrates how use of self (understood as countertransference) plays an inadvertent role in maintaining disrespectful relations of recognition, thereby constituting a problem of justice because it violates the integrity of a human being. I will then situate the concept of use of self in a kind of broad critical ethics, of which social work is one arena, rather than the application of professional technologies. In the former, I understand such ethics to ultimately be in service of a practice of respectful recognition as a condition of justice. In the latter, social control prevails over respect.

I would like to offer my reading of an article by Eastwood et al. (Eastwood, Spielvogel et al., 1990). I want to work against this article in order to articulate why I understand the conventional concept of use of self as countertransference to be a problem of justice.

The article exemplifies the way use of self is conventionally taken up in clinical literature. The authors are women staff on an in-patient psychiatric team who encounter female patients who arouse intense feelings of hatred and contempt. The authors are concerned about their inability to achieve a kind of feminist rapport with these female patients. Their conclusion is that they see such patients as instances of stereotypes of bad or feared women (i.e., the "aggressive woman," the "sex trade worker," the "dependent woman," and the "bad mother"). In team meetings, staff work to acknowledge their feelings about these patients and to become aware of their own fears of being like the "bad" women. The result of this acknowledgement is that "we learned to manage these reactions better" (p. 273). This formulation is the prototypical frame for use of self as countertransference.

I will explore the first case vignette, entitled "The Aggressive Woman." I am concerned that the lens of countertransference supports the construction of a story about staff and patients that precludes awareness of the operation of relations of domination, so that disrespectful relations of recognition are hidden from view. In short, this use of countertransference when it is the dominant explanation for therapists' reactions to clients is a problem of justice. I am particularly interested in how the case vignette works up a view of the patient that is severed from social relations in the context of the hospital psychiatric unit. My contention is that use of self, understood as countertransference, is a story about how individuals turn to *themselves* — to their individual biographies and proclivities, which add up to "who they are" — as the source of their reactions to others, whose behaviour also emanates from "who they are." This notion of the self makes their location within relations of power in psychiatry unavailable for reflection, and in so doing makes the problem of power and resistance disappear. The result is the exercise of domination over the patient that is taken for granted, unnoticed because it is read as correct professional behaviour.

The vignette concerns Ms. S, the "aggressive woman," who is described as a "38-yr old, married, Caucasian woman." Here, the patient is identified in terms of race, age, and marital status. However, no similar information is provided about the social location of psychiatric staff. This begins to set up a hallmark of domination: the gaze from nowhere or, in Donna Haraway's (Haraway, 1988) terms, the "god-trick" (p. 581). Here, the patient is the marked person while staff remain unmarked. The patient is described by staff from an invisible yet powerful location where power itself renders the observers' location irrelevant. This power comes from the status and meaning attributed to professionals. The normalization of professionalism allows the authors to escape an intersubjective dimension: Their actions are not connected to Ms. S's behaviour. In this way, practices associated with use of self can enable the reproduction of domination.

Implicit here is the assumption that the social locations of staff are irrelevant to the behaviour of the patient. The professional self is not presumed to carry the weight of historical baggage, making it possible to overlook the effect, for example, of class dynamics in the professional encounter. The relationship itself is individual and ahistorical. Staff are not *of* the relationship: they are outside it, looking at patients whose behaviour is autogenetic: not constructed, not developed in context and in history, but the sum total of the observers' observations. Domination takes place when the dominator has the power to define the Other from within the dominator's frame of reference and interests. It takes place when the dominator's power to construct the definition of the dominated is unacknowledged. Such a gaze from nowhere precludes respectful relations of recognition because it leaves the misrecognition (e.g., stereotypes, assumptions, disregard) that is constructed through power relations unexamined.

Let us see how relations of recognition play out in the case vignette. Ms. S is associated with the stereotype of "the castrating bitch" (p. 66). Staff's negative reactions to her are understood as based in their fear of being like her, and their sense of paralysis in "managing" her is generated by this fear. The article outlines Ms. S's situation: She has had many admissions to hospital due to "poor outpatient compliance." She is pregnant, and determined to keep the baby. Her three older children are in foster care. Staff's attempts to "return Ms. S to the community failed and she was hospitalized throughout her pregnancy." With respect to her relations with the staff, "If the treatment team would disagree with her she would become loud, hostile, and threatening. Although receiving therapeutic levels of medication and free of delusional ideas, she steadfastly held to distorted beliefs of reality and had no insight into the effects of her threats on others" (p. 66).

We can see the thrust of the staff's story about Ms. S. She is not compliant. She is not polite to the team. Her belief that she can keep the baby is "distorted." She has thwarted the staff's attempts to "return her" to the community. There is a great deal of unexamined power being exercised in this account. Take, for example, the comments that if the team disagreed, the patient became "loud, hostile and threatening," and she had "no insight into the effects of her threats on others." There is no awareness of the effects of "disagreeing" within relations of power. There is no connection made between Ms. S's loud hostility and her disadvantaged status as a poor, disabled woman facing a "disagreement" with middle-class professionals who hold considerable statutory power over her life.

When she is described as thwarting staff's efforts to return her to the community, the staff position themselves as the active agents who assume direction of Ms. S's best interests. Here, Ms. S's own understanding of her interests, her narrative about her needs, is absent and unknown. Her desire to keep her baby is not even seen as legitimate, if doomed. Instead, it is "distorted." The evidence selected for the vignette is presented as the truth from a neutral vantage point, and the staff's reactions are notably absent, but somehow justified without requiring any argument. This can be seen in the description of Ms. S's behaviour, which is taken to warrant the staff's hatred of her:

> Ms. S took a position in the day room of the unit where she could oversee all the activities. From her "throne" she attempted to direct the action, offering a loud comment whenever a staff person entered the ward. Often she observed special characteristics or actions of the staff and would develop a denigrating comment to the individual. One

of us had recently assumed the role of senior attending psychiatrist, responsible for the medical and psychiatric care on the unit. One day she brought a crate of apples from her garden for patients and staff. Soon Ms. S greeted her every day, calling her "Apple Annie," a dramatic character who is a street saleswoman but passes as a society woman with the help of a group of bootleggers. Another of us was told by Ms. S that she should be home with her children, raising the underlying conflict most working mothers feel. (p. 66)

Following this account, the central question of the vignette is raised: "What gave this woman with a serious psychiatric disorder and meagre success in work or relationships such power over us" (p. 274)? The authors' answer lies in the countertransference problem: She triggers feelings in staff due to their own fears about aggressive women. However, the question itself hides the overlooked operation of power. The question signals that a "serious psychiatric disorder and meagre success work or relationships" are grounds for warranting their unquestioned power over Ms. S, but this signal is hidden from view by the conceptualization of the staff's reactions in terms of countertransference. Staff investigate their fears of being like Ms. S rather than searching for the immediate intersubjective context for triggers to her behaviour, a search that would need to take account of the operation of power as it affects respectful recognition. Such a search, at minimum, would need to acknowledge the existence of different narratives that arise from social subjects who are differently located in power/knowledge relations.

The account offers us a glimpse of another source of the staff's hatred of Ms. S: She actively resists their power over her at every opportunity. Ms. S refuses any sort of obedience to the staff's psychiatric narrative of her, which marks her as non-compliant, holding distorted beliefs, and unaware of her best interests. Indeed, Ms. S goes to great lengths to level the power structure by introducing the metaphor of Apple Annie to suggest the illegitimate nature of the chief psychiatrist's power. She levels power by pointing out the status of mother, which she shares with them, and by finding them negligent, as they have found her. Her comments about staff unmask their invisible location. She seeks to mark them as she has been marked. In short, the text offers us a view of Ms. S as resistant — as refusing domination.

There are many accounts of the problem of power in psychiatry, from Ken Kesey's popular version to the intricate examination of power by

Michel Foucault. Indeed, the consumer survivor movement was inspired by the damage to the identity of people with mental illnesses by virtue of the medical model in psychiatry as it harnessed science to social control. Yet these critiques do not disturb the working of power as it operates in the article in question. Sensitivity to power is not the stuff of reflection at a day-to-day level of conventional psychiatric units. Instead, discourses like that of countertransference constitute a perspective that makes it possible for individual workers to do away with problems by locating and fixing their internal faults through processes of individual awareness. Power and control are protected while staff feel they have engaged in enlightened practice through their self-awareness. This is perhaps why progressive social work has come to eschew the concept of use of self.

At this point, defenders of "use of self" might protest that I am setting up a straw dog. They might argue that the conventional notion of use of self as countertransference is a thing of the past — that more intersubjective, more holistic versions of use of self have replaced the past convention (Basescu, 1990) — indeed, that notions of anti-oppression have infiltrated the use of self. We can certainly see this in the Eastwood article as it claims to use a feminist perspective on the need to eschew the view of women's assertion as aggression.

But, as we see in the article, the problem isn't solved by recourse to feminism, or to intersubjective views, because the problem is the invisibility to themselves of the power they wield. I suggest that this problem is due to the conception of "self" at the heart of the conventions of "use of self," and, further, that such a concept must change from self to subjectivity.

SELF AND SUBJECTIVITY

The Liberal Humanist Subject

In general, helping professions such as psychiatry, social work, and psychology have historically depended on a liberal humanist subject as the conception of the self. Here, the self emanates from a unique essence, a core self, a place not socially constructed. Development of self proceeds *from* that essence. The liberal humanist subject is a unified, rational subject who chooses, decides, and acts as an individual who is the author of her place in society.

Liberal humanism is at the heart of the vignette discussed above. The patient's internal state is seen to be the origin of her behaviour, and that internal state exists as a function of an essential self, not developed within a historical context that potentiates and constructs selves in response to that context. In this way, the patients are viewed as the lone origin of non-compliant behaviour, which, in the context of psychiatry, is managed as pathology. The problem of justice here is that the social relations of psychiatry, with their productive role in patients' subjectivities, fall from view, leaving power and domination undisturbed. "The liberal-humanist assumption that the individual subject is the source of self-knowledge and knowledge of the world can easily serve as a guarantee and justification of existing social relations" (Weedon, 1987, p. 84).

In this vignette we see the operation of power, dependent as it is on the liberal humanist conception of self, working through the concept of countertransference. The staff come to knowledge of themselves as individual actors so that they can better manage patients, and the question of power is outside the discourse. The inability to raise the question of power is a function of their position in discourses of use of self based on countertransference. In such a way, countertransference acts as a nodule for the micropolitics of social power. Nikolas Rose refers to this in his investigation into psychology:

> ... I argue that the growth of the intellectual and practical technologies of psychology in Europe and North America over the period since the late nineteenth century is intrinsically linked with the transformations in the exercise of political power in contemporary liberal democracies. (Rose, 1996, p. 11)

My contention is that use of self, born as countertransference, has been unable to address practice based on justice defined as respectful relations of recognition because it rests on a liberal humanist subject and therefore cannot address issues of power and domination.

THE SELF AS SUBJECTIVITY

I would like instead to move from the liberal humanist concept of the self-contained and constant self to a postmodern understanding of self as subjectivity. In my view, one of the crucial contributions of postmodernism to professional practice has been its critique of the liberal humanist subject and its insistence on understanding the construction of subjectivity as an effect of power. Indeed, the term "subjectivity" signals a rejection of the

[handwritten: discourse of SW. shitty experience for tenants can't escape that; even student. go]

liberal humanist subject in favour of a social subject where individual and social are co-constructed through language.

The concept of subjectivity implies the dependence of the subject on language. Language, already social, can be understood as discourses — language boundaries that include some things and exclude others — which create positions for identity. In such a way, the individual and social are not split, as in liberal humanism, but are co-constructed. Here, the end of an individual/social dualism makes way for a "theorization of subjectivity which starts with the recognition that it is a socially constituted product" (Venn, 1984, p. 149). As a socially constituted product, subjectivity operates within discursive positions, which are always historical. As historical positions, they embody the operation of power. Chris Weedon (1987, p. 134) makes the connection between language, individual, and institution as follows:

> Discourses, in Foucault's work, are ways of constituting knowledge, together with the social practices, forms of subjectivity, and power relations which inhere in such knowledges and the relations between them. Discourses are more than ways of thinking and producing meaning. They constitute the "nature" of the body, unconscious and conscious mind and emotional life of the subjects they seek to govern. Neither the body nor thoughts or feelings have meaning outside their discursive articulation, but the ways in which discourse constitutes the minds and bodies of individuals is always part of a wide network of power relations, often with institutional bases. (Weedon, 1987, p. 108)

Taking up the concept of self as subjectivity insists that discourses, as media of power, have to be understood as having constitutive effects on identity. It is not possible to see the psychiatrist as a monad improving her inner self and the patient as self-producing her own dysfunction. Rather, the field of power in psychiatry, and the ways that such power constitutes subjectivities in the social relations of psychiatry, give access to a view of psychiatrist and patient as selves positioned in complicated histories in which care and domination are interpenetrated. And it is because of the continuous interpenetration that concern for the ethical relation is the primary imperative of practice.

Conventional forms of use of self can be seen as active forms of resistance against acknowledgement of power. This is because the power that shapes the identities of professionals, if evident, threatens to undo our conceptions of self as "professional," a term that itself depends on being innocent of the use of power and of domination. Speaking of the problem of the notion of subjectivity for professionals, Couze Venn says: "I have demonstrated that for the logocentric subject of psychology the social and the cultural is a contingent embarrassment, which needs to be watchfully disciplined" (Venn, 1984, p. 149).

The liberal humanist self of countertransference/use of self discourses seals off analysis of the social constitution of staff and patients, as we see in the Eastwood article. The self as subjectivity demands an understanding of how subjects are produced in ways that transcend the individual/ social divide. This demand opens us to the inevitability of power in social relations and therefore to the necessity of practice as an ongoing search for justice in relation to power. The presence of power is a demand for ethics. In this view, ethics is the continuous search for the operation of power and the inevitability of both domination and justice in practice.

I want to explore the notion that the concept of subjectivity opens us to the problem of power and that this opening enjoins us to a concept of use of self as ethics. Because power inheres in language and discourse, there is no possibility to circumvent it. There is no system that puts us outside power — indeed, such a system can only become another form of power. Yet as practitioners, we must act within the shattering knowledge that our subjectivities are implicated in relations of domination that is our historical legacy through the development of professions within the rise of modern forms of power.

CONCLUSION

I want to conclude by discussing the implications of the turn from self to subjectivity and the consequent possibilities for respectful recognition as a frame for "use of self." Here, I am interested in exploring how conceptualizing subjectivity as a site of power relations leads us to theorize a justice-based practice accomplished through an ethics of self-interrogation: in other words, a new conception of use of self for social work.

I am interested in such a conception because of the need to take account of the "whole self" of the practitioner. My critique of conventional frames for use of self is that "whole self" frequently stops at "personal" reactions, which is taken to mean feelings and responses to clients that must be traced to the internal state of the therapist. There is no question that this is a necessary part of use of self: People in the helping professions are obligated as a matter of ethics to reflect on their responses to others, and to ascertain the origin of those responses. Clearly, we will respond based on our own experiences, values, expectations, etc., and that use of self fairly asks us to differentiate our responses from the needs and realities of our clients. However, the liberal humanist conception of self stops the investigation at the "personal," while a concept of use of self as subjectivity allows for a "whole self" that is thoroughly social, invested in power relations, given through history. This concept of self complicates use of self by asking us to interrogate our responses in light of our social selves. I argue that such a use of self facilitates greater possibility for respectful recognition, and thus orients practice in justice.

How might this have worked in the Eastwood vignette? Such a revised use of self asks that we understand how our relationship with clients might be socially constructed, and how our behaviour and that of our clients might be organized through that construction. Let's start with the feeling of hatred staff had toward the "aggressive woman." It is quite possible that such feelings arise from fears associated with the socialization of woman regarding aggression and assertion. It is reasonable to consider whether such feelings are at the root of the sense of disgust at the client. But this cannot be the end of the use of self. The following suggest the kinds of question associated with a use of self as subjectivity:

- What is the nature of the language used regarding the client, and how does it constitute power? What stories (discourses) are told about the client, and how does power operate in them?
- What is the effect of psychiatric discourses on the construction of staff and patient's subjectivity?
- Whose story is legitimate and whose is not? How does delegitimation of the client's story occur?
- What other readings of the aggressive woman are left out by the dominant story of aggression?
- How can we understand the behaviour of staff and client as a contest for control? Whose control is legitimate, and whose is not?
- What is the distribution of power in the status of the professional and the status of the client?

- How does the word "aggressive" position staff? Are they excluded from the possibility of being aggressive?
- How does the social class of staff and patients get reproduced through the vignette?
- What is the effect of the medicalization of patients regarding the inclusion of their social circumstances—what aspects of the patient's context disappears in medicalization?

Such questions as these allow us to consider the relations of power/ knowledge as we engage in helping. It is this consideration that increases the potential for respectful recognition of people needing help because it forces us to interrogate the forms of power that produce misrecognition as a problem of justice. If we address such questions, we might find a way to construct new narratives about Ms. S, a narrative that could problematize the use of power and, in so doing, might cease to trap Ms. S within the identity of a "castrating bitch." In other words, a narrative that gives Ms. S. the respectful recognition that is her *right*. We might then begin to develop an understanding of Ms. S's self-narratives out of a belief that recognition of her narratives about her life is a primary form of respect. Such recognition, in its capacity to sustain human dignity, better serves justice in practice.

As professionals, continuous questioning about how power works through our subjectivities is critical reflexive practice as ethics, and I assert that this ethics is the first concern of practice—not theory, not technique, not knowledge. This ethics is enacted by an ongoing responsibility for constituting the worker/client relation as an ethical relationship. I do not seek truths about ethical relationships, only ways to keep its primacy at the forefront of my thinking during practice.

I want to suggest that critical reflection as ethics is the interrogation of our whole selves, understood as subjectivity (Miehls & Moffatt, 2000) with a view toward establishing relations of recognition with clients. There are no stories of "how to," nor techniques, nor solutions. There is only self-questioning and hesitation—a hesitation before knowing and acting in the micro spaces of practice that I am always/already implicated in forms of power and powerlessness, as is my client, and that these forms will be present in our contact. There is self-questioning about the stories I employ in practice and how those stories constitute recognition of the client. There are questions about how the relationship between us permits or inhibits recognition. How do I, as a middle-class White woman, reproduce domination through my relationships with others — domination that acts as misrecognition, thus injuring dignity?

Critical reflexive practice constitutes the use of self as ethics that references the "whole self" where the personal — which is always/already social — can be used in service of human well-being, understood as an always out-of-reach, incomplete, shifting, and momentary search for justice found in relations of recognition.

REFERENCES

Basescu, S. (1990). Tools of the trade: The use of the self in psychotherapy. *Group 14*(3), 157–165.

Benjamin, J. (1988). *The bonds of love.* New York: Pantheon.

Eastwood, J., Spielvogel, A., et al. (1990). Countertransference risks when women treat women. *Clinical Social Work Journal 18*(3), 273–280.

Fraser, N. (1995). From redistribution to recognition. *New Left Review, 212,* 68–93.

Haraway, D. (1988). Situated knowledges: The science question in feminism and the privilege of partial perspective. *Feminist Studies 14*(3), 575–599.

Honneth, A. (1992). Integrity and disrespect: Principles of a conception of morality based on the theory of recognition. *Political theory 20*(2), 187–201.

Honneth, A. & Margalit, A. (2001). Recognition. *Theory, Culture & Society 18*(2–3), 111–126.

Miehls, D. & Moffatt, K. (2000). Constructing social work identity based on the reflexive self. *British Journal of Social Work, 30,* 339–348.

Rose, N. (1996). *Inventing ourselves: Psychology, power, and personhood.* Cambridge: Cambridge University Press.

Rossiter, A. (2000). The professional is political: An interpretation of the problem of the past in solution-focused therapy. *American Journal of Orthopsychiatry, 70*(1), 1–12.

Rossiter, A. (2005). Discourse analysis in critical social work. *Critical Social Work, 6*(1). Retrieved from http://www.criticalsocialwork.com.

Venn, C. (1984). The subject of psychology. In J. Henriques, W. Hollway, C. Urwin, C. Venn & V. Walkerdine, *Changing the subject: Psychology, social regulation and subjectivity* (pp. 119–152). London: Methuen.

Weedon, C. (1987). *Feminist practice and poststructuralist practice.* Oxford: Basil Blackwell.

CHAPTER 3

THE MO-HEBREW CONUNDRUM: HOW ANTI-SEMITISM IN THE ABORIGINAL COMMUNITY CHANGED MY PROFESSIONAL AND PERSONAL IDENTITY AS A SOCIAL WORKER

Jeff D'Hondt

I do not know who I am... *Ntaktanena nahpiaw.* I do not know what language I should use to write this chapter... *Ntaktanena nlixsuwsi nleekhiikeewsi.* I know that I'm tired of being called "too Indian to be White" and "too White to be Indian"... *Nweewiiheewsi npeeksutaweewsi wshinnzuwaaleewawa "machii-shuwanakw" wak "mataakanii-lunaapeewak."* Such words have created pain for me... *Niawweendam eel-nshiingsutaweewsi.*

Voss, Douville, Little Soldier, and Twiss (1999, p. 228) found that the Lakota people were suspicious of written words, which could be exploited in ways not intended by their authors, and while I am not Lakota, I understand their caution. The sentences above, which I have translated myself from English to Lenape, may contain errors. In addition to this potentially faulty translation, I could be preparing a manuscript with concepts that might be misunderstood by those who read them. Nonetheless, Voss et al. (1999) chose to publish an article because the absence of scholarly writing discussing Lakota world views perpetuated the invisibility of American Indian people. In the same spirit, I continue to type, not wanting to insult people with careless remarks.

Yet it is difficult to avoid carelessness without a firm grasp of a language. I am not bilingual, and neither are the sentences I wrote in the opening paragraph. Rather they are bicultural. The world of a heterosexual, able-bodied, middle-class male Canadian social worker has combined with the experiences of a heterosexual, able-bodied, middle-class Lenape man, and the result was a paragraph that was emotionally and linguistically difficult to write—I want to be bilingual and bicultural. In my opinion, I am not a "half-breed." I am not Métis. I am Canadian, *and* I am Lenape, even though accepting both roles at the same time can be agonizing. Can I actually be two people if I know that one of them has historically harmed the other? In fact, I might be a third person—a social worker comfortable in both Aboriginal and non-Aboriginal worlds, and at times comfortable in neither of those worlds.

Sadly, throughout my career, I have encountered numerous scenarios that not only made me want to leave my profession, but also forced me to reconsider who I was. In one such incident, I was confronted by anti-Semitism in the Aboriginal community. After hearing a full-blooded Aboriginal community member berate a half-Jewish/half-Mohawk man, I found myself in a moment of crisis. Part of me was frustrated by my sudden inability to stop a potential fight between the two men. My exact thoughts were "I'm a social worker. I should know what to do!"

In fact, I did have an idea of how to help these angry men. After one man slapped another on the chest, I was able to intervene in the situation and prevent more serious violence. However, in the moments before my partner arrived, my own feelings were hurt by the harsh words uttered to the Jewish man, and the sometimes clear line between my Aboriginal, Caucasian, and professional identities was blurred to the point that I did not know how to act. This chapter will describe the incident in detail, and critically analyze the thoughts and feelings I had as events unfolded.

Before continuing, I should clarify two additional points of my own. First, to protect confidentiality, I have disguised the name, age, First Nation, medical information, geographic location, and possibly the gender of some people that deeply touched my life many years ago. Second, my intent is not to stereotype or condemn my own decisions or the actions of the people I once served. Instead, I hope to discover why this event, nearly a decade old as I tell the story, had me questioning my abilities as a social worker and my identity as a Canadian and Lenape man.

THE INCIDENT

I come now to the incident that is at the heart of this reflection, beginning with a brief summary of what occurred. At the time this incident unfolded, I was working at an Aboriginal health centre as an addictions counsellor. The day in question began when I was greeted by "Jim," a self-described "Mo-Hebrew" man. He developed this term to describe his mixed Mohawk and Jewish heritage. One morning, he approached me, wondering if he could use the television in the centre's lobby to watch a documentary. His cousin had mailed him a film that discussed the Holocaust, the genocide of European Jewry during World War II. I encouraged him to view it at his leisure, and he told me he'd watch it after he met with the traditional healer he had come to visit.

A few hours later, after lunchtime, Jim took the chance to use the VCR. My office was steps away from the lobby, and I was sitting at a desk, preparing a workshop on substance use. My co-facilitator was reading over the notes, suggesting changes as I typed at the computer. Our conversation was frequently interrupted by the sound blaring from the large television that rested only 20 feet outside my door. The stories we heard were powerful, and finally we gave up our work to watch the film. As the film progressed, six other men joined us, each quietly walking into the room, standing for a few minutes as survivors of torture described their pain, and finally taking a seat to view more.

One of these men was "Wes," a full-blooded Aboriginal fellow from a reserve in Western Canada. I had known him for over a decade, having encountered him at other agencies, powwows, and cultural workshops. He had a taste for wild rice, lacrosse, experimental theatre, pugilism, and theatre history, and viewed himself as an activist. He had often busked at street corners, singing songs about the oppression of indigenous peoples worldwide. I used to pass him on the street during my lunch hour, if only to laugh at his acerbic lyrics. Eventually, he started to chat with me, and learned that I was a social worker. Days later, he had arrived at the health centre in search of addictions counselling, specifically asking for me to be his case manager.

Wes and Jim participated in the support group I was supposed to be organizing while I watched the film, though only Wes had approached me for individual counselling. Nonetheless, I knew both men well enough to recognize their habits. Neither had raised his voice in the time I had shared with them. They shared tobacco with each other, exchanged jokes, and travelled together to watch hoop-dancing exhibitions. When I came to work, I would pass a coffee shop where the two of them would be sitting inside, telling stories about their families or discussing politics.

On the day of the incident, Wes started sighing as the film progressed. As he shifted in his seat, his foot nudged magazines on a nearby coffee table onto the floor. I asked him if he was okay, and he told me to leave him alone.

For the first time, I heard him scream.

"Why are we watching this garbage!" he shrieked. "Aboriginal peoples are murdered right here in Canada to this day, and we're crying about folks who died in Europe decades ago."

Jim, who was sitting on a nearby couch, turned to Wes.

"We watch stuff about Native rights everyday," started Jim. "I want to hear something new."

"Like it's news people want to kill Jews, you worthless kike."

My co-worker and I looked at each other, and neither of us said a word. My jaw was agape, just like hers, our eyes wide and brows furrowed. Frozen with a look of confusion, we each struggled as a man, hardly known for his temper or prejudiced views, passionately screamed hateful, oppressive language.

"I'm a social worker," I thought. "I should know what to do."

Somehow, I had entered one of the nightmare case scenarios that were discussed in my social work practice classes. In the final year of my undergraduate program, 20 students sat around a table, talking about situations that had occurred in field placements. We critiqued each other's practice, providing emotional support alongside an analysis of our professional actions. It was easy to hear other people tell stories, and ask for advice. For a moment, I imagined myself back in school, listening as a colleague told me about a client that made anti-Semitic remarks. Wes's words seemed a fantasy, one a friend made up so that he could tell the most sensational story of the school week. Yet, my pounding heart and queasy stomach belied any notion that I had imagined the event. I realized that my breathing had stopped. I was terribly angry and afraid.

Suddenly, I was very aware of how large these two men were. Jim was 6 feet 5 inches, and weighed 250 pounds. His pectoral muscles always tested the elasticity of the T-shirts he wore. Wes was taller and thinner, but just days before, I had watched him move an upright piano with his bare hands without assistance to make room for a new couch.

Both men were standing now, and I noticed the veins in their forearms bulge as they clenched their fists. I checked over my shoulder, and watched my co-worker get out of her chair, which was between the two men, and back away. I was sitting on the other side of the room as my thoughts slipped into the "fight or flight" impulses I heard about in an introductory psychology class. For what felt like several seconds, I felt my entire body go numb as my knees trembled. Even while I feared for my own safety, not to mention the health and well-being of the other clients and staff in the room, I felt the impulse to punch Wes in his anti-Semitic mouth.

Wes's epithets continued, and the two men were nose to nose. The community members, who had gathered to watch the film, all stood up and stood in a semicircle around the two men. Some of them looked at my co-worker, who was shaking, her face ashen. The others looked at me, sitting several feet away, my face still showing little feeling except confusion.

Wes's hands smacked Jim in the chest so forcefully that the blow echoed as one giant tried to intimidate the other.

The noise startled me to action. Two people could be hurt if I did nothing! I found my legs and jumped out of the chair.

"You two are friends!" I howled as I got on my feet. "Don't get yourself barred from here because you forgot that!"

I made this remark for two reasons. First, both men continually told me how much they cared for each other. I hoped that by reminding them, especially Wes, of their feelings would stop the incident from escalating into a fist fight. Second, they had told me that they had nowhere to go during the day. If their concern for each other had been forgotten in a heated moment, I hoped that the threat of losing the focal point of their social life would stop them.

"He's a fucking prick," sobbed Jim, his eyes full of tears.

He'd been knocked back a few steps by the shove, and took a few more away from his opponent. Suddenly, my co-worker appeared with another staff member, and they asked Jim to walk away with them, so they could talk about the situation in a room where everyone was safe. I was so shaken I failed to notice her leaving the room to get help.

"Jim, go with them," I spoke evenly. "Wes, come with me."

There was little thought put into my words because I was still too scared and angry to think clearly. I simply recalled the drill that the staff practised every two months to ensure we could react swiftly to situations like these. If possible, one participant in a near fist fight was moved to a counselling room at the front of the building. The other was taken to a quiet room at the back of the facility, a place where people normally went to relax or offer thanks to the Creator.

Removed from conflict, it was easier for the angry men to calm down. Another staff member had joined me as I walked Wes to the calm space out back, where he resumed his bloodcurdling anti-Semitic remarks. I choked back tears. Someone very close to me happens to be Jewish, and I was imagining that person hearing these hurtful words.

My distress grew as Wes's tirade damned my loved one. I recalled hearing him speak about his spiritual teachings. His Elders had told him to combat prejudice by promoting co-operation between races, and each word betrayed that ideal, bringing me closer to tears. My co-worker was already crying.

Suddenly, I had a thought: We're watching a brother die.

The Wes I knew had been murdered by this anti-Semitic monster who refused to shut his mouth, even as his "family by choice," the name he gave to the community members and staff who helped him, were reduced to tears and fear. For once, I was not the "phony Indian" in the room. Although no Aboriginal peoples have disputed my claims to be Native, I have often worried that my white skin and Eurocentric education could disqualify me from membership in First Nations. Without actually meeting someone who refuses to accept my heritage, I fear being labelled a part of the oppressive society that harmed so many of my Native brethren, even while I identified with my Aboriginal heritage to wash my hands of any guilt that had stained them. However, as this horrible anti-Semitic incident unfolded, I decided that Wes's racism trumped my participation in Canada's middle-class society as a possible betrayal of the ideals of Aboriginal cultures. My vision of Aboriginal belief systems pictured them unadulterated by racism, and viewed these paradigms as healing cultures that made people strong and just. This man was a traitor to those ways, and I wanted no more of his outbursts.

It was far easier to reject him than to consider the numerous ways that hatred filters into any culture. If he was not Aboriginal, I still had an ideal to aspire to. If he remained a part of a Native culture, indigenous ways of life could be just as nasty as that of the colonizer. Suddenly, I knew that I had romanticized one part of my heritage by calling it prejudice-free. That discovery crushed me, alongside the pain Wes's words had created for Jim. I did not want to think about the agony I felt — my heart was breaking, and frankly, the agony I felt still overwhelms me. I have been asked many times to examine my own prejudice at this moment alongside Wes's, and I remain unable to rise to the task. I cannot say how hate infiltrates a mind or a culture, just that it does. I will say that the impact of knowing that no one person or culture is free from oppressive behaviour took away my willingness to practise social work, to identify as a Canadian, or to associate with Aboriginal peoples. For a moment, I had no identifiable concept of self.

Five minutes or so passed as Wes spoke. Neither my colleague nor I said a word. We stood on the other side of the room, next to the door, listening to him scream. Each outburst made me shake. I hid my hands behind my back as I leaned on the wall, not wanting to show him the fists clenched so tightly that my forearms ached. I breathed slowly, trying to control my temper. I also wondered how I could get away with punching a client.

"You're more than angry," I told myself and soon started crying as vigorously as my colleague. Wes yelled for a few moments, but went silent after my co-worker wiped her eyes with her sleeve. He watched us cry, and gulped. Shaking, he fell into a nearby chair.

"I didn't mean to explode," he started. "I was watching that movie, and I knew that my family didn't get murdered. No one deserves to die. What happened to them was horrible, but what about us Natives? My whole family was sent to residential schools. Watching that video, I knew someone would use it as an excuse to take the spotlight off what happened to us. We need help, bad. The Holocaust is over, most Jews are rich, and we Indians rot on reserves."

I had no idea how to reply, so I just listened, yet I knew I wanted to say something. What silenced me? Partly, I was listening for any sign of insincerity that revealed a feeble attempt to avoid the penalty for discrimination. The facility had a non-discrimination policy, and his outburst would result in a one-week suspension from service if he was unable to convince staff to accept his apology and overlook the incident. Another part of me was hoping to hear genuine words of regret, a retraction for every awful word. I wanted Wes restored to innocence; he had seemed like a good man committed to Aboriginal teachings of unity and well-being, and that image comforted me. After all, why would I want to be Aboriginal if they were just as angry and filled with hate as the oppressor my social work education identified?

At the same time, he was unaware that I loved a Jewish person. I wanted to tell him about my loved one, so he could understand the impact that careless words had on people. Yet, Jim—not my loved one—was the target of the vitriol. Adding my own discomfort to the mix might turn the discussion to a debate about how Wes had harmed me, diverting the focus from the incident that was about to get him barred from the service he so fondly used.

Concerned about appropriating the incident for my own purposes, I decided to avoid self-disclosure. However, there was a less altruistic reason for my silence—I was struggling with disappointment. To that point, I had not heard an Aboriginal person make anti-Semitic comments—this incident predated the remarks made by David Ahenakew, a Native leader who has stated publicly that the Holocaust was justified. I was mortified that my Aboriginal brethren were capable of such prejudice.

As the conversation with Wes continued, I continued to say very little, though as it turned out, there was no need for me to speak — he punished himself. After an hour of debriefing, he voluntarily left the health centre, promising to stay away for a week. While leaving, he stopped to offer an apology to the group that was sitting in the television room, still taken aback by his outrage. Jim was absent, so Wes left an offering of tobacco with another service user, asking the man to hand it to Jim when he returned. Wes explained that he wanted to thank Jim for his friendship, and to restore it eventually.

After Wes left the building, Jim returned to the television room to thank folks for preventing a fight. Eventually, the typical laughter and teasing of an afternoon at the centre resumed, and all staff gathered for a debriefing session. I was told that the "Mo-Hebrew" had felt guilty when Wes spoke. One of Jim's great fears was that he would overshadow the harm of Aboriginal oppression by sharing stories of the Holocaust.

Two men, one argument, and the same reasons for having it. I still had little to say, other than to report that Wes would be absent from programming for seven days, according to centre policy.

ANALYSIS

My silence continued for days after the incident, and I spent a great deal of time reviewing articles from my social work and Aboriginal education, hoping to reclaim a sense of who I was, and how I should have responded to the situation. Strangely, some articles by non-Aboriginal authors found their way onto my reading list too. For example, Pease (2002) found that social workers often shoehorn clients into a powerful-powerless dualism. Workers sometimes imagine that they have power to give to clients, and clients can be perceived as powerless to act independently of the workers. This characterization of power is not liberating as it promotes the authoritarian nature of the professional-client relationship — by definition, change cannot occur unless the professional gives permission for it to occur by "empowering" a client. In reality, clients have access to various sources of power that the worker does not control. Pease suggested that workers should encourage the use of those resources by helping clients tell their own stories, in their own words. Doing so would validate the knowledge that clients already possess and allow them to revive suppressed knowledge that challenges the dominant world view.

Wes told his own story, in his own words, without my permission, and went so far as to propose and administer his own punishment, with little input from any worker. Yet Pease imagined a dialogue wherein the client identified a source of oppression and constructed a new language that liberated people from domination. Wes used his words to harm another person, and I initially used few of my professional skills to prevent or change the conversation. In a moment of crisis, I abandoned my professional identity because I was upset with my brother by choice, and because I was angry with a minority group that seemed as hateful as the colonizer that had harmed him.

Yet Scott (1992) found that it is just as necessary to critically examine marginalized values and beliefs as it is to challenge dominant beliefs. Historians who recorded the history of oppressed people often wrote down a subject's own account of what he or she had lived through without contextualizing it or analyzing the narrative for signs of the prejudices and oversights that often tainted dominant views of history. By failing to contextualize marginalized accounts of history, authors failed to identify the sources of strength that allowed marginalized knowledge to persist, while also failing to explore how a difference between subordinate and dominant groups helped to facilitate the control of subjugated people.

Haraway (1988) also noted that the subjugated are not immediately innocent of the misdeeds commonly attributed to the dominant society. Moreover, some authors acknowledged that no truth exists, yet spent their life trying to find it, only to be fooled by people claiming to speak the truth, marginalized or otherwise. To describe this phenomenon, Haraway conjured an image from Southwest Native American teachings: the Coyote or Trickster. The Coyote has been characterized as a creature of mischief in many Aboriginal nations, including my own. He/she/it was a powerful spirit, gifted with powers beyond reason. The beast regularly visited humans, clumsily causing mishaps until it was forced into exile. Harraway applied the Coyote metaphor to feminist authors, idealistically seeking out an oppressed group that presented a completely factual view of history, unfiltered by prejudice and judgment, all the while knowing the task was impossible. This metaphor could easily be expanded to my analysis of this incident—Wes and I were tricksters.

By now, I tried to view him as a new client, previously unknown to me, one less coloured by an idealized lens. I invited him to tell me about his experiences with alcohol, although he rarely chose to talk about the topic himself. He similarly discussed prejudice at my request. However, the pattern would occasionally shift, showing the numerous identities I hid. He would try to re-narrate my story, either using his stunning musical talent to write unflattering songs about my lacrosse playing or by teaching me to dance. He wanted me "to be better than I was," as he liked to inform me. His challenge to me was fair; I also wanted him to be better than he was. I thought he could be a great man if he quit drinking, changed his racist thinking, and became a professional musician. He thought I could be a great social worker if only... I could be a great husband, if only... I could be a great athlete, if only.... His "unwanted advice" irritated me, and I missed the irony of that thought. He was imitating my behaviour and, by acting like me, he was trying to stop me from behaving in the way that I was.

A thought occurred to me as our relationship continued. Ife (1997) claimed that social workers understand technical jargon and legal language, and are able to translate it into plain language so that clients can learn the concepts and speak for themselves. The professionals are "street-level intellectuals."

Wes was an autodidact, familiar with literature, classical music, popular culture, and colonial history, among other interests. He gave me a birthday card that read, "Life is a cesspool, and the young are in the prime of their existence. Congratulations." He would often sit with other service users and explain what legal documents meant, the context of a news event, or how to successfully apply for welfare benefits. Ife applied his metaphor to social workers, though Wes himself embodied the metaphor, but as a client, not as a worker. We even discussed this metaphor during a supper program — I was taking evening courses and he would read my textbooks before I left for class. The experience was odd. For a time, we were both so taken by our discussions of Ife that we both remarked that we were two different types of "brainiacs with street cred" trying to define our roles in life, in lieu of identifying ourselves as Aboriginal.

Nonetheless, my thoughts would not allow me to shelve the incident. I still considered myself a professional failure, and I hoped that another worker had faced this dilemma. My reading continued, this time focusing on material dealing with Aboriginal social work. I noticed many questions that I had ignored in my first examination of the material. For example, how would I define Aboriginal social work? Could it be a form of cross-cultural Eurocentric social work practice that incorporated Aboriginal teachings?

Or was it a new practice perspective that was different from both social work practice and Aboriginal healing? Perhaps it was a distinct style of helping that existed in the Americas prior to the arrival of Europeans, a style of helping that was experiencing a renaissance in the age of post-colonialism. Maybe it was a combination of these possibilities.

My ability to answer these questions was compromised because, as I've said, I had not mastered my Aboriginal language. Still, I had learned some terminology that could start my journey. The word "Aboriginal" was used to describe treaty and non-treaty Native peoples, the Métis, and the Inuit—nations that had different languages and cultures that called for different forms of helping. If over 650 nations and 100 languages were encompassed by the word "Aboriginal," and many of these nations were still struggling to define who they were, how could I identify what "Aboriginal" social work was?

Moreover, Canadian social workers have been a historical tool of oppression in Aboriginal communities. The helping professionals were involved in the "Sixties scoop," an era in which numerous Aboriginal children were removed from their families and placed in White homes (Blackstock & Bennett, 2003). Some Aboriginal nations prefer to refer to social work as *Mino-Pimatisiwin* (The Good Life), which was a system of healing predating colonization, and which has been associated with the revitalization of First Nations' cultures. In so doing, they not only apply an Aboriginal term, but refer to an indigenous concept of what helping individuals and communities is about. This is a different view of social work from the one used in professional mainstream social work in North America:

> Helpers [on a life journey to *Mino-Pimatisiwin*] raise and maintain an awareness of their personal histories. They understand the histories of their own family, community and nation and how they are influenced by these histories. The helpers' values, which include respect and sharing, are clear to them. They model such values by sharing their knowledge, experiences and abilities in a way which respects the gifts and abilities of others.... They strive to learn from the hardships they have faced and caused, and use what they have learned for healing and growth. They recognize difficult situations, problems and pain created by the structures in our society and by people in distress. They also see the beauty of discovery, healing and growth within themselves and in the universe around them and as such pull

out the opportunities for healing and growth that these difficulties, problems and pains provide. They acknowledge the role that rituals and ceremonies have in this process and they utilize them for help and support. They also seek out support and guidance from Elders and other people who have traveled further along their own life journeys. (Hart, 2002, p. 106)

I reviewed this passage, and realized that I had ignored any mention of ritual in my time with Wes. Furthermore, Morrissette, McKenzie, and Morrissette (1993) found that Aboriginal social work differed from other forms of social work practice because it educated Aboriginal peoples about the impact of colonialism. As frequently as Wes and I labelled ourselves as "street-level intellectuals" dedicated to creating social reform, our frequent analyses of Aboriginal politics never included an analysis of colonial attitudes that informed racism or stereotypes. In fact, I noticed that I was relying on stereotypes to describe my time with Wes. I introduced him as the "anti-Semite" during the weekly staff case management meetings. The label was useful. When he was Wes, I was conflicted — he was a good man with unjust views about millions of people. As an anti-Semite, he was a fool I could freely dislike. Finally able to plainly label him as immoral and disgusting, my own discomfort with the incident dissipated.

Yet I knew there were many factors that my flippant remarks failed to discuss. For instance, Clarkson, Morrissette, and Regallet (1992) also noted that Aboriginal social workers should be involved in environmental protection because of Aboriginal peoples' strong ties to their physical, spiritual, emotional, and mental environments. Social workers could draw parallels between this notion and systems/ecological theory — both paradigms described how people could shape and be shaped by their surroundings. However, unlike systems/ecological theory, indigenous views of the environment did not view their surroundings as socially constructed. Rather, everything had a living spirit that must be treated with love. There had been no mention of the environment in any of my discussions with Wes.

No wonder I no longer felt Aboriginal; I was avoiding key aspects of that culture out of a disgust for the actions of someone who apologized for his behaviour, and was working to atone for his mistakes. Why was I still judging him so harshly when every indication suggested that he was legitimately remorseful? As the days passed after Wes returned to my caseload, I gathered some tobacco so that I could offer it to an Elder. I approached a humble woman, who has always asked me not to identify her in my writing, but I feel comfortable noting that she has knowledge of social work literature, acquired as she practised as a medicine person in her First Nation.

"I think I failed to act properly," I told her before I explained the incident.

"Perhaps you should've stepped in earlier," she commented as I recounted my hesitant reactions to the outburst. "Yet the way you intervene is as important as the timing of your intervention. If you barged in righteously, as if you were the only smart and morally adept person in that room, you would've violated the principle of non-interference. You've read folks like Brant (1990) and Goodtracks (1973). They indicate that it is inappropriate to label, command, or persuade Native clients — they will view these actions as coercive and dismiss your actions as disrespectful. As I see it, you adhered to the principle actions by providing a respectful ear humbly capable of hearing all perspectives, while modelling a path others could follow. In spite of Wes's reluctance to address the issue, you continue to respectfully ask questions of your client, and thank him when he answers. You aren't there to argue, but to hear words, learn what caused him to speak so angrily. As you find that moment, so will he."

I bit my tongue. I was practically told that it was okay to tolerate racism, provided I eventually talked about it. What if someone pulled a knife and carved his opinion of a race onto someone's face? Would there be a discussion then?

"Yes," she replied, "once safety was restored. It might take years for the healing process to gain steam, but healing rituals or counselling would be offered to all involved, victim or aggressor. Words would be spoken there, and used to develop a series of actions and thoughts that helped someone recover from that horrible trauma. However, that didn't happen here. Why do you insist on complicating the matter?"

She grinned at me and that simple grin put a thought in my head. In a moment of doubt, I had turned to an Elder for guidance. I associated with Aboriginal folks throughout my entire self-reflection. When I thought that I misunderstood something about professional practice, I reviewed notes from Aboriginal instructors. In fact, I explicitly called myself an Aboriginal social worker instead of a "social worker." However, none of that helped me. In the moment of crisis none of my chosen identities helped me know what to do. I wasn't looking to hear I'd done the right thing; I wanted to hear what I could've done differently. Part of me was in great distress as an unresolved identity crisis left me wondering who I was, and if that person was of any value to the community I served. Whatever label I called myself, I sat still and watched two men prepare for a fight, and could do nothing until they separated themselves. Frustrated, I prepared to leave the old woman and what I condemned as her passive nonsense. I felt contempt for her teachings.

Part of me still screamed for Wes to get a lifetime ban in lieu of a calm discussion about inappropriate remarks, even as I watched Wes and Jim laugh as though nothing had happened. Fed up by the recurring thought, I undertook a reanalysis in order to resolve the dilemma, since nothing I had read or heard was easing my sense of having failed professionally.

I recalled Wes was furious that the suffering his family had endured had been trumped by the misery that Jim's family experienced: murder and forced participation in unethical medical experimentation. When confronted about his flare-up, his anger gave way to shame and, strangely enough, my own anger similarly metamorphosed into a sense of guilt and then back to anger, creating a cycle of ambivalence. I hated the man, yet I felt obligated to support him as an Aboriginal person in the professional manner expected of a social worker. With each cycle, the emotions I felt — anger, ambivalence, sadness, confusion — grew more distressing, and I wanted to spare myself a repeat of this relentless agony.

Once again frustrated, I suddenly had an insight. Wes's outburst was terribly bewildering because I had never heard my people talking like that. However, my "people" were both the colonizer and the colonized, and Aboriginal peoples were certainly not the only folks from whom I have heard anti-Semitic remarks. Why had I been focusing so exclusively on my Aboriginal identity to the point that it overwhelmed other aspects of myself? The answer came to me.... I found that it was more beautiful than the culture of a colonizer.

Why? I had images of Aboriginal peoples creating beautiful crafts, co-operating, living off the land. My stomach turned as I relived my thoughts. My view of what my Aboriginal heritage represented had been twisted by the views of a colonizer. The flawless, loving, spiritual man I once saw in Wes was a reconstruction of the noble savage (Duran & Duran, 1995), an idealized view of Aboriginal peoples as physically fit protectors of the environment, in tune with nature and possessing great artistic gifts. Yes, some Aboriginal peoples craft thought-provoking art, and regularly participate in environmental crusades, but many of us prefer to buy dream catchers instead of wasting sinew as we struggle to tie it on a hoop ourselves.

Aboriginal peoples are complex humans, not static cultural symbols. Duran and Duran (1995) noted that stereotypes could lead to social problems — it was thought that people struggling with their identity drink, so many Aboriginal peoples believed that drinking was the way to define their heritage. Somehow, I had adopted the image, automatically viewing my chosen brothers and sisters as kind, caring, and deeply in love with all of humanity. Wes's comments uncovered two sets of prejudices: his own and mine. For too long, I had craved simplicity. Being two people, one Aboriginal and one White, hurt for many years. I wanted to believe that this pain was the result of a vicious oppressor saying that I was less than a human being because of my mixed blood, and of an oppressed nation rejecting me because I was part of the society that colonized them. Yet most urban Aboriginal peoples are bicultural. They often have jobs outside the Aboriginal community. They live in cities like I do. They frequently speak English more commonly than their Aboriginal tongue. Yet they may also go to powwows, make traditional crafts, and spend much of their time socializing with other Aboriginal peoples. If I were the only bicultural Aboriginal person in North America, rejection would make sense to me, yet why would people shun me for being similar to them? Furthermore, most non-Aboriginal people I have encountered have been thankful for my insights into Canadian history, my ability to connect ideas in unique ways, and my ability to promote a balance of mind, body, spirit, and emotions, a balance they often lack themselves.

Flax (1992) wrote that many feminist thinkers have sought a set of behaviours through which humans can learn to act for the benefit of all. The attraction of this truth view, outside of the fact that humans would learn to help everyone, is that it offers a position of innocence. Someone could live with the absolute knowledge that they are working exclusively for the common good and doing the right thing. Flax critiqued this notion from a postmodern perspective, and I noticed some ties between her views and my self-perception. I viewed myself through the lens of the noble savage stereotype. Instead of an environmental protector, I perceived myself as the innocent professional selflessly working for others. This ideal had numbed my mind to the hidden oppressions surrounding me. I was pursuing innocence by calling myself a social worker instead of White or Aboriginal. In fact, I was donning a false face and colouring it red with blind pride in my Aboriginal nation, White with the distortions created by the colonizer, all the while perpetuating the prejudice that had me reaching for masks in the first place.

CONCLUSION

I have long hoped that such realizations would silence the litany of questions that plague me daily. At best, a breakthrough could bring a day or two of silence before unforeseen circumstances reminded me that I am not immune to life. Genocide was not ended by a world war in Europe, as conflicts like those in Rwanda, Darfur, and Bosnia have demonstrated. Anti-Semitism has not been limited to Nazi Germany, and nor has Canada recognized Aboriginal political autonomy, nor granted First Nations sufficient socio-economic resources necessary to govern themselves effectively.

My desire for a definitive ending even put images in my head. If Wes eradicated his prejudice, and then taught others to do the same, I would be ecstatic. Equally satisfying would be the final resolution of my identity conflicts, or even the fall of discrimination worldwide.

Truthfully, I will probably die with these dreams unfulfilled. Tidy endings have been rare in my life, let alone in my social work practice. Wes was on my caseload until I finally resigned my position in order to pursue graduate studies in social work. He was never involved in another incident at the centre, nor was Jim. Both men eventually secured permanent housing and steady employment via programs at other agencies. Occasionally, staff would discuss the incident, especially the agony we had gone through as we heard the obscene tirade, though most of us chose to forget it.

Still, in my time as a worker, I have never seen someone fully recant prejudice. At best, community members, including myself, followed Wes's example and kept their opinions to themselves. I cannot speak for him, and I do not know if his views caused him any discomfort, other than the moment when he temporarily excluded himself from service. Nonetheless, I thank him now for keeping his promise to remain silent when he felt like voicing his opinion about other minorities and the insights he gave me in the time that I knew him.

This chapter was intended to provide a case example of how I have used critical self-reflection in social work practice. I do not want to suggest that my words here should be viewed as a description of best practice, or to pretend that I answered all of the pertinent questions herein. For example, are any of my identities truly independent of all the others? I have described myself as an "internalized colonizer" (i.e., a White Canadian) mixed with someone who was "internally colonized" (i.e., an Aboriginal person). But how could someone be a colonizer if someone else was not colonized, and vice versa? I have often treated some of my identities as separate entities when in fact my various notions of self exist in tandem.

Is critical self-reflection the most effective way to mediate the discussion of identity sparked by my discussion with Wes? Some authors suggested the use of ritual and talks with Elders (Duran & Duran, 1995; Hart, 2002), yet neither of these resources was available at the moment that an impromptu movie day went sour. Instead, my actions were determined by personal history, self-concepts, and by my experiences of oppression. My thoughts, memories, and values accompany me everywhere and are always available for my use.

Still, in the absence of sufficient time to think carefully, many stories, and probably some identities too, were probably missed in the moment. I have since accepted that the journey that began with Wes's insults will truthfully never end, not while I live in a world filled with contradiction and a history preserved in customs, stereotypes, language, beliefs, and values.

Put another way, I recognize that part of me is neither Caucasian, Native, nor social worker. This fourth identity asks several questions. Why should the other paradigms just named fight each other? Even more, why should I be at war with myself? Simple. There are injustices hidden in the paradigms and in my life. I am no more noble than the savage image I used to stereotype a brother.

I apologize to anyone reading this chapter looking for clear answers. Instead, I ask you: What are you trying to hide, or hide from? Name your worst fear, or your biggest regret, and start your journey now.

REFERENCES

Blackstock, C. & Bennett, M. (2003). *National Children's Alliance: Policy paper on Aboriginal children*. Ottawa: National Children's Alliance.

Brant, C. (1990). Native ethics and the rules of behaviour. *Canadian Journal of Psychiatry, 35,* 534–539.

Clarkson, L., Morrissette, V. & Regallet, G. (1992). *Our responsibility to the seventh generation: Indigenous peoples and sustainable development*. Winnipeg: International Institute for Sustainable Development.

Duran, E. & Duran, B. (1995). *Native American postcolonial psychology*. Albany: SUNY Press.

Flax, J. (1992). The end of innocence. In J. Butler & J.W. Scott (Eds.), *Feminists theorize the political* (pp. 445–461). London: Routledge.

Goodtracks, J.G. (1973). Native American non-interference. *Social Work, 18*(6), 30–34.

Haraway, D. (1988). Situated knowledges: The science question in feminism and the privilege of partial perspective. *Feminist Studies, 14*(3), 575–597.

Hart, M.A. (2002). *Seeking Mino-Pimatisiwin: An Aboriginal approach to helping.* Halifax: Fernwood.

Ife, J. (1997). *Rethinking social work: Towards critical practice.* Melbourne: Longman.

Morrissette, V., McKenzie, B. & Morrissette, L. (1993). Towards an Aboriginal model of social work practice: Cultural knowledge and traditional practices. *Canadian Social Work Review, 10*(1), 91–108.

Pease, B. (2002). Rethinking empowerment: A postmodern appraisal for emancipatory practice. *British Journal of Social Work, 32*, 135–147.

Scott, J.W. (1992). Experience. In J. Butler & J.W. Scott (Eds.), *Feminists theorize the political* (pp. 22–39). London: Routledge.

Voss, R.W., Douville V., Little Soldier, A. & Twiss, G. (1999). Tribal and Shamanic-based social work practice: A Lakota perspective. *Social Work, 44*(3), 228–239.

CHAPTER 4

STRUCTURING SOCIAL WORK USE OF SELF

Jill Grant

In this chapter, I aim to extend the currently limited scope of the concept of use of self to create space for expansion by considering the importance of reflecting on particular contexts and the relationships within them when we consider our interactions with those we support. Because of my own location, I also consider how our own life experiences may both inform and challenge our work. I construct this discussion from a unique position — that of a former support worker in community mental health services who has also received mental health services (a prosumer[1]).

During my Master's in Social Work training, I had a course called "Differential Use of Self," which attempted to move beyond the traditional focus on transference and countertransference to a broader discussion of how our views of the world influence the ways in which we work with and are perceived by clients. While I learned some important values, such as understanding our sources of power and attempting to understand clients' situations from their perspective, I experienced two major weaknesses in this training: It ignored the contexts of the practice of social work and it ignored the question of the use of social workers' own experiences as recipients of service. With regard to the latter, I received both implicit messages (for example, talking about "those people") and explicit messages (silence when I spoke of my own relationship with mental health difficulties) to subjugate any knowledge that I had attained through my own experiences with the mental health system in favour of professional knowledge. I was taught to silence my experiences so that they would not "contaminate" the therapeutic relationship. This teaching did not correspond well with my sense that my knowledge from these experiences was just as valid as my knowledge from published texts. I also found within this message of detachment a subtle message of "othering" our clients and the knowledge derived from the experiences that lead one to being in the position of client. Throughout my Master's training and the concomitant community mental health work I was doing, I struggled to find a place for my insider knowledge of the mental health system and the ways in which this particular system influences how we interact with others.

This chapter, through illustration of an example from my practice, explores some of my journey toward understanding and owning the unique insight that my own experiences with the mental health system can bring and the impact this may have on my practice and on the mental health system. For me, the key to understanding this was to understand that a therapeutic relationship unfolds within a broader context, within certain power relations and taken-for-granted rules that impact on our relationships (Giddens, 1984, 1993). I would assert that, rather than ignoring our knowledges of these relations and rules, as social workers we have a responsibility to reflect on them and to find ways to challenge those rules that may be disempowering to those we serve. In doing so, I hope to encourage social workers to honour our own experiences of service use and to consider the importance of reflecting on the context within which we practise, the ways in which it impacts upon ourselves and our clients — in other words, to consider that the therapeutic relationship is much more complex than two people interacting in a sterile environment.

As mentioned, I construct this argument from a unique perspective: that of someone who has been both a recipient and a provider of mental health services. This prosumer aspect of my identity, however, interacts with various other identities that impact upon my understanding of mental health services, those who use them, and those who provide them. Along with having received and offered services in mental health, I am a woman of privilege. I am White, middle class, physically able, heterosexual, and university-educated. These sources of privilege have protected me from many of the sources of oppression common among those who are labelled with mental illnesses. I have never experienced the distress of having nowhere to live, no income, no support system, and no food to eat. I believe it is primarily because of these sources of privilege that I have had mostly satisfactory experiences with mental health services, and have successfully used these experiences to support those experiencing mental health challenges similar to mine. As a result, it is necessary for me to constantly remind myself that others without such sources of privilege experience the system from a much more disadvantaged position and thus often have less satisfactory experiences. The simple state of shared mental health experiences, then, does not necessarily lead to similar experiences of the system in which one receives support; it is impacted by a myriad of other factors, including our social locations. The story I will tell presents some challenges in keeping this awareness at the fore.

The sources of my privilege also impact upon my positioning within the mental health system. They allow me the automatic respect from professionals that usually comes with them — respect that may become diminished if someone learns of my mental health status, but respect that comes with being able, in most professional situations, to "pass." They also, however, separate me from many who are labelled with mental illnesses; as a result, what may be considered insider knowledge in many ways comes from the outside as well — the privileged outside. In the story that follows, this rather ambiguous positioning creates conflict for me as I try to determine with whom I will align myself, experimenting with which aspect of my identities will take the lead in my choices about behaviour. We all have various identities forming us and make decisions, however automatic they may seem, based on our understanding of situations and our previous experiences of others' reactions to our choices. As will be seen in the example from practice that I present, in order to sensitively support someone, I needed to change my choice regarding which aspects of my identity were leading my behaviour.

Before sharing my story, I will provide some background on users of service who are also providers of service in the mental health context. This discussion is framed through the theory of Anthony Giddens (1984, 1993), a British sociologist, who identifies that the relationships into which we enter (what Giddens calls "the system") are affected by certain taken-for-granted rules and the resources available (what Giddens calls "structure") *and* that these relationships can also affect the rules by interacting in ways that challenge them. For example, the characteristics of the mental health system, as described below, form one part of a structure that both constrains and enables the relationships (or systems) within it. Another example of structure constituting these relationships is the conceptualization of valued knowledge in social work: that professionals have traditionally been accepted as the experts who control the knowledge base of the profession (Grant, 2004). Examining a practice experience from this theoretical perspective requires us to consider that having insider knowledge about a structure may, in fact, give us important sensitivities to the relationships (system) constituting that structure. Giddens (1984, 1993) in fact, recognizes this ability of insiders to better understand or *penetrate* the system. Giddens notes that those who do not have this insider understanding often reproduce relationships in a non-reflexive way that maintains the structure (or rules). This recognition that those experiencing a structure have insight into its workings helps me to better understand the role that prosumers may bring to mental health services: sharing this insider perspective with others who may have a less nuanced understanding of the power relations within it in order to augment their understanding of their roles. My hope is that the reflection I demonstrate in my practice example will encourage all of us to reflect on those times when we non-reflexively reproduce relations of power and to discover ways to challenge oppressive structures.

SERVICE USERS AS SERVICE PROVIDERS

It has long been accepted practice for those who have received services in fields of helping related to hearing and vision impairment, HIV, substance abuse, and spinal cord injuries to be employed within the field of their own struggles. It is, however, a newer development in the field of mental health (Carlson, Rapp & McDiarmid, 2001; Chinman, Rosenheck, Lam & Davidson, 2000; Moxley & Mowbray, 1997; Solomon & Draine, 1998; Zipple et al., 1997). Some authors (e.g., Carlson et al., 2001; Cavanaugh-Daley, 1997; Mowbray & Moxley, 1997) contend that, having experienced mental health services, one brings to mental health support greater empathy and understanding of issues and experiences, and that these qualities lead to a greater ability to build trusting relationships with other psychiatric survivors. I agree with these contentions — these qualities are abundantly important.

The important contributions of prosumers in mental health, though, are also evident beyond this relational interaction. Understanding them requires dissolution of the traditional artificial dichotomy in social work between micro and macro practice by understanding that our relationships constitute and are constituted by our structures. Because we bring an intimate knowledge of the mental health system, different than that of most professionals, prosumers can offer leadership to the system by drawing attention to the importance of understanding and reflecting on the impact of structure on the relationships we enter while envisioning the impact on structures that our relationships can have.

A discussion of critical use of self in social work requires recognition of the particular structures, or rules and resources, of the context within which we practise, as well as the system, or reproduced relations. Prosumers can supply leadership toward integrating this macro perspective within the mental health context because of our intimate acquaintance with the mental health system. The next section will discuss the context of the mental health system and particularly its rules, resources, and relations.

THE MENTAL HEALTH CONTEXT

Paul Carling (1995), in his examination of the past, present, and future of mental health services, and Harvey Simmons (1990), in his review of the history of Ontario mental health policy, present narratives of change within the mental health system. In the first half of the 20th century, according to Carling (1995), North American mental health systems focused on protection of the community from those labelled with mental illness; thus, separation from society via institutionalization was the primary response. Finding itself the battleground for the struggle for legitimacy of psychiatry, mental health treatment became increasingly medicalized as psychiatrists fought to establish their specialty as a legitimate medical practice (Simmons, 1990). Psychiatric "hospitals," offering little more than custodial care (Carling, 1995), were established and various medical interventions were experimented with (Simmons, 1990). Medical professionals, led by psychiatrists, defined the nature of mental illness as well as its treatment and prognosis. The prognosis was poor: Those diagnosed with mental illness were expected to spend a bleak life of dependency on medical treatment and public financial support (Carling, 1995). Thus, treatment, for the most part, focused on management of behaviour (Simmons, 1990) and separation from the community.

In the 1960s, as the incarceration of those with mental health issues became a financial burden and new psychotropic medications made those labelled as mentally ill seem much less threatening (Simmons, 1990), both Canada and the United States began to experiment with ad hoc deinstitutionalization (Carling, 1995; Simmons, 1990). Although at the outset (and I would argue at the present), neither country was prepared for the sudden release from institutions of individuals taught to be dependent on institutions (Simmons, 1990), eventually a continuum of community services was developed (Carling, 1995). Rather than maintaining the role of the mental health system as simply providing custodial care, the emphasis of service changed to rehabilitative care (Carling, 1995). Slowly, more services emerged, and a myriad of professional groups, from case managers to vocational rehabilitation workers to mental health workers to residential support workers, became involved in the care of those diagnosed with mental health issues. Social workers have become the most highly represented professional group in the community mental health service system (Dewees, 1999). This proliferation of professional supports is undoubtedly viewed by many as an entirely positive outcome. A prosumer perspective, though, may help to underline its drawbacks. While the network of people involved in a psychiatric survivor's life broadened, life in the community came to mean, for many with severe mental health difficulties, life surrounded by paid support people (Carling, 1995), with little value given to establishing natural support networks. Thus, professionals appropriated a great deal of influence on the lives of survivors. My experience as one of those *surrounded* as well as one of those *surrounding* is that the professional, especially the medical, view retains the power in this network. While we speak of self-determination and empowerment in our current community mental health service system (Carling, 1995; Nelson, Lord & Ochocka, 2001), the centre of our medicalized system continues to be the professional (Carling, 1995), especially the psychiatrist. Those who comply with the demands of these experts are considered to be the "good" patients and clients, while those who assert their independence more frequently are labelled as "resistant" or "incompetent" (Carling, 1995; Colom, 1981).

A review of current Ontario mental health legislation confirms the assertion (Beresford & Wilson, 2002; Carling, 1995; Cook, 2004; Moxley & Mowbray, 1997; Rose, 1996) that the mental health system continues to perform a social control function: Assertive Community Treatment Teams provide "treatment" when it is not welcomed (Government of Ontario, 1999) and Community Treatment Orders mandate treatment in exchange for avoiding incarceration in an institution (Ministry of Health and Long-Term Care, 2000). Many lament the dependency created by the professionalized nature of our array of supports (e.g., Capponi, 2003; Carling, 1995; Cook, 2004; Cook, Terrell & Jonikas, 2004; Simmie & Nunes, 2001), even while the ex-patient or consumer-survivor movement is asserting itself and demanding that we allow survivors greater control (Capponi, 2003; Carling, 1995; Nelson et al., 2001). In many interactions within our mental health system, professionals make decisions *for* psychiatric survivors, create services that *professionals* decide will be helpful, and encourage dependency by determining survivor needs and directing the services that *professionals* establish to meet them. These interactions, rooted in an imbalance of power predicated on the constructions of professional knowledge as expert knowledge, create and support conditions, probably in most cases non-reflexively, that emphasize the dependence and need for control of psychiatric survivors. In short, they *reproduce relations* that both divide survivors from the rest of the community (Foucault, 1994a) and reinforce the power of professionals.

The above discussion is likely uncomfortable for those of us who provide service within the mental health system. It is uncomfortable for me. We prefer to talk about the successes and improvements made through adoption of a recovery framework (Anthony, Cohen & Farkas, 1990; Nelson et al., 2001) and through attempting to recognize the importance of self-determination and empowerment (Carling, 1995; Nelson et al., 2001). Undoubtedly, these successes and improvements are real. Those diagnosed with mental illnesses have more rights and make more decisions today than has ever been the case. We are also viewed with more optimism than the bleakness of the early prognoses.

There is much room to grow, however. As Giddens (1993) helps us to understand by noting our tendencies to reproduce relations, the system of relationships as described above is not intentionally harmful. In fact, I believe that it is the opposite: Most professionals that I have encountered in the mental health system truly want to help and likely truly believe they are being helpful. As Webb (2000, p. 2) states in an examination of social control in social work:

> Many, if perhaps most, uses of power in social work are intended to produce good ends, but this should not obscure the most important point that they are nevertheless uses of power, and as such, as a matter of good practice and not mere theoretical whim, should be critically evaluated.

Despite the impressive efforts of many mental health professionals to be helpful, the reproduced relations of power described above weaken the efforts that we make. The effects of dependency and social control created by our uses of power can be understood as the "unintended consequences of intentional conduct" (Giddens, 1993, p. 98) that Giddens discusses as the outcome of non-reflexive and repetitive relationships. We *intend* to be helpful, but the "unintended consequences" are that we control others and create dependency. Psychiatric survivors that I have worked with recognize that this dependency is not helpful to them. Further, in interviews with psychiatric survivors living in a shelter in the United States, Cohen (1998) found that none preferred an authority-based relationship; all preferred either a partnership or a relationship based on mentorship. Adding to our use of self by reflecting on our reproduction of relations has the potential to alter these relations and reconfigure them into more helpful ways of connecting, which in turn alters the dominant structure.

Those with an intimate insider understanding and experience of the relationships within the mental health system are in an ideal position to provide leadership for this reflection. It is necessary for prosumers to bring a high level of reflexivity to our work. As Mackey and Mackey (1994) report, many of those who have experienced similar challenges to those they support use their own experiences of service as a model for providing services. Considering the particular case of the prosumer in mental health services, this is a frightening prospect when we contemplate the lessons learned from receiving service in a mental health system as described above. In short, by receiving services from our mental health system we run the real risk of learning that support for those diagnosed with mental illnesses means encouraging dependency and controlling psychiatric survivors through a well-meaning paternalism/maternalism based on the assumption that professionals know best. This paternalism/maternalism, while well intentioned, has the unfortunate outcome of teaching those receiving services that they are not competent. Practitioner reflexivity is one way to mitigate this risk. Giddens (1984, 1993), by recognizing our agency, provides an excellent framework to guide this reflexivity. One approach to identify and then challenge the rules that shape our structures is to bring them to the forefront of our consciousness and to reflect on the meanings of our behaviours and assumptions in light of larger structural conditions (Kondrat, 1999). Building on Giddens's work, Kondrat (1999) argues for the use of *critical reflectivity* in social work practice to avoid reproducing, and to encourage challenging, undesirable structural relations. It provides an excellent extension to traditional formulations of use of self by encouraging us to consider not only the dynamics between practitioner and client, but also the effects of the context within which we practise, the rules we have learned, and the relations we are reproducing.

KONDRAT AND CRITICAL REFLECTIVITY

Kondrat (1999) argues that the reproduction and production of social structures that Giddens presents can be moderated through the use of *critical reflectivity*. Recognizing that we all have the potential, indeed are likely to reproduce social structures through unreflective practice, she suggests a way to become more reflective in our approaches to others. In her model, critical reflectivity mediates between the individual and social structures, creating a mirror for the individual's practical knowledge, or the assumptions guiding our actions, that can mitigate the reproduction of oppressive structures and thus reconfigure them.

If we can make more explicit the implicit knowledge we hold, which influences our actions, then we can identify the implicit knowledge that is guiding undesirable actions or outcomes and challenge it. Bringing oppressive conditions and their rules to consciousness and choosing to act in ways that are inconsistent with them allows us to dispute these conditions. Kondrat (1999, pp. 465–466, 468–469) presents some questions for a clinician to consider with the goal of becoming more critically reflective by examining the iterative relationship between structure and practice. Becoming more critically reflective, Kondrat tells us, involves a process of gaining awareness of one's self, of society, and of how they intersect: "… self-reflection is always a reflection on society and vice versa" (1999, p. 465).

A case example from my own practice as a community mental health worker will highlight the dangers of acting non-reflectively. It will also demonstrate the possible changes to practice, to systems, and to structures when one applies critical reflectivity to social work practice, along with the leadership possible by a prosumer.

THE ADMISSION DEBACLE[2]

As a community mental health worker I supported Tom, a 50-year-old individual diagnosed with schizophrenia. Tom was an intensely private person whose belongings were sacred; he always carried a large bag full of his personal items with him. Although he presented himself as an angry, abrasive, and loud individual, I also knew Tom to be generally frightened of most other people. He successfully maintained distance from others with his wall of protective fury. Tom's housemates were frightened of him and mostly stayed away, except for the occasional swearing matches when they had had enough of his violent verbal outbursts.

To me, there was intense sadness behind Tom's angry facade, and I was determined to let him know that I was willing to share in it if he chose; I took a supportive approach instead of the behaviour management and discipline that Tom's previous workers had used. Some would criticize this approach as one that had the potential to encourage lack of responsibility in Tom for his behaviour and one that put Tom's own self-protection at risk. Certainly, it rested on my assumption that accessing and expressing the pain behind Tom's anger would be an important step in his recovery, as it had been for me. This assumption had the potential to backfire, but I trusted my instincts, which led me to listen to the implicit messages I heard from Tom. I considered the fact that Tom had been angry and verbally aggressive for 10 years, resulting in a loss of support from, even connection with, any family, friends, or housemates. I noted the sadness in Tom's eyes and his hesitant attempts to connect with me in our rare moments of privacy—in my car on the way to his psychiatrist appointments (the only time I could convince Tom to leave the house and interact privately with me). In addition, I listened carefully to his complaints, and especially the ever-present "But you probably don't care," and perceived them as expressions about injustice rather than as "symptoms" of schizophrenia as others had. When he began his yelling, rather than immediately trying to stop it, I simply stood by and listened. While I was trying to understand, I noted that Tom fairly soon both lowered his voice and used less colourful language, which made it easier for me to hear his complaints about the ways in which he had been hurt by others. Many of the complaints Tom had, in fact, were also evident to me. By taking the time to understand them, I moved beyond Tom as an illness and toward Tom as a person, allowing me to see his suffering.

This approach very slowly began reaching Tom, and in tiny steps we began to form a tentative relationship. Did the fact that I had experienced intense sadness similar to that which I perceived in Tom enable me to recognize his presentation as requiring more than disciplinary intervention and to connect with him in a meaningful way? Considering the uniqueness of my approach, as compared to others who had worked with Tom, I believe it did. I believe that my experiences with the mental health system also helped me to understand the social control function that these disciplinary approaches reinforced.

After a year of improvement, life became somewhat more emotional for Tom, as he experienced some losses within tentative relationships he was reforming with his family. He found himself grieving intensely and believing that his housemates were violating him in various ways. His verbally violent outbursts increased and he stopped eating and sleeping. Finally, after I had made the suggestion several times, he asked me to help admit him to the hospital. Tom, understandably, was terrified. I was impressed by Tom's courage. I do not believe that someone who has not experienced the sense of relinquishing of control that comes with the decision to enter a psychiatric ward can understand the enormity of this kind of decision in the same way as those of us who have. If you have not experienced the powerlessness that comes with admission, it is difficult to understand the significance (and risk) of this decision.

Tom and I had called ahead to the hospital staff to arrange a convenient time for his admission and, at their request, we arrived at 4:00. We were directed to a room to await the nurse who would do the intake assessment, where we waited for what seemed like a very long time. I went to see what the delay was, and I was told that the nurse who was doing the intake had gone on a break and would be with us shortly. I looked at the clock. It was 5:45. We had been waiting for close to two hours. I went back to Tom, who was clearly becoming agitated and told him the news. He said, "Well, let's just leave then." I considered his suggestion, said in a half-hearted way, as simply an objection to waiting, and rather than giving it attention, I assured him that the nurse would be with us shortly and asked him to be patient. This response, I believe, was influenced by the fact that I was optimistic about the potential for improvement of Tom's mental health through an environment that could provide 24-hour support. I also believe that I was so happy that Tom had decided fairly independently to reach out for support that I wanted it to work out.

At 6:45, I returned to the nursing station and reminded them that we were still waiting. At that point I was told that it was almost time for a shift change and that it would be another half hour. I countered that it was unacceptable to expect Tom to wait any longer. Sighing, the nurse followed me to the room, and Tom let out a string of profanities, which sent her racing from the room. "You're going to have to calm him down," she told me. "I'm not interviewing him until he settles down." I explained to her the effect of the length of wait on Tom and the lack of respect it signified. After I spoke with Tom she reluctantly agreed to interview him if a psychiatric assistant could be present for her safety.

The nurse re-entered the room, saw Tom's oversized bag and said, "Why do you need all that stuff? I'll have to search it." A 15-minute battle ensued, with Tom refusing to allow her to touch his belongings and the nurse responding that they would be taken away in that case. I intervened several times, trying to explain to Tom the importance of safety and to the nurse the importance of his privacy. There was no compromise. Tom began bellowing and swearing, to which the nurse responded that she would not be present with him in that state. Once again, she ordered me to "settle him down." She also informed me in private that she was going to call the psychiatrist and have Tom committed. "This is a voluntary admission," I reminded her, "and there is no need for that to change." I implored her to ask the psychiatrist to allow Tom to keep his belongings, at least until he was more comfortable. I went back to Tom, who was in tears and pleading with me to take him home. I reminded him of his desire to come to the hospital and why, and tried to assure him that once the admission process was over, things would get better. Even though I was beginning to seriously doubt that, I continued, as explained above, to hold onto hope that this step in Tom's recovery would be positive. In addition, the ante had been increased, with the threat of an involuntary admission. I knew from past experience that one is treated with much more respect when an admission is voluntary.

"Please," he begged, "just get me out of here." Finally I "heard" him and realized I had been ignoring the primary player in this situation. I asked Tom to give me a few moments and I went outside to consider the situation. I thought about what I was doing and recognized an important dynamic. I was making the assumption that the hospital was going to be positive for Tom as it had been for me: that, like in my life, the pain and anger created by the perceived need for a stay in hospital and the repercussions of that would be outweighed by the eventual relief of overwhelming and painful symptoms. I was identifying with Tom, and this identification led me to make assumptions that related to the ways in which I had experienced mental health services rather than understanding Tom's experiences of services. This is an example of a traditional micro-level reflection that may be discussed in the use of self literature. I was using my experience to judge Tom's current and future experience. I had to remind myself of the need to focus on what Tom wanted and needed. My reflections, though, needed to deepen, and I had to also consider the situation from a macro perspective. I reflected on my place within the structure and system in which I was an actor. I asked myself some questions similar to the following, which are an adaptation of the questions that Kondrat suggests practitioners of clinical social work ask ourselves (1999, pp. 465–466, 468–469).

- What have I been taught about Tom's capacity to decide on his own "treatment"?

- Does the evidence uphold this teaching?
- How can I challenge these rules about who makes "treatment" decisions?
- What are the rules that contribute to the way I am reacting to this situation?
- How am I contributing to social control and dependency by my actions and words?
- How can I resist these dynamics?
- What have I been taught about the structure of the mental health context that is affecting the way I am interacting with Tom?
- How can I challenge this structure?
- How are these rules affecting the way I am interacting with the nurse, and how can I change that?

As I thought about the oppressive relations within the mental health system, I realized that I was adhering to the hierarchical relationships I had been taught in the medical environment by relenting to the nurse's demands and then recreating this hierarchy between Tom and me by ignoring his requests to leave. I was also acquiescing to that part of my social work training that separated me from the people I serve—in this case, I had aligned myself with the nurse and had upheld the view that professionals know best. Worst of all in my eyes, I was reinforcing the social control of the hospital by placating Tom when he was clearly telling me that he wanted to leave. I was acting on the erroneous assumption that I knew what was best for Tom and that my knowledge of the situation was somehow more valid than his. This was a clear reproduction of the assumption that those with mental health diagnoses are incompetent, and an action that encourages dependency and ignores the fact that those caught in a service system are able to penetrate and understand that system. Disappointed in myself, I returned to tell Tom that I realized I had been wrong to ignore his requests, that he had the right to make his own choices and that if he wanted to go, I would take him home. We discussed our experiences of our roles within the system and had a much more productive conversation after that about what he wanted.

STRUCTURATION THEORY AND POWER

My actions in this example demonstrate the dangers of acting non-reflexively. Until I reflected on the situation, not only was I using my own experiences with the mental health system to make decisions about Tom's potential experiences, I was reproducing oppressive social relations within the structure of the mental health context. By reinforcing the hierarchical relationships, disregarding Tom's ability to make his own decisions, and believing that I knew better, I was contributing to the dependency and the social control that the mental health system creates: I was reflecting (reproducing) as well as creating (producing) these effects. As Giddens (1984, 1993) points out, human agency means that we can always choose to act in different ways (Lazar, 1992). Once I took time to consider my role in enacting the structures that constitute me, I was able to choose less oppressive action. The questions I asked myself during this reflection directed my attention to the larger questions of the system and structures that constituted the nurse, Tom, and me. As a result of my reflection, and Tom's willingness to help me understand my role, Tom and I were able to collaborate rather than to compete for power over his well-being.

The above scenario portrays an example of our use of power over Tom. Giddens (1984, 1993) refers to domination as those moments when we achieve outcomes through affecting the actions of others. The nurse and I had both made attempts to dominate. The nurse had used me to achieve her desired outcome of restraining Tom. I had used Tom in turn to attain my desired outcome of his being treated for a mental illness. These outcomes were based on our solipsistic notions that the hospital would be a helpful place for Tom and on our reproduction of the hierarchical relations, based on our assumptions that we had the right to exercise our power over Tom. Exercising this power over Tom meant that we decided whose knowledge was valid and whose was not. As Foucault (1994b) says, defining which form of knowledge is legitimate allows those of us in positions of power to maintain these positions.

Power, Giddens (1984, 1993) tells us, can also be used in positive ways to change the outcome of events and to influence structures. This "transformative capacity of agency" (Giddens, 1993, p. 110) is the power social workers can access to advocate with and for those who use services, or to resist oppressive structures. Prosumers can use it to illuminate and challenge disrespectful treatment they and those they support have received. Determined to use my resources of power in a more positive way and to attempt to "intervene in a series of events so as to alter their course" (Giddens, 1993, p. 110), I met at a later date with the director of Inpatient Psychiatry to outline my concerns with the unfolding of events at Tom's admission (Tom declined to join me, but supported the meeting). From this meeting came a new protocol for admissions, including acceptable time frames for intake assessments. Power used in a transformative way made a positive difference in the admission process, as I came to experience in later involvement with others' admissions.

Discussions with my co-workers after this event highlighted for me the fact that having experienced the mental health system had given me deeper insight into the sequence of events than those who have not had this experience. It required quite a bit of explanation on my part for my co-workers to understand fully the harmful repercussions of my actions, the ways they reproduced the structure, and for them to be able to learn from my experience. I believe that many of my co-workers joined me in reaching a new level of understanding through my commentary on this experience.

The above scenario represented a turning point in my mental health career. I reflected on whether I wanted to reproduce social practices shaped by our structures or to utilize my unique position as a prosumer to positively affect both the individuals I was working with and the mental health system. After faltering by reproducing relations that encouraged dependency and enacted social control, I chose to act on the basis of critical reflectivity. It was at this moment that I chose to combine my insider penetration of the mental health system with my desire to be helpful to psychiatric survivors and to the mental health system. By reflexively honouring the knowledge I had of the mental health system and of the relationships within it, I was able to recognize my subjugation of another's knowledge. This illustrates well the applicability of Giddens's structuration theory and Kondrat's critical reflectivity to responsible social work practice that combines both macro and micro views and considers the helping relationship within the context of the structure. It was also at this moment that I realized my contribution as a prosumer: to examine and challenge, while helping others to examine and challenge the reproduced relations that constitute mental health services. Adapting Kondrat's questions to our own practice contexts provides social workers with one way to become more reflexive in our practice.

CONCLUSION

If social workers are going to make a difference in the support offered to those with mental health diagnoses, we must make a decision to examine our own "reproduction of institutionalized practices" (Giddens, 1993, p.

101). Adding reflexivity to our practice allows social workers to highlight for other professionals the deleterious effects of dependency and social control within our mental health system through reflexive critical use of self. Social workers who have experienced services are especially well positioned to do this: Having experienced these outcomes ourselves, through critical reflectivity we are clearly capable of recognizing when they are being reproduced and produced by ourselves and by our colleagues (Giddens, 1984, 1993). Further, we are positioned to demonstrate the importance of considering the context of practice in our reflections on our social work relationships. Neither of these comes automatically, and both require a process of critical reflectivity and a willingness to confront our own complicity in the reproduction of power relations. By noting that the "here and now" constitutes the structure, we can move toward more respectful relationships that challenge conditions we do not wish to replicate. Integrating a critical understanding of the contexts within which we practise and honestly reflecting on our own practice, the structures, and relations of the contexts in which we work and the iterative effects of them, social workers can extend traditional conceptualizations of use of self to positively affect rules and relationships.

NOTES

1. "Prosumer" is a combination of provider and consumer, signifying an individual who has both received and provided services. This term is not a commonly used one, but has been used by Frese and Davis (1997); Davidson, Weingarten, Steiner, Stayner & Hoge (1997); Salzer (1997) and its use has been noted by Solomon (2004).
2. The name of the individual involved has been changed, as has certain information that may be used for identification of the situation or of the individual.

REFERENCES

Anthony, W.A., Cohen, M.R & Farkas, M.D. (1990). *Psychiatric rehabilitation*. Boston: Boston University, Center for Psychiatric Rehabilitation.

Beresford, P. & Wilson, A. (2002). Genes spell danger: Mental health service users/survivors, bioethics, and control. *Disability & Society, 17*(5), 541–553.

Capponi, P. (2003). *Beyond the crazy house: Changing the future of madness*. Toronto: Penguin.

Carling, P.J. (1995). *Return to community*. New York: The Guilford Press.

Carlson, L.S., Rapp, C.A. & McDiarmid, D. (2001). Hiring consumer-providers: Barriers and alternative solutions. *Community Mental Health Journal*, 37(3), 199–213.

Cavanaugh-Daley, L. (1997). From patient to provider: The quest for equity in an unwilling world. In C.T. Mowbray, D.P. Moxley, C.A. Jasper & L.L. Howell (Eds.), *Consumers as providers in psychiatric rehabilitation* (pp. 279–291). Columbia: International Association of Psychosocial Rehabilitation Services.

Chinman, M.J., Rosenheck, R., Lam, J.A. & Davidson, L. (2000). Comparing consumer and nonconsumer provided case management services for homeless persons with serious mental illness. *The Journal of Nervous and Mental Disease*, 188(7), 446–453.

Cohen, M.B. (1998). Perceptions of power in client/worker relationships. *Families in Society*, 79(4), 433–442.

Colom, E. (1981). Reaction of an angry consumer. *Community Mental Health Journal*, 17(1), 92–97.

Cook, J.A. (2004). *Values and systems change in self-directed care*. Paper presented at the SDC Mental Wellness Conference, Orlando, Florida, June 30, 2004.

Cook, J.A., Terrell, S. & Jonikas, J.A. (2004). *Promoting self-determination for individuals with psychiatric disabilities through self-directed services*. Paper presented at the SDC Mental Wellness Conference, Orlando, Florida, June 30, 2004.

Craib, I. (1992). *Anthony Giddens*. New York: Routledge.

Davidson, L., Weingarten, R., Steiner, J., Stayner, D. & Hoge, D.A. (1997). Integrating prosumers into clinical settings. In C.T. Mowbray et al. (Eds.), *Consumers as providers in psychiatric rehabilitation* (pp. 437–455). Columbia, MD: International Association of Psychosocial Rehabilitation Services.

Dewees, M. (1999). Application of social constructionist principles to teaching social work practice in mental health. *Journal of Teaching in Social Work*, 19(1–2), 31–46.

Foucault, M. (1994a). The subject and power. In J.D. Faubion (Ed.), *Michel Foucault: Power* (pp. 326–348). New York: The New Press.

Foucault, M. (1994b). Truth and power. In J.D. Faubion (Ed.), *Michel Foucault: Power* (pp. 111–133). New York: The New Press.

Frese, F.J. & Davis, W.W. (1997). The consumer-survivor movement, recovery, and consumer professionals. *Professional Psychology: Research and Practice*, 28(3), 243–245.

Giddens, A. (1984). *Constitution of society: Outline of the theory of structuration*. Cambridge: Polity Press.

Giddens, A. (1993). Problems of action and structure. In Phillip Cassell (Ed.), *The Giddens reader* (pp. 88–175). Stanford: Stanford University Press.

Government of Ontario. (1999). *Making it happen: Implementation plan for mental health reform*. Toronto: Queen's Printer for Ontario.

Grant, J. (2004). Embracing an emerging structure: The employment of psychiatric survivors in mental health service delivery. Unpublished manuscript.

Kondrat, M.E. (1999). Who is the "self" in self-aware: Professional self-awareness from a critical theory perspective. *Social Service Review*, (December), 451–476.

Lazar, J. (1992). La compétence des acteurs dans la "Théorie de la structuration" de Giddens. *Cahiers internationaux de Sociologie*, 93, 399–416.

Mackey, R.A. & Mackey, E.F. (1994). Personal psychotherapy and the development of a professional self. *Families in Society* (October), 490–498.

Ministry of Health and Long-Term Care (2000). *Mental health: Brian's law (mental health legislative reform)*. www.health.gov.on.ca/file:file:/Brian's%20law%20overview.htm. Retrieved April 18, 2004.

Mowbray, C.T. & Moxley, D.P (1997). A framework for organizing consumer roles as providers of psychiatric rehabilitation. In C.T. Mowbray et al. (Eds.), *Consumers as providers in psychiatric rehabilitation* (pp. 35–44). Columbia, MD: International Association of Psychosocial Rehabilitation Services.

Mowbray, C.T., Moxley, D.P., Jaspar, C.A., & Howell, L.L. (Eds.). (1997). Consumers as providers in psychiatric rehabilitation. Columbia, MD: Internatiional Assoication of Psyhcosocial Rehabilitation Services.

Moxley, D.P. & Mowbray, C.T. (1997). Consumers as providers: Forces and factors legitimizing role innovation in psychiatric rehabilitation. In C.T. Mowbray et al. (Eds.), *Consumers as providers in psychiatric rehabilitation* (pp. 2–34). Columbia, MD: International Association of Psychosocial Rehabilitation Services.

Nelson, G., Lord, J. & Ochocka, J. (2001). *Shifting the paradigm in community mental health*. Toronto: University of Toronto Press.

Rose, N. (1996). Psychiatry as a political science: Advanced liberalism and the administration of risk. *History of the Human Sciences*, 9(2), 1–23.

Salzer, M.S (1997). Consumer empowerment in mental health organizations: Concept, benefits, and impediments. *Administration & Policy in Mental Health*, 24(5), 425–434.

Simmie, S. & Nunes, J. (2001). *The last taboo*. Toronto: McClelland & Stewart.

Simmons, H. (1990). *Unbalanced: Mental health policy in Ontario, 1930–1989*. Toronto: Wall & Thompson.

Solomon, P. (2004). Peer support/peer delivered services: Underlying processes, benefits, and critical ingredients. *Psychiatric Rehabilitation Journal*, 27(4), 392–401.

Solomon, P. & Draine, J. (1998). Consumers as providers in psychiatric rehabilitation. *New Directions for Mental Health Services*, 79, 65–77.

Webb, S.A. (2000). The politics of social work: Power and subjectivity. *Critical Social Work*, 1(2). www.criticalsocialwork.com/00_2_politics_webb.html. Retrieved April 27, 2004.

Zipple, A.W., Drouin, M., Armstrong, M., Brooks, M., Flynn, J. & Buckley, W. (1997). Consumers as colleagues: Moving beyond ADA compliance. In C.T. Mowbray et al. (Eds.), *Consumers as providers in psychiatric rehabilitation* (pp. 406–412). Columbia, MD: International Association of Psychosocial Rehabilitation Services.

CHAPTER 5

POWER AND STATUS CONTRADICTIONS

Paul Morrel

This is an exploratory account of the "divided self" experienced as a child protection worker, and the struggles encountered as I mediated between the institution and the client, fraught with the experience of feeling caught between the two. Often the work of child protection is carried out in isolation and the worker must engage in a juggling act to establish a balance between the mandate of the institution and the needs of the client. At the same time, striking a balance between the two often becomes elusive.

The power vested in the child welfare system enables child protection workers to help bring about changes in the lives of clients. The system is vested with legislated power and enacts that power along with policies and standards. For the purpose of this chapter I am defining the holder of power as the party or individual who has greater access to and possession of resources. The individual or party who has fewer resources is subject to the will of the party or individual who possesses, controls, or has access to resources that facilitate desired outcomes.

Margolin (1997), in *Under the Cover of Kindness*, states that, "one of the characteristics of power generally, is to hold the weak accountable for transgressing rules established by the powerful for their own advantage. Social Work's unique contribution is to get others, the weak and powerful alike, to agree that it is the weak who are acting inappropriately in situations in which they are dominated" (p. 123).

In the field of child protection, the use of language becomes a form of power; whether in written form or spoken language, it regulates how things are said, interpreted, and acted upon. Language gives relative weight to things, and thus becomes a very powerful resource. Margolin (1997) states that "social work frames its intervention in the language of helping, [and] it is freed from the responsibility of taking political position or performing political action" (p. 72). On the other hand, the specific area of intervention that we call child protection service often involves struggling families with multiple problems and because there is, according to Bishop (1994, p. 48), "power over" embedded in service delivery to these groups of people, social work controls the lives of recipients and creates roles of power and authority.

In child welfare systems, clients are expected to trust the agency, work co-operatively, and make all the changes deemed necessary to their lives; this gets framed as "client empowerment." However, should a client attempt to achieve empowerment in his in her own terms, and not comply with the prescriptions of Children's Aid policies and standards, then such a client is viewed as hard to serve, resistant, and non-compliant.

As a former child protection worker and an agent of change within this frame of reference, I was responsible for a diverse caseload, providing services to clients from different multiracial and cultural backgrounds with varying and multiple needs. Relying on the agency's mandated power vested in me, I was expected to promote changes in the lives of clients while promoting agency policies and standards, and upholding the legislative end of the Child and Family Services Act. The story I offer in this chapter of my work with one family highlights conflicts between client, institution, and worker. As the worker, I question whether I myself was empowered, or disempowered, or both at once. Or was it "token" power – which creates a status contradiction caused by a misleading perception of having power – intersecting with different statuses relative to shifting social identities? This example is intended to illustrate the interaction of the complex power dynamics between institution, client, and the worker's personal and professional selves.

The clients in this story are Mrs. Smith (45), mother of Mary (21), Peter (17), Casey (15), and Joan (13); Mr. Smith (47), father of Casey and Joan and stepfather to Mary and Peter; and Mary's four young children.[1] Mrs. Smith had limited education; her source of income was social assistance. Mrs. Smith's two older children were from her previous marriage. Mrs. Smith experienced difficulties early in her parenting, and her two older children were subsequently apprehended by Children's Aid and made wards of the Crown, with access to the parents. Mrs. Smith's two younger children are from her present marriage, and they remained in the home. Mr. Smith, college-educated, possesses good parenting skills, which facilitated his children remaining in the home. The Smiths did not believe in public education; they did not send their children to school, nor did they have a formal plan for home schooling registered with the Board of Education. The family did not believe in conventional medicine and took care of their medical needs through their own traditional home remedies.

Mrs. Smith's eldest daughter, Mary, had become a mother of four children by four different fathers, who were all on the periphery of this family. Mary had difficulty parenting as a single mother. Her source of income was social assistance. The four children were apprehended from Mary's care due to a determination of parental neglect, and made wards of the Children's Aid. The two-year period of society wardship was up for status review by the child welfare court. The Children's Aid recommendation to the court was for Crown wardship for all four children for the purpose of adoption. Mary disappeared from the lives of the children, and she was deemed to be incapable of parenting. Mrs. Smith, the maternal grandmother, learned of Children's Aid's recommendation to the court and decided that she would present an alternate plan for her grandchildren with the help of her husband.

The Child and Family Services Act for the province of Ontario (OCFSA) supports the principle of relatives presenting a plan to child welfare court to provide care to children under the age of 16. Section 57 (4) of the Act reads as follows:

> Where the court decides that it is necessary to remove the child from the care of the person who had charge of him or her immediately before intervention under this Part, the court shall, before making an order for society or crown wardship under paragraph 2 or 3 of subsection (1), consider whether it is possible to place the child with a relative … with the consent of the relative or other person.

However, when Mrs. Smith came forward with a plan to the court to parent her grandchildren, it came under the scrutiny of Children's Aid because of her own previous involvement with Children's Aid when she was a young mother. It would require great skills to mediate between the institution and Mrs. Smith in order to develop a plan that would be in the best interest of the children. Mrs. Smith's limited parenting skills were well known to Children's Aid and created concerns in the agency over her ability to care for four small children. Given these concerns, the court ordered that a court clinic assessment be done to determine Mrs. Smith's capability to care for her grandchildren. The recommendation from the assessment would assist the judge to determine whether or not it was in the children's best interest to be placed with the grandparents.

While the matter before the court was on adjournment, the worker who had responsibility for carrying the case left the agency abruptly. Mrs. Smith demanded that the new Children's Aid worker who would take on the case be racially and ethnically matched with her family. The previous worker, although not racially matched, had shared the same culture, and there appeared to have been a working relationship between the worker and the Smiths. As a person who originates from the Caribbean, I fit the profile of a racial match with the family, and my supervisor assumed that I would be culturally sensitive to the needs of the Smith family. Both the family and I are immigrants from the Caribbean, although Mrs. Smith is from a different island, while Mr. Smith and I are from the same island. Despite the fact that I was an intake worker and the Smith family case was a Family Services case, I was assigned responsibility for it. Management's instruction to me was that Children's Aid would go along with whatever recommendation would result from the court clinic assessment. As a representative of Children's Aid I would be called upon in court to present some evidence regarding the case. My role, therefore, was essentially relegated to "babysitting" the case. This limited role I was asked to take on necessarily limited my effectiveness as a child protection worker, and curtailed any independent decision making on the case.

The first problem that I encountered in taking over the case was that there had been no closure between the previous worker and client, there was no summary of the work done, and there was no introduction made between the family and myself. I entered into Mrs. Smith's life solely on the strength of shared racial and cultural heritage. My initial experience with Mrs. Smith and her family was one of inherent mistrust from Mrs. Smith toward me. Mrs. Smith's stated opinion was that the previous caseworker had intended to recommend that the children be placed in her care; this belief was, however, inconsistent with the recommendation put before the court by the previous worker. Mrs. Smith maintained that the worker was removed from the case on account of her intention to support the grandparents' plan, and that I was introduced to carry out the agency's agenda: to keep the children away from her. Unfortunately, I had no way of knowing what contractual agreement, if any, had been made between the previous worker and the family because of the incomplete documentation. I had to pick up where the previous worker left off and seek the best intervention point to begin the work with the family.

My role as case manager began to emerge as I handled the issues at hand regarding the misgivings and mistrust inherited in the case. I accepted the Smith family unconditionally for who they were, refraining from judging their unconventional social values, beliefs, and practices and I began the process of working with them. Mrs. Smith had powerful lingering feelings about her own prior experience as the mother of children who had been placed in the care of Children's Aid and were made wards of the Crown. Now she saw her grandchildren faced with the similar possibility of being made wards of the Crown. The difference this time was the threat of Crown wardship for the purpose of adoption. I made a conscious decision to take on a meaningful role in the case rather than act out the role of "babysitter." I adopted the role of a worker with a purpose and a clear vision of a desired outcome. As my role evolved with the family, it became necessary – if I was going to work toward getting closer to a plan for the grandchildren – to spend time exploring Mrs. Smith's feelings and the loss of her own children when they were made Crown wards. Through weekly talks, Mrs. Smith was able to mourn having missed out on her children's growing up. She began to focus on her desire to make things better for her grandchildren. It was that second chance that she wanted so badly: to rewrite her life, which society deemed a failure.

The context of my involvement with the Smith family included office visits, foster home visits with the grandchildren, visits at the Smith family home, and attendance at court. The level of contact between the grandparents and the grandchildren was court ordered. I assumed the role of supervising these contacts to facilitate smooth reintegration and to be of support to the grandchildren and grandparents in their interactions because the children did not know the grandparents. Supervising this interaction gave me the opportunity to observe and assess the level of comfort between them and the grandparents' capacity to parent. There were times when I had to intervene between the children and their grandparents and provide structure to the visits. For example, a day at the park proved it was too difficult for Mrs. Smith to handle four children: When one child took off on her, she went after the runaway and forgot about the other children. In that instant, I assumed dual roles – one to protect and the other to supervise – as I gathered up the other children and went after the escaped child and the grandmother. Mrs. Smith saw my interventions as manipulative and meant to sabotage the visits. Her interpretation was that I was determined to prevent the children from coming to live with her.

The children had a close-knit relationship with each other, and any inappropriate behaviour of one child could trigger the behaviour in the other children, and the children could become destructive in their behaviour and difficult to manage. Mrs. Smith found these challenges too much for her. On the other hand, the children had adjusted well in the foster home in which they were placed. The caregiver was very affectionate to the children. Mrs. Smith's grandchildren were the first to be placed in that foster home, and the attachment between the children and caregiver grew from the start. Steinhauer (1991) states that, "among the most important and developmental hazards faced by children within the child welfare system are those related to problems of attachment and separation, and to children's difficulty in mourning their losses" (p. 13). These children appeared to have done their mourning and it appeared they were now able to move forward and form a good attachment with the substitute parent.

Mrs. Smith's grandchildren had not been placed according to racial criteria, i.e., they were not placed in a Black foster home, which became a major struggle between Mrs. Smith and Children's Aid. Because I worked for and represented the institution, I got caught between the two. Mrs. Smith wanted the children moved from the foster home without appreciating the importance of the established bond between the children and the caregiver. The urgency with which Mrs. Smith demanded that the children be moved from the foster home showed a lack of understanding of the children's needs, and posed a threat to her wish to have her grandchildren returned to her by the court. It is my contention that the underpinning issue with which Mrs. Smith struggled was the fact that the caregiver's social location was very different from her own family. Mrs. Smith felt that because the caregiver's socio-economic situation was so very different from hers that the caregiver stood a better chance of adopting her grandchildren. I weighed the attachment between the children and the caregiver against racially matched placement. At that point in time, attachment was very critical in the children's development. I felt that because of their need for competent, affectionate parenting—needs that were not met in their own home—this was what was most important at that time. The difference in their foster family's race was, in my judgment, less of a priority. Saleebey (1994) states: "culture insinuates its patterns on us, and [those patterns] become embedded within us" (p. 352). I believe that culture is a way of life: it governs and dictates behaviour; it manifests in music, song, dance, literature, history of a people, and certain lifestyles.

Culture is what defines and sets one group of people apart from the other, and for these children it was important to be aware of their own cultural identity. I believed, too, that there were other ways in which the children could remain effectively connected to their cultural heritage without losing their beneficial placement. A plan was developed and adopted in the foster home to afford the children exposure to their Caribbean culture. The children maintained regular appointments at a hairdresser where they had their hair groomed in a traditional Caribbean manner; age-appropriate literature with Caribbean content was made available to the children in the foster home. The children were given toys that were representative of their culture, they attended cultural events, and they lived in an environment that was rich in ethnic diversity. They attended schools where there were other Black pupils, and they did well in that environment.

The children's progress and development became noticeable to all those who were involved, and those who provided treatment to them. Mrs. Smith was satisfied with the efforts that were made for the grandchildren to give them a good understanding of their cultural heritage, and the working relationship between Mrs. Smith and me grew to the level where we were able to work, talk, and plan for the children. Mrs. Smith's hostility toward Children's Aid and the caregiver dissipated over time, but this peaceful interlude would not last for long.

There was soon a twist in the relationship between the foster caregiver and me. As I made my assessments of the contacts between the children and their grandmother during visits, and as feedback about the grandparents' interaction with the children grew more positive, the caregiver feared that my recommendation would be in favour of the children going to live with the grandparents. The caregiver's contention was that because I shared the same racial identity and cultural heritage as the grandparents, I would be unduly sympathetic toward them.

There was no denying that there was an emotional investment between the caregiver and the children. She had invested time and energy into caring for these children, whom she treated not as foster children, but as children of her own. There was a sense of pride and accomplishment for the caregiver that she had nurtured these children to a level where they were able to function like children who had not experienced neglect. The caregiver was not prepared to give up these children without a good fight, and I was the one whom she fought with. There were two competing interests operating side by side, and those two opposing interests brought on a conflict between the caregiver and me. The caregiver's interest was to find the children a new family, different from and better than their family of origin. She believed the best family for the children was her own. My interest was buried in maintaining kinship ties; I wanted the children to be with family, a value that the CFSA recognizes in acknowledging the need to preserve kinship. From my vantage point, I saw the Black family breaking down and apart in the surrounding community; children growing up without having a sense of their identity, void of their history and heritage. My preferred outcome was for the Smith children to grow up in their own culture, and the best way I saw to make this possible was for them to grow up in their own family. However, I was not prepared to compromise their safety solely on the grounds of culture, and a middle ground would have to be sought where they could be safe even if it meant that they would not be able to return to their family of origin.

The level of confrontation between the caregiver and me grew to a point where management became involved in the case. The caregiver wanted to assume the role of case manager. For example, there were times when she denied visits to the grandparents, which was outside of her role, as these were court-ordered visits. There were also unprecedented meetings that went on between management and caregiver and from which I was excluded. The caregiver became instrumental and empowered as management seemed to take her side, gave in to her, and offered unscheduled meetings without informing me. This made me feel that I was excluded as a relevant party to case proceedings. I resented what appeared to be "back door" dealings between management and caregiver, which caused me additional frustration in the handling of the case. My reaction to what appeared to have happened in the case made me feel as if I was an outsider, isolated, and a loner; it further added to my professional disempowerment.

The power structure in the child welfare institution has always, in my experience, maintained a top-down approach in decision making and the dissemination of information. Management tried to give staff the impression that we were part of the decision making by engaging us in discussions when in fact management made the decisions as they saw them. This incident fit the pattern. Management was intending to make the decisions on the Smith family case without any client contact, and I was expected to carry out the instrumentals. I was led to believe, by virtue of my professional role, that I actually had "power," but at the same time, power was taken away from me. I often wondered if the case was given to me as a "test," and whether or not I did pass the "test." I was put in an awkward position, and one could easily perceive that it was "Black against Black." In fact, from Mrs. Smith's perspective, the fight was hers against the institution and its power; I became a small part of the equation when I was caught between the "client" and the institution.

An underlying theme that I struggled with was the issue regarding the agency's perception of my professional competence as a Black man. Management never acknowledged my skills, knowledge, and long years of experience in practising in child welfare. Therefore, the question that I still try to find an answer for is whether or not the institution knowingly tried to set me up to test how competent I was in managing cases that had racial components. Likewise, I wondered if the same would have been asked of a White worker: to assume case manager responsibility of a very complex case and be instructed merely to "babysit" in anticipation of the recommendation of the court clinic assessment.

The client's request to be serviced by someone from her culture was quite reasonable. However, what if the institution could not find a representative from the client's ethnic and racial background to take over case management responsibility? In this situation the institution can boast about its capacity to meet the needs of a diverse client population, and equal opportunity for workers from diverse backgrounds; however, I question how much of that stance is only lip service. As it turned out, race and culture became a wedge that caused a split between worker, management, and caregiver. In child protection it is often said that the worker wears "many hats." In this story it is more than wearing many hats: It is having different levels of consciousness, and identifying the need to relate to clients at one level, management at another level, other professionals at still different levels, and all the while maintain a sense of balance. It might indeed have been easier for me to relate to Mrs. Smith since both of us are Black immigrants from the Caribbean, and faced with similar social, economic, and adjustment issues. Similarly, perhaps there was a kind of gravitational pull between management and foster caregiver, who shared the social identities of whiteness and membership in the middle class. I was left feeling isolated, an outsider, and the "bad guy" until my assessment went along with the recommendation that the institution had put before the child welfare court.

For me to appear in child welfare court and speak to the recommendation that was before the court, I needed to gather information and make my own assessment, irrespective of the volumes of information contained in the record of Children's Aid. Both the caregiver and I had genuine interest in the children, and wanted what was best for them. An accord was reached between the caregiver and me, whereby it was established that in order for me to speak to the matter in court, I would need to carry out my own independent assessment. It was important that I remain neutral and non-judgmental, and collect factual data about the grandparents' parenting ability. Once role clarifications were established between the caregiver and me, we were able to function as a team working to achieve what was in the best interest of the children, and favouring to the grandparents was of less importance than the needs of the children.

During the early stages of my involvement, my assessment of the Smiths' plan to parent the grandchildren was that it would be satisfactory. However, as the court periods of adjournment (meant to facilitate the court clinic assessment) became lengthy, the Smith family began to show signs that they were not, after all, able to take on the role of parenting four small children who had special needs. The grandmother suffered physical and emotional setbacks and my support of the plan to have the grandchildren go to the grandparents began to wane. That influenced my decision to support the recommendation that was already before the court.

When I shared my assessment with the Smiths and informed them of my decision, I experienced what turned out to be the full force of Mrs. Smith's wrath and verbal abuse. The exposure to and first-hand experience of Mrs. Smith's rage sent me into flight mode. She moved through her house like lightning: Cupboards were emptied, drawers pulled out, things fell on the floor, and pieces of furniture were knocked over. Mr. Smith sat motionless while Mrs. Smith went on a rampage. Mrs. Smith resorted to calling me names that chilled my spirit, and forced me to examine whether the words used were an accurate reflection of me.

In *On Self and Social Organization*, Cooley (1998) writes:

"... each to each a looking glass, reflects the other part that doth pass. As we see our face, figure, and dress in the glass, and are interested in them because they are ours, and pleased or otherwise with them according as they do or do not answer to what we should like them to be; so in imagination we perceive in other's mind some thought of our appearance, manners, deeds, character ..." (p. 164).

I wanted the Smith family to see that I was one of them. Instead, I was told that I was a "Black man with a White man's heart"; "Uncle Tom"; that I had "sold out" and was "one of them"; that I had forgotten who I am, and from where I had come. I can still hear those words as if they keep step with me. Those words became a dagger that pierced my very soul, and I was wounded emotionally and spiritually. The wounded and divided self that I experienced at that point almost caused me to feel that there was no hope of redemption for me. I was not sure that I was prepared to pay the price required of me as a worker in becoming involved with this family.

I was able to maintain my sense of equanimity and worked through the racial tension with the support of a supervisor who was not directly involved in the management of the case. I became a member of a race relations and peer support group in my agency, which provided me with added support and where I, in turn, was able to offer support to others. The many years of experience that I had as a protection worker were an asset as I was able to share my experiences with new workers on working with difficult and hostile clients. Despite this, I concur with Kottler (1993), who, in his work *On Being a Therapist*, points out that the impact upon the therapist of working with clients can be powerful indeed:

> If we really considered the possible risks in getting involved with a client, we would not do so for any price. Never mind that we will catch their colds and flues, what about their pessimism, negativity, and psychopathology? You just cannot see somebody week after week, listen to their stories, and dry their tears without being profoundly affected by their experience. There are risks for the therapist he will not recognize until years later. Images stay with us until the grave. Words creep back to haunt us. Those screams remain deafening. (p. 8)

In retrospect, the risk of sustaining physical harm was very real when I informed the Smith family that I would not support their plan. I was very vulnerable: I was in the client's home with no added support, and no other voice to tell what might have happened to me, or what went on before to cause the outrage from the client. But on the other hand, it was evidence to share with the court about the grandmother's behaviour. Of primary concern was the safety of the children, who had special needs and demanded attention. They were very active children who could easily provoke someone like Mrs. Smith to outright rage when the need was for her to remain calm and attentive to their needs.

Mrs. Smith's anger and frustration were a response to the system that took away her grandchildren, placed them in foster care, and was about to make them Crown wards for purposes of adoption. I became an object to Mrs. Smith, a vehicle for the system to operate against her; in her words, I was "one of them" and her anger toward the system was displaced onto me as a representative of the institution. My way of dealing with the verbal and racially focused attacks on me by Mrs. Smith was to externalize the assault and tell myself that it was not meant for me but was aimed at the system; in so doing, I was able to carry on my work. I arranged to have visits between the grandparents and grandchildren shifted to the office. Mrs. Smith refused to attend at the office or to work with CAS, but remained committed to her plan for the children. Mr. Smith, step-grandfather, continued to attend visits with the children at the agency office.

I came to realize that people from the same racial and cultural background can appear to be just as racist as people from foreign or different cultures. I have difficulty internalizing and coming to grips with people who share identities of race and heritage, who have been marginalized and oppressed by mainstream society, themselves victimizing others who share the same culture. As a Black man from the Caribbean, I was told that I was a "Black man with a White man's heart," which was intended to destroy my sense of self. Mrs. Smith was saying that my allegiance and sensitivity was with the White world. She believed I could not understand what she was experiencing because the colonial past had shaped me to think White. Bishop (1994), in *Becoming an Ally*, states that, "we are oppressors in some parts of our identity, and oppressed in others" (p. 61). This concept is far more complicated than Bishop's statement of it sounds. I did not identify with the oppressor; I saw myself as experiencing oppression in a way similar to how Mrs. Smith might have perceived and experienced it. By virtue of my role as child protection worker, though, I was perceived to have power — or *should* have had; Mrs. Smith believed that I had power to make crucial decisions over her life and the lives of her grandchildren. From Mrs. Smith's perspective, that made me an "oppressor." She believed that as a Black man from the Caribbean, I should not be wielding that kind of power over my "own kind." However, what Mrs. Smith did not know was that at the same time I had actually been rendered powerless by the agency. The only semblance of power that I had left was to do what was best for the children. She perceived me to be part of an oppressive system that had caused her to suffer social injustices and disempowerment, and I was destined to experience her wrath. The Smith family struggle was bound up with my own struggle: We shared a racial identity and a cultural and historical past. Nevertheless, I was alienated by the family because of other status contradictions. The Smith family saw me as privileged, in a different socio-economic class, with higher income, education, and with better access to resources and power than they. In the larger scheme of things, I experience oppression by society just as much as they, or anyone else, through gender, skin colour, being an immigrant, or speaking with an accent. When I had worked across race with some White clients, I was told to "go and find your own kind." I had now been rejected by people of my own ethnic and racial origin, as well as by others.

My only way to proceed was to hang on to my identity as an ethical social worker. As such, my responses to client behaviour and situations are prescribed by the Social Work Code of Ethics, College of Social Workers and Social Service Workers, the institution's policies and standards of practice, and my own values. Although clients may have said hurtful words to me over time, I was still expected — and expected of myself — to carry out my responsibility with integrity and a sense of professionalism.

My legal and professional responsibility was to the grandchildren. It became clearer to me that they were my primary clients. I became the voice through which the children would speak, and I became an advocate for them. The grandchildren were at a level of maturity where they were able to give instruction as to their wants and wishes. My instruction from the children to the court was that while they enjoyed their visits with the grandparents, they did not want to live with them. The children wanted to live with their "psychological mother," the foster mother, and her family.

My challenge was to convey the children's wishes to the court and legal system when, in fact, the court clinic assessments recommended that the children be placed with the grandparents. Again, kinship ties between grandparents and children weighed heavily in this instance, plus the fact that the grandparents had never harmed the children. The grandparents were presented as teachable, and whatever parenting skills that were lacking could be ameliorated by their attendance at parenting classes in the community.

The lawyer for the children supported the grandparents' position, and did not take into account the instructions from the children. The challenges that I faced were many, especially coming from the legal system that was put in place to advocate and protect the desires and wishes of the children. The lawyer representing the grandparents used race in an attempt to discredit me as to how insensitive I was to the plight of the grandparents. The "race card" was played out at the highest level in court when the legal representative for the grandparents questioned my knowledge on the Zulu tribal system. The grandparents had made it their lifelong ambition to pattern their lifestyle after the Zulus. My education was rooted in the colonial system, and Eurocentric thinking was the order during that period. Afro-Caribbean culture and literature had not developed to its height, as it is today. My lack of familiarity with the Zulu caused me to be labelled by the council for the grandparents as indifferent to the grandparents' value system and beliefs. It would have been easier to "go with the grain" and agree with the legal representation that favoured the grandparents' wishes against those of the children. I was prepared, however, to be led by the children. I advocated on behalf of the children that they be made Crown wards for purposes of adoption, which was the Children's Aid original recommendation and later became my own independently reached conviction. I believe the granting of Crown wardship was the best outcome for the children. It provided them with stability, safety, and predictability, while keeping open the door for them to have some contact with the grandparents via letters. The foster parent presented a plan to the court to adopt the children. I supported the foster parent's position to adopt all four children. The plan put forth by the caregiver was the least disruptive to the children's lives; it would keep all four children together and would protect the bond between children and caregiver. In the Black community there is not a high demand for adoption of Black children as Black couples without children often seek to adopt within family, or sponsor relatives from overseas. The ages of the children were another factor, as most couples seeking to adopt prefer younger children with whom they can bond.

Out of chaos and uncertainty, a permanent plan was achieved for the children to be with their foster mother and her family. However, while the children are settled in the place they call home, and where they wanted to be, years later I find myself still struggling with the issue of Black children being adopted into White culture. The struggle is whether these children will have to go in search of their culture to find their true identity. As a professional, I often felt caught between the White power structure and the many clients with whom I share the same history and a sense of community, and wonder what it might be like for Black children who grow up in White culture to take on their own identity and experience the Black culture. The issue regarding Black adoption is thought-provoking and raises many questions, and for some of these questions, there are no wrong or right answers, simply judgment calls, which make striking a balance very elusive at times. Sometimes attempting to achieve this balance can cause deep personal struggles for the worker, as it did for me in this instance.

In conclusion, the struggles in this case were many. Some were very painful and unpleasant; some left deep emotional scars as I navigated between the many layers of power structures within the institution, the legal system, and other subsystems that impact human lives. I still grapple with my own status contradictions, being in a position of relative power and being able to facilitate change in the lives of clients. In retrospect, looking back on the many clients with whom I have come in contact, some lives touched successfully – and others not so successfully – I conclude that clients are the ones who make change to their lives, even when child protection workers come armed with mandated power in hand, and as enforcers of protection laws. I believe the balance of power still rests with the client.

NOTE

1.   All names are fictional in order to protect the identity of the individuals.

REFERENCES

Bishop, Anne. (1994). *Becoming an ally: Breaking the cycle of oppression.* Halifax: Fernwood.

Cooley, C.H. (1998). *On self and social organization.* Chicago: University of Chicago Press.

Kottler, J. (1993). *On being a therapist.* San Francisco: Jossey-Bass.

Margolin, L. (1997). *Under the cover of kindness: The invention of social work.* Charlottesville: University Press of Virginia.

Ontario Child and Family Services Act, R.S.O. 1990, c. C.11, s. 57 (4) p. 55.

Saleebey, D. (1994). Culture, theory, and narrative: The intersection of meanings in practice. *Social Work, 39*(4), 351–359.

Steinhauer, P. (1991). *The least detrimental alternative: A systemic guide to case planning and decision making for children in care.* Toronto: University of Toronto Press.

CHAPTER 6

ENCOUNTERS IN
SOCIAL WORK PRACTICE

Martha Kuwee Kumsa

TRYING OUT THE "USE OF SELF"

Rocky beginnings shook my early encounters in social work practice. My unshakable certainty in who I was and how I would relate to clients with unflinching empathy and utmost sensitivity to issues of power were put to trial from the very outset of my journey. I came to social work from a life tarnished by human cruelty and violence, but I came with the conviction that I would heal from my own wounds through helping others heal from theirs. It was not clear to me how this process of mutual healing might play itself out in actual practice. But I believed and still profoundly believe that the healing of Self is intimately intertwined with the healing of Other and whatever I do for Others is also what I do for my Self at one and the same time. Little did I know, however, that my firm belief in this solid Self of mine and how I would conduct it in relation to an equally solid Other would be so deeply shaken by my encounters in social work practice.

One of these early unsettling encounters was with a refugee woman. I will call her Claire for the purpose of this chapter. Claire's case grabbed my attention as I was going through the client waiting list of the feminist organization I was working for. From what I could piece together from bits and fragments of information on the brief assessment sheet, Claire was a refugee woman experiencing serious difficulties adjusting to life in Canada. She had seen the ugly faces of violence, death, separation, and loss. She was tortured, raped, and forced to witness the violent murder of her young son and husband. She did not know the whereabouts of her daughter. She did not even know whether or not her daughter was alive.

And she was having difficulty getting along with her youngest son, the only child and the only family she brought to Canada.

I felt deeply moved. My eyes welled as I pulled out her file and phoned Claire to set up an appointment. Surely she needed help immediately; she should not sit in that waiting list. Besides, Claire was a person with whom I felt I shared a lot and, therefore, with whom I could be deeply empathetic. My supervisor agreed that I would be the best person to work with Claire. I had no doubt in my mind — been there done that after all! I knew what it meant to raise estranged and traumatized children in a new country. I had experienced violence, separation, and loss. I had struggled hard in recapturing some of the lost meanings of life and in reconstructing a new sense of Self in Canada. I knew what it meant to be uprooted and dislocated. I knew what it meant to lose total control over one's own life and body. I knew what it meant to feel utterly helpless. But I also knew what it meant to feel hopeful and trusting once again. Who could be a better social worker?! My supervisor had repeatedly reassured me that I had everything it took to become a caring and empathetic social worker. The only thing she warned against in this case was the possibility that I might overidentify with Claire and lose objectivity.

I took my supervisor's warning to heart and repeated to myself that, although Claire and I had gone through somewhat similar predicaments, she would still experience them differently. I promised myself to honour Claire's uniqueness as an individual. I reflected on my own experiences and took deeply reflexive notes to help me provide detached empathy. To attune to her generic reality without falling into the trap of stereotyping, I did background research on the history, culture, and politics of Claire's former country. I attempted to minimize the weight of my institutional and professional power by using several strategies. First of all, I booked an appointment with Claire on her terms. Instead of asking her to come during regular office hours, I stayed behind my colleagues after work to make my services accessible to her. True to my training, I also reflected and self-talked to conduct my Self with utmost humility and respectful curiosity. Anticipating that Claire might be intimidated by my institutional and professional power inscribed in the physical setting of the office, I moved the chairs around and removed some barriers to effective communication. In short, true to my commitment to social justice, I attended to the repressive forms of power that might turn the helping and caring relationship into a space of further oppression and targeting of the refugee.

I went to the lobby well ahead of time and spotted Claire the moment she came through the door. When we booked the appointment on the phone, Claire and I had exchanged details of individual signifiers that two strangers needed to recognize each other from among a crowd. But, as it turned out, Claire and I were neither individuals nor strangers. I approached her and asked if she was Claire. She was indeed. I told her I was Martha. A flash of recognition flickered and almost as automatically a cold curtain descended between us. It seemed to me that Claire was literally taken aback. I thought I saw horror in her eyes as her body pulled away from mine. Perhaps I reminded her of somebody untrustworthy. I could relate to that experience very well. I knew trust was a major issue for traumatized refugees. I smiled sweetly, hoping to dispel the contagious unease I too was beginning to feel. "I came to see Martha," she said. "I'm Martha. We talked on the phone the other day, remember?" I said. "Martha the social worker!" Claire snapped back. "I am Martha the social worker!" I insisted. Claire looked away. I followed her gaze as it landed on the woman cleaning up the messy winter floor. Something hit me. My knee-jerk reaction was to hit it right back, but I wasn't sure what hit me and I had no time to reflect on or process it. Instead, I pushed it down and focused on maintaining the sweet smile I had initiated. "The counselling office is upstairs. Would you like to come?" I asked bluntly. Claire followed me reluctantly.

Back in the office, I let Claire choose where to sit and I sat on one of the chairs she left empty. I did my ritual of a well-rehearsed role clarification, talked about confidentiality, and praised Claire for taking the courageous step to seek help and to actually come in on a cold winter evening. I stated matter-of-factly that this was an opportunity for her to check me out; that nothing was carved in stone and if we were not a good match, she could try other counsellors who would be very happy to work with her. I had sensed her hesitation and wanted to get across the clear message that she was not stuck with me. Claire sat through it all nodding, but without initiating much or consenting to our working together. I guessed and second-guessed at the possible meanings of Claire's silence. I let the silence dance in the space between us for quite a while. But instead of providing space for making sense and understanding, that silence enhanced the cold discomfort I felt earlier. In my own silence I took a quick peek inside myself and found that I was extremely eager to "help" Claire. I felt that perhaps I was pressuring her to consent to my services. Now, that would go against the grain of my own commitment since it would reproduce the coercive power of the violence Claire had lived. Attempting to curb my overenthusiasm, I asked Claire if she would like to think about it and call again. She felt relieved, or so I thought. She said sure, she would call back and jumped to her feet. My eyes welled once again. I felt a deep urge to scream: "Please don't go away with that pain!" I wanted to hold her. I was certain I could "help" her, if only she stayed, if only she came back. But something told me Claire would not come back. And she never did.

That evening, I locked the door and left the office, but I could not lock up the disquiet of the encounter in that office. I cradled it and took it home with me. I realized I was crying, tears streaming down my cheeks, but why? I knew those were not tears of relief or joy, but I did not know exactly where the pain was coming from. Was I vicariously experiencing Claire's pain? Was it the reliving of my own pain through Claire's pain? Was it Claire's rejection of my help? I was not even sure if what happened was a rejection at all. I knew Claire needed help so desperately or she would not have come on that cold and dreary winter evening. What did I say? What did I do to turn her away from the help she so desperately needed? I could swear to all the gods I knew that I conducted my Self appropriately for the situation. I could swear that I was warm in my welcoming. Whatever it was that made Claire reject my help, assuming that it was a rejection, it must have been what I did unconsciously. It could also be what I did not do or say! What was it that I failed to do or say that turned Claire away? Or could it be something totally beyond my control since I felt I was totally innocent? This last train of thought grew bigger and bigger in my mind as my reflexive eyes meandered back to the moment of tension when Claire recognized and misrecognized me simultaneously.

I knew there was some sort of a misunderstanding when Claire said she came to see Martha the social worker and looked away from me, but I didn't know where that was coming from. I knew something hit me when my glance followed Claire's eyes and fell on the woman cleaning the floor, but I did not realize the full depth of what that meant. For me, realization often comes long after I leave the situation and immerse myself in a quiet reflection. Too many noises distract me while the situation is unfolding — perhaps the long-term effect of my own traumatization, people tell me. I went to bed with a heavy heart that night and the encounter kept bothering me far into the night. As I tossed about, putting back together and remembering the encounter, the light bulb suddenly went on! And I realized that I was not alone. An echo from other times and other places reverberated through the room. "I came to see Martha the social worker" and images of eyes roaming and falling on the cleaning woman — it had all happened to someone else before! It must be so widespread because I could hear it so clearly and loudly, almost word for word! Did somebody share an experience with me? I couldn't remember a face or a name. Did I read it somewhere? I jumped out of bed in the middle of the night and started digging up boxes of copied articles. I was sure somebody had named it before; I just couldn't find it in my pile of readings. What good was reading it anyway? I didn't heed it until I started experiencing it myself! Well, I told myself, tracing it is not important any more. I'm experiencing it now and I need to work my way through this now. Everybody experiences it differently, anyway. But one thing was clear. No amount of training in the "Use of Self" could have prepared me for the insights I gleaned from that encounter and the years of reflexive journey that followed it.

TOWARD AN ALTERNATIVE CONCEPT

My "Use of Self" crumbled on me when I failed to strike a helping relationship with Claire, but I did not know an alternative approach that would help me understand the situation, so I kept going down the same path time and again, trying to revive the encounter and develop it into a relationship. I called and left Claire several phone messages. She must have been astonished by my persistence, but she did not respond. Doesn't that make her a more stubborn person? It takes two to create a relationship, after all! I felt very angry and frustrated with Claire. A part of me was telling me this was a misplaced anger, but I couldn't place it anywhere else. Once again, I pushed it down and continued to play the kind and understanding social worker. I had other clients who needed help and were benefiting from the empathy I could provide, but for months, I continued to agonize over Claire's need for help. I brooded over the role I played in turning away a person in distress. I nagged my supervisor to check in with Claire so she could get help from other counsellors. My supervisor told me that Claire was in counselling in another agency closer to her neighbourhood. She reassured me that why Claire was not coming to our organization had nothing to do with the encounter; it had to do with Claire's choice and convenience. That may be true, at least partially, but I still had a sneaky feeling that my supervisor told me that story just to put to rest my raging anxiety. Claire still came in and saw me before she made her choice. My nagging question lingered.

When I was preparing to meet with Claire, I felt my healing Self was ready for the encounter. When I say healing, I mean to blur the transitive and intransitive aspects. That is, the blurring of my Self in the experience of healing an Other and my Self in the experience of healing Self. When I came to social work, I came seeking such a space of mutual healing through encounters with Others. In my understanding, the "Use of Self" makes the claim that there is a healer inherent within each individual, professional, or client. The role of the professional then is to facilitate the awakening of the client's internal healer. Healing itself is viewed as the process of making whole by integrating both the good and the bad Self. While I value such acceptance of Self, I would also like to move beyond psychological healing and conceptualize the process of healing as a process of social justice and liberation. Oppression is a form of violence that cuts deep wounds in people's sense of Self, whether that Self is individual or collective. Yet, this social wound cannot be healed by simple acceptance of the "bad" Self. Indeed, it perpetuates violence since "bad" is itself a social category constituting a social wound. Healing requires creating space for the mutual liberation of Self and Other through encounters of unlearning oppression. It requires an understanding that the healing of Self is intimately intertwined with the healing of Other.

When I was preparing to meet with Claire, I was confident that my professional Self was solid enough and ready to "take on" and "help" the client. Yes, it was a Self cultivated through critical introspection and sensitivity to power but, all the same, it was lurking there fully formed and readymade, waiting for me to just roll it out and "use" it. At least that's what my skills in the "Use of Self" prepared me for. I was particularly sensitive in how I could minimize the potentially oppressive power vested in my professional Self. After the encounter with Claire, however, I found that even the most critical versions of the "Use of Self" were deeply flawed when it comes to the formation of the subject. Yes, they address the repressive power that oppresses, but what about the creative power that produces identities and subjectivities? What about the power that continues to produce new subjectivities through encounters in social work practice? Yes, they dig deep into the biographies of Claire and Martha, but what about their relational histories and historicities? Yes, they assume pre-existing identities of "the professional" and "the client," but what about the social processes that produce these identities in the first place? Yes, I can be reflexive and try to minimize my oppressive power once a helping relationship is put in place, but what about the power that creates the relationship itself?

The helping relationship does not drop from the sky, nor does it happen in a vacuum. Historicizing "the professional" and "the client" shows that the same historical processes that produced multitudes of the dispossessed also produced the profession of social work at one and the same time. One does not exist without the other. Both historically and in the here and now, then, the helping relationship is necessarily a relational process whereby both the professional Self and the client Other are produced simultaneously. I am not a professional and Claire is not a client until we both take part in co-creating the helping relationship. We are mutually constitutive and become professional and client only as we mutually create and simultaneously are created through the very helping relationship we co-create. Our subjectivities come into being only through the encounter and last only as long as the encounter lasts. After that, it is only the traces of the encounters that we hang on to—as I am now remembering and hanging on to the traces of the encounter with Claire many years after it had happened. Yet, remembering is never a quiet act of introspecting and retrieving a memory neatly tucked away in the past. Remembering (and forgetting!) is a deeply constitutive work of putting together that very past in a new way to meet the needs of our subjectivity now. Remembering is a labour of constructing the newest subjectivity of the fleeting present.

Attending only to oppressive power and neglecting to weave in the creative power that produces a multiplicity of subjectivities, we risk reproducing "the professional" and "the client" as mutually exclusive monolithic categories of the powerful and the powerless. This view assumes that power is vested in me as the professional and that Claire is powerless as the client. It does not take into account the power that produces Claire as a Subject, thus enabling her to choose or refuse help. Nor does it address the power that produces me as an Other, thus disabling me from making some choices. Nor does it address the possibility that individual choices are mediated by processes beyond the individual and that there are no pure undetermined choices. Power does not exist in an empty professional vessel called the professional Self. Power exists only when it is exercised. Outside practice, power is meaningless; it is only a potential waiting to happen. In this encounter, my professional power was rendered meaningless the moment Claire refused to submit her Self to the relationship. No amount of my solo preparation or professional readiness could produce the helping relationship that must happen only through the mutually constitutive labour of the social worker and the client.

Yet, the "professional" and the "client" and, indeed, the generalized Self and Other are not created in a vacuum. They happen in the context of webs of power relationships producing multiple other subjectivities that mediate encounters and criss-cross in helping relationships. When a boundary is drawn to define Self, what is left on the constitutive outside becomes the territory of the Other. Self and Other are thus produced and reproduced simultaneously. And this holds whether Self and Other are individual or collective. Indeed, there is no individual without the collective and no collective without the individual as the two are so intimately intertwined. By assuming an individual Self, however, the "Use of Self" masks the social relations through which Claire and I were simultaneously produced both as individuals and as collectives. But, when Claire and I met, it was not two strangers who met; it was two deeply ingrained relational histories that met. Embodied non-verbal communication of centuries of history took place in that split second when Claire simultaneously recognized and misrecognized me. Ages of values and beliefs were distilled and crystallized into just one glance in that split second. They are internalized, embodied, and deeply woven into our sense of Self, but they are also placed beyond the grasp of our consciousness. Invisible they may be, but they determine our choices and shape our likes and dislikes at the most mundane level of everyday living, including our professional encounters. Encounters make them visible through emotions like shame and guilt, shock and disbelief, love and happiness. For me, then, the social origins of such encounters are what are missing in the "Use of Self."

Whither the "Use of Self" then? I have repeated the term "encounter" enough times that my preference seems obvious. Yet, it seems to me that a word or two is in order to develop "encounter" as a concept. For this, I draw on Ahmed (2000). She develops the term "encounter" as a concept in the context of the post-colonial Self and Other. Yet, it seems to me that it is a generic enough concept that works so well in the context of the encounters between the social worker Self and the client Other as well.

Indeed social work practice is a space of constant encounters between Self and Other in their multiple criss-crossing subjectivities. Encounter makes visible social processes through which Self and Other are mutually constituted and intimately interwoven. It suggests a meeting of Self and Other that is only partially determined and remains full of surprises. Encounter hesitates between the one and the many (the individual and the collective), the particular and the general, the conscious and the unconscious, the past and the future. I see social work practice as encounters between social actors with multiple subjectivities who continue to mutually constitute each other throughout the helping relationship.

The journey is filled with colourful surprises and discoveries each time unfolding subjectivities criss-cross and interweave. Encounter addresses the multiplicity and fluidity of Self and Other so well. Also, rather than examining some inherent Self or Other, encounter focuses the emphasis on the interaction between the two. That is, it breaks down the oppressor/oppressed binary and focuses attention on the oppressive relationship, thus disputing essence and making visible the relationality of oppression. The following quote so eloquently explains my encounter with Claire.

> If encounters are meetings, then they also involve surprise. The more-than-one of such meetings that allow the "one" to be faced and to face others is not a meeting between already constituted subjects who know each other; rather the encounter is premised on the absence of a knowledge that would allow one to control the encounter or to predict its outcome.... [I]n doing so, they shift the boundaries of what is familiar. Encounters involve both fixation and the impossibility of fixation.... [W]hen we face others we seek to recognize who they are, by reading the signs on their body, or by reading their body as a sign.... [S]uch acts of reading constitute the subject in relation to the stranger, who is recognized as out of place in a given place.... The encounters we might yet have with other others hence surprise the subject, but they also reopen the prior histories of encounter that violate and fix others in regimes of difference.
>
> Encounters are meetings, then, which are not simply in the present: each encounter reopens past encounters. Encounters involve, not only the surprise of being faced by an other who cannot be located in the present, they also involve conflict ... requires that we consider the relationship between the particular — this encounter — and the general.... [H]ow the particular encounter both informs and is informed by the general: encounters between embodied subjects always hesitate between the domain of the particular — the face-to-face of this encounter — and the general — the framing of the encounter by broader relationships of power and antagonism. (Ahmed, 2000, p. 8)

SOCIAL WORKING WITH REFUGEES

It is this spirit of encounters that I take into examining my social working with refugees. I use social working in its active and processual form to dispute a professionalized and frozen identity and to release its creative energy into the encounters of Self and Other. Now that I have mapped out social structural factors that mediate helping relationships, I can turn to examining the ugly underbelly of my own social working. In the above pages, I painted a saintly picture of my Self — so kind and empathetic, so self-righteous. Well, except that I felt a deep urge to project my good Self, I know I am not that saintly person. Looking deep inside, I see a landscape full of embarrassing surprises. I also painted a rosy picture and romanticized the notions of surprises and encounters. Yes encounters of Self and Other are full of surprises, but some surprises involve facing deeply hidden faces of Self and Other. Especially hard is the experience of facing an oppressor Self. Sometimes surprises involve bitter hurts and pains. Sometimes the shifting of the familiar is not a comfortable journey. Indeed, many a time, the personal growth that comes out of encounters comes at a cost. But it is growth and blossoming nonetheless. The surprises I share here are only the ones I have been able to process and embrace. I find other surprises that still hurt not amenable for sharing at this point.

I will start with the now familiar encounter with Claire. Please note that what I share here may not be how Claire sees the encounter; it is how I interpret it from my very specific location in the webs of power relationships. In this encounter with Claire, our multiple criss-crossing subjectivities were thrown into a sharp profile the moment we faced each other. I will name just the most relevant ones. Claire was a refugee from an East European country. She was White. She was a potential client. I was a refugee from an African country. I was Black. I was a potential social worker. Claire said she came to see Martha the social worker and looked away from me to the cleaning woman. I felt a jolt. My racialized Self was peering at me from the face of the Black woman cleaning the floor. My Black face was peering at Claire from a space that belonged to a social worker. In that instant, the familiar shifted for both of us and we were both surprised. Claire did not expect Martha the social worker to be Black. I did not expect to see my Self as a cleaning woman. There was "an absence of knowledge that would allow us to control the encounter or predict its outcome." We had to "read signs on the bodies and bodies as signs" to recognize Self and Other. For me, Martha the cleaner was a body out of place. For Claire, Martha the social worker was a body out of place. We both pulled our bodies back, away from the strangers, away from the bodies out of place.

Yet, this encounter was not an isolated encounter unfolding just on its own. It was an echo of other encounters from other places and other times. It was a reopening of prior histories of encounter. It was a particular encounter informed by the general informing back the general. Our surprises at what we saw as bodies out of place come from our prior embodied knowledge, knowledge deeply ingrained through other encounters in other times and places. While this encounter claims fixity in this sort of continuity, in its own particularity, the encounter itself has already interrupted that very fixity and shifted the territory of the familiar. This interweaving of the particular and the general makes visible the interweaving of the individual and the collective. Surely Claire and I were not relating just as individuals but as embodied histories of collectivities as well. So this was also an encounter between relational histories of generic Whites and Blacks and of the poor and the middle class, to name but a few. In the absence of this new territory of knowledge, at the time of the encounter, the assumption was that Claire and I were two full-blown solid individual strangers coming together to create a helping relationship. Gleaning from this analysis, Claire and I were neither individuals nor strangers.

If I could put to words the jolt I felt at Claire's misrecognition of my professional Self, it would say: "How dare you insult my professional Self!? You are a mean-spirited racist!" I felt I was symbolically relegated to the role of a cleaning woman and that was a terrible assault on my professional Self. That must have been what hit me in the face and what I must have pushed down in utter disbelief. I felt it repeatedly as I tossed about in my bed far into the night. Again, I kept pushing it down repeatedly. I felt rejected not because of my professional inadequacy but because of who I was. It must have been so hurtful that I needed to "forget" and erase it out of existence. I felt resentment and anger toward Claire. But, this too, I pushed down immediately. How could I harbour such a cruel thought toward a woman experiencing serious difficulties? I couldn't berate my Self enough for that thought. My empathy for Claire and her need for help towered above all feelings and I embraced it dearly. That was what I felt when I was phoning Claire and nagging my supervisor. Claire needed help!

Submerged and hidden beneath all these talks of kindness and empathy, though, were other voices silently narrating my most embarrassing encounters with my oppressive Selves. The first was how, in my desperate bid to elevate my disparaged professional Self, I was, in turn, disparaging my cleaning sister's worker Self. It was so embarrassing and disgusting to realize how my body was shrinking away from her in fear and disgust, so the contagious germ of contempt would not get to me. The tears I shed on my way home that evening must have been tears shed to wash away that contagion. It must have been to cleanse my professional Self that almost got lumped and thrown together with that worker Other. It was my privilege that was hurting so badly. Intertwined with this is another submerged narrative of privilege. Recall how many times I repeated how I wanted to "help" Claire, how I wanted to create a "helping" relationship, how Claire desperately needed help. "Help" is such a nice sounding word too. It was so easy for me to indulge in it. That must be why the profession appropriated the word — to obscure its own function of control. Helping an Other, especially an Other that hurt me, makes my hurt Self look very good. Taking a peek inside, however, I found my hurt privilege desperately seeking revenge. Claire refused to submit her Self to my services, but I so desperately wanted to subject her to those very services. I would scream to her, "Did you think your White ass was too good to lower itself to a Black professional? Here is how I can help you with a competence far beyond your imagination!" Yes, indeed Claire needed my help and I needed to rub it in so that my professional Self could be elevated.

To further complicate the matter, there is a flip side to this need for help. Whose need is this need for help? Who needs help so desperately? Was it Claire or me? I was going out of my way to phone Claire myself and was nagging my supervisor to call her. Why all this running around? If Claire didn't want to come in, then she didn't want to come in, period! Whatever happened to client self-determination? Claire knew her choices and she had chosen what she wanted. So what's all this fuss about? Surely more than Claire's needs are at stake here. Upon reflection, I realized there was another client who desperately needed help but turned away from it, rebelling and refusing help. Amazing how an encounter echoes events from other times and other places. This Other client was Martha the refugee who came to Canada, escaping years of torture and violence and was having serious difficulties getting along with her teenaged children. So it wasn't Claire that I wanted to help. There is a merger of Self and Other here! Claire was me! Claire the stranger was only my estranged Self, a Self Othered and forgotten.

I remember pouring out my soul and my counsellor sitting there and nodding warmly. I would tell her about the violence of oppression I was facing in the here and now; she would keep referring back to the violence I endured back in Africa. She would not even acknowledge people would be oppressed here. For her Canada is a paradise of peace where there is no violence. I would tell her how I long to belong here; she would tell me how difficult it must be that my place of real belonging was so war-ravaged and so far away. Several sessions of that and I was utterly frustrated. She would sit there nodding, telling me how she tried to understand what I was going through. It felt so hollow and phony. I sat there staring at her and wondering whether she knew anything about retraumatizing refugees. That's what the session felt like to me. No, I didn't have a feeling she knew anything at all. I burst into tears. I saw her face open up. She must have felt that she really helped me access and get in touch with some of my buried feelings and release some tied up energy. She kept saying, "I know, I know, I know," capping it with an empathetic nod each time she said it. She must have repeated it a hundred times. "Shut up!! You have no clue!!" I heard myself scream quietly inside. No word came out of my mouth. And I never went back. She called several times and left me phone messages. I didn't bother to call her back.

It's amazing how what goes around comes around! I can now understand why Claire chose not to come back to me. Of course she did not believe I could help her! While that does not take away from my suggestion that our beliefs and choices are shaped by wider inequities and power relations, it does implicate me in those same structures of power. However, with an activist background and rigorous social work training, I thought I would be armed with a sharp axe to go out into the forest of inequity and chop down all the trees! Perhaps that was why I was running after Claire — to do the job and do it right! That was why I was trained after all. If all the years of my professional training were not in vain, then my expertise needs to be put to practice. And that was why I was preparing for my meeting with Claire in the most ethically sensitive way available to me. But alas!

When I wanted to become a social worker, I vowed not to be like my counsellor. What I needed as a refugee was to heal from the wounds of the nation. I needed a nation to belong to. I did not come seeking the wealth of Canada. I came seeking a sort of respite from oppression. A refugee is a refugee because of the violent exclusion from the nation. A refugee longs to belong. I know what they mean when people call me a refugee years after I became a Canadian citizen. Refugee is a space of Otherness and exclusion, a space of perpetual unbelonging. I was certain I understood the refugee experience because I had lived and worked through it. To my chagrin, I discovered that, like all categorical identities, "the refugee" is also a contested territory heavily marked and deeply engraved by age, class, gender, race, religion, sexuality, and many other forms of social cleavage. To my utter chagrin, I found that even the space of my own intimate community of refugees from my own national background is mediated and shot through by multiple criss-crossing subjectivities of the wider society. Claire was not the only refugee that contested my professional Self. Members of my own community have also contested my oppressive practice. My encounters in community practice are equally rife with shameful surprises and embarrassing discoveries.

BEYOND CONFESSION: VICISSITUDES OF ETHICAL PRACTICE

I see two pitfalls in sharing confessions. One is that people distance themselves from it. It runs the risk of people pointing to me saying what a terrible person I am, rather than pointing to Self and reflecting on how this terrible Other might be their very Self. It is much easier to point to Others and say, "That's their experience; it has nothing to do with me." I have seen that happen time and again. True, everybody's experience is different, but there is a powerful continuity in that very discontinuity. As long as Self and Other are intimately intertwined, there are lessons for Self in the experiences of Other. That is my whole argument in this chapter or I would not have taken all the pain of mapping out some of the shameful territories just for the simple love of sharing my individual experience. The other pitfall of sharing personal reflection concerns my own Self as the narrator. Now that I have confessed, I can rest and relax. Now that this is off my chest, I can breathe easily. I have talked about it; I have done my duty, and that's it! Indeed, that is what I see in many well-meaning proponents of social justice. Well, that's not it! The social world is still immersed in webs of unequal power relations. Inequities permeate our lives. Confessing is excellent, but it is only a torch lighting the path of ethical practice toward healing and liberation. I will conclude this chapter by discussing what ethical practice means to me and how I believe it sits at the heart of healing and liberation.

But what is ethical practice in the first place? For me, ethics are not those cut-and-dried, one-size-fits-all standards of practice frozen into institutional and professional codes. For me, ethics are fluid principles brought alive and navigated within the surprising twists and turns of encounters. For me, then, ethical practice is calling to question those very frozen codes and particularizing their universalist claims. Ethical practice is locating those codes and positioning them within historical, cultural, and political specificities. Yet, ethical practice is not a rejection of continuities and generalities. It is a practice of navigating the interweaving spaces of the general and the particular, the collective and the individual, the conscious and the unconscious. Indeed it is a practice of making visible the fluidity of those seemingly cut-and-dried principles by making visible how the past is deeply ingrained and embodied in the rolling present and the anticipated future. And for me, this is what makes ethical practice a practice of justice, a practice of freedom from oppression. That is what makes it a practice of healing and liberation.

If ethical practice is a practice of healing and liberation, then, it involves a process of unlearning oppression. And a process of unlearning oppression involves rethinking and reconceptualizing oppression as a relational process of Self and Other. Unfortunately, both my activist experience and my social work training focused my attention on either Self or Other, either personal agency or the agency of social structures. When it comes to oppression, I was taught to look for the culprit either in the person or in the society. So, for example, racism was lurking in either the racist person or the racist system rather than in the relational processes of racialization. I was taught to locate oppression as an essence either in the oppressed or the oppressor rather than understand it as a relational process that is brought to life only through encounters. I now see why trying to unlearn oppression through the anti-oppressive lens of the oppressed/oppressor binary is like a blunt knife that doesn't cut oppression. Indeed, I see this essentializing binary as a system of practice put in place to perpetuate oppression. People embrace and defend these rigid, mutually exclusive categories with emotionally charged debates. Usually these debates are empty rhetoric, contributing more to perpetuating oppression than to unlearning it. To unlearn oppression and engage in the practice of freedom, we need to break down the frozen binary. We need to understand how oppressive relation shifts through the surprising twists and turns of encounters, how the interweaving of different subjectivities facilitates or impedes ethical practice.

In my experience, breaking out of this oppressed/oppressor aspect of the Self/Other binary requires an almost superhuman feat. I have attempted to initiate processes of unlearning oppression through encounters. I find, however, that both sides of the binary defend it with such an incredibly powerful emotionality. I have observed this both in my Self and in Others in the context of activism around human rights and social justice, in the context of liberation movements, in the context of community and clinical practice, in the context of classroom teaching and learning, and in the context of institutional social work collegiality. Those who consider themselves privileged and feel accused of being oppressors tell me how deeply hurtful my words are. Some totally deny their oppressor Self and pose as allies of the oppressed – even as they are deeply engaged in colonial and exploitative relationships with the very oppressed they consider allies. Those who see themselves as marginalized and feel they can never be oppressors tell me how I hurt them so profoundly by pointing out encounters in which they are oppressive to some Others. Some totally deny their oppressor Self even in the face of concrete and glaring examples. If they are oppressed, how can they be oppressors? They tell me if I am not with them as the oppressed, then I am with the oppressor. There are liberation strugglers and colleagues who totally avoid any kind of encounters with me because I want us to challenge ourselves in breaking down these absolute Self/Other boundaries.

Gleaning from such experiences, then, the biggest roadblock to ethical practice is this absolute sense of the binary relationship between Self and Other. Especially powerful is the denial of the oppressive aspects of Self as that is where people feel deeply hurt. Wearing our oppressed Self entitles us to self-righteousness whereas wearing our oppressor Self denies us these entitlements. Who wants to be seen as an oppressor? Thus, breaking out of the absolutist binary of Self/Other is only the first baby step since the denial of an oppressor Self needs to be tackled even in the context of multiple subjectivities within individuals. Oppressive relationships are deeply embodied and woven into our sense of Self. Perhaps that is why people feel deeply hurt and angry. In the context of ethical practice, though, we need to make a distinction between the anger of our oppressed subjectivities unleashed to right a wrong and the anger of our oppressor subjectivities unleashed to maintain privilege. Oppressive relationships are held together, put in place and defended through unleashing high emotionality.

For me, then, this marks emotions as targets for ethical practice. Encounters are scary for people because the surprises of facing an oppressor Self are so hurtful. Therefore, the tendency is to deny and fly away from the hurts and pains. The tendency is to repress and forget them. However, at least in my experience, forgetting or denying does not bring about healing or liberation. Forgetting is precisely what it is—forgetting and not healing. There are people who argue that forgetting is healing. In the context of ethical practice, however, neither forgetting nor remembering constitutes healing in and of itself, at least not in my experience. Devoid of actions to end oppression and bring about liberation, empty forgetting and remembering of oppression perpetuate injustice. It ends up in constructing memorials of oppression rather than ending oppressive relationships. I suggest instead that we use forgetting and remembering as tools for accessing and working through those emotions we tend to fly away from. Emotions are signals through which the Self is made visible. I suggest, therefore, that we stay with those hurts and pains. In my experience, this is a path to healing and liberation. And this is happens only through the encounters of Self and Other.

To conclude by singing a mantra that I feel captures the spirit of ethical practice, I will here remember two deeply revered thinkers. Indeed, their words resonate with me at a deeply spiritual level. In the words of Paulo Freire (2003) the Brazilian educator, "liberation is not a gift, not a self-achievement; it is a mutual process." Liberation is also a mutual process in the words of Lilla Watson, an Aboriginal woman from Australia, who said (quoted in Faith, 2000): "If you have come here to help me, you are wasting your time. If you have come here because your liberation is bound up with mine, then let us work together." That is the essence of ethical practice for me too.

REFERENCES

Ahmed, S. (2000). *Strange encounters: Embodied others in post-coloniality*. London: Routledge.

Faith, K. (2000). Reflections on inside/out organizing. *Social Justice*, 27(3), 158–167.

Freire, P. (2003). *Pedagogy of the oppressed* (M.B. Ramos, Trans.). New York: Continuum.

CHAPTER 7

HOPE HAS TWO DAUGHTERS: CRITICAL PRACTICE WITHIN A WOMEN'S PRISON

Shoshana Pollack

> Hope has two beautiful daughters. Their names are anger and courage; anger at the way things are, and courage to see that they do not remain the way they are.
>
> —St. Augustine (AD 354–430)

This chapter is not the one I set out to write. I began by writing from a position of comfort and ease: I drew on familiar (tired?) frameworks for standard academic papers, synthesizing what we know about women in prisons and the current state of theorizing on critical approaches to social work practice. I began situating myself within this literature and providing an analysis of how my own practice fits into these theoretical perspectives. The chapter, had I continued along that vein, would likely have been adequate and perhaps moderately interesting. However, as I wrote I felt a growing discomfort. I felt disembodied. Distant. *Hidden.* I was writing a chapter about use of self from behind a shadowy version of *my self.* I realized that I was reproducing a distancing process with which I was very familiar. This was how I originally began this piece:

> This chapter explores use of self issues within the context of a women's prison. The central dilemmas discussed in this chapter relate to issues of power, control, and surveillance that permeate correctional institutions. The interventions of social workers and mental health professionals, however well intentioned, often support the logic of the correctional agenda, thus reinforcing relations of dominance and control. This chapter explores these tensions and examines strategies for using one's self in ways that challenge, rather than reproduce,

disciplining correctional practices. The central questions addressed in this chapter are: What are some of the tensions confronting critical social workers within women's prisons? What are some practice strategies for dealing with these tensions and contradictions within the context of a punishment regime?

Reading it over, I see there is nothing particularly wrong with this introduction; it does, in fact, reflect one story that I do indeed want to tell. Yet I am conspicuously absent from that version of the story. I suspect my academic training has helped me to create this shadow version of myself that I produce in written scholarship. I have, though, also seen this type of distancing occur time and time again in clinical practice settings where social workers position themselves as distant experts, armed with specialized knowledge about a given population. So, I decided to write a different kind of chapter, one in which I deploy parts of myself that both academic and practice contexts usually encourage me to conceal. Here is what I really want to say.

MY FIRST TIME AT THE KINGSTON PRISON FOR WOMEN (P4W)

People often ask me why I decided to work in a women's prison and with women prisoners. Generally, I respond with something about how working with imprisoned women was a logical extension of my residential work with young girls; both groups are typically survivors of childhood abuse and often find themselves in conflict with the legal and mental health systems. Another equally true response that I sometimes supply is that my politicization as a feminist within the anti-violence against women movement motivated me to support women who had survived childhood abuse and sexual and physical violence as adults. Since a majority of incarcerated women have long histories of abuse, working with them was a good place for me to place my energies. Less often, I tell another story about what motivated me to work in a women's prison. This relates more to my subjectivity, social location, and experiences that, in addition to being informed by and related to my professional and political values, are also deeply personal. I have decided to tell that story here.

My first time into the Kingston Prison for Women (known as P4W) was in the fall of 1991. I had just begun the Master's of Social Work program at Carleton University and one of our instructors had organized a visit to the P4W. This was my first time in the P4W, which was kind of intriguing given the fact that I was raised in Kingston and had lived there for 17 years of my life. I certainly knew the prison was there; it was impossible to ignore the tall grey wall that went around a large city block. And the women's prison was but a 15-minute walk from my house. Yet somehow, despite growing up in Kingston, I had always thought of the prison as having absolutely nothing to do with me. I did not know anyone who was incarcerated there or anyone who worked there. My parents' friends worked at a different institution: Queen's University. From time to time I would hear about my mother's friends perhaps teaching a course in P4W, but that was the extent to which I heard or thought about the women locked behind those grey limestone walls. *They had nothing to do with me.*

So in the fall of 1991 I was excited to be making the trip from Ottawa back to Kingston and to enter P4W for the first time. We met the women who were hosting our visit in the prison auditorium. We sat in a large circle around a group of Native women who opened the day with drumming, singing, and dancing. My strongest memory of this moment was their powerful singing of the "Strong Woman's Song." This was followed by several of the women sharing their life stories in order to educate us — budding social workers — about the oppression that their culture, their families, and they themselves had experienced. Some of the Native women talked about cultural genocide and how they had learned about their heritage and traditions for the first time while incarcerated. One woman described this process of connecting to her history while imprisoned as ironically liberating: She said, "I heard a wolf call my name. And then I was free." Other women shared their poetry with us. Many told stories of abuse they had experienced by caretakers and professionals within institutions, such as residential schools, detention centres, and psychiatric hospitals. One woman who had been incarcerated for well over a decade said that, at the age of 42, she had just recently learned how to smile. This comment had a powerful impact upon me, and when I got home that day I wrote the following poem about his woman. I've changed the name of the woman here in order to protect her identity.

Sasha's Smile

I'm glad you learned to smile,

Sasha

Your eyes cast downward and inwards
When you thought no one was watching.

Your face—a puzzle of pain
Untold stories of hurt
Seared into your face.

They scatter, these stories, when your lips gently part
And a smile pulls your cheekbones high.

So many years behind silent walls
Seeing who knows what
You get no news.
A tomb of silence.

In solitary, there is even more to be silent about.

I'm glad you learned how to smile,

    Sasha

Your courageous lips part,
Your cheekbones rise high and proud,
Gum snapping and pen scrawling nervously,
As you try not to absorb your sister's words.
They thunder through your body but you cannot invite them in.

Later, you reveal a hopeful flash.
A life reaches out and grabs in its fist my heart
                                                    November, 1991.

In one of my MSW classes at the university I was attending, our professor had told us that we should consider it a privilege and an honour when people entrust us with their stories of suffering, oppression, and survival. So when our day at P4W was coming to an end, I told one of the women who had spoken to us that I felt privileged to hear her story. This woman stood up tall and replied, "Good. You *are* privileged. When you earn that trust, you are indeed privileged. Walk with that knowledge."

I was deeply affected by my first visit to P4W. I was blown away by the humour, strength, and goodwill of these women; the laughter and warmth they extended to us and their openness to sharing and advising. I was struck by the pain that seemed to lie just below the surface of their smiles and the stories of loss and anger that sprang from their lips. I was taken with what I thought to be their "kick-ass" attitude – tough women who would no longer let themselves be hurt, taken advantage of, or exploited. I was aware of our vastly different social locations – I grew up in a White, middle-class home in Kingston, primarily raised by my mom, who separated from my father when I was eight years old. Both my parents were professors. I was currently doing my MSW at a university, receiving training to "help" women such as those teaching me in the prison auditorium that autumn day. Yet, suddenly, these women had *everything to do with me.* I identified with a presentation of strength and security that masked a hurt and angry self. I knew that I too had shoplifted and used drugs, although despite several run-ins with the police, my class and racial positioning most likely protected me from entering the criminal justice system. I, too, wrestled with identity issues such as being bicultural, from a broken home, and wondering at that time about my sexual orientation. I too felt judged, stereotyped, and misunderstood. I also knew that I perceived myself to have strengths and gifts despite mistakes I had made and hurts that I carried. I imagined myself making a connection with these women, a connection that would be healing and would represent a struggle toward justice.

So what do I make of this? I am struck by a number of things as I reflect upon my reactions from that first day at P4W. I constructed an image of these women through my own lens. I seem to have constructed them as victims of institutional and interpersonal violence who had fought back. It was their resistance that was being punished. In so interpreting, I implicitly took a position regarding the events that landed them in prison. I saw them as surviving oppression rather than as bad women who had done bad things (as the criminal justice and correctional systems generally perceive them). This also implies a viewpoint regarding punishment: the idea that they were being punished for being socially marginalized and abused. I positioned myself as their ally. I saw their situations as representing the destructive effects of such injustices as racial, class, and gender oppression. I saw allying myself with them as reflective of my commitment to social justice. I also believe I romanticized their struggles and pain in an attempt to validate my own.

Is it wrong or inappropriate to experience these reactions? We all have views about the people with whom we work and on what we think are the sources of their troubles. Sometimes we do not recognize these as views, but consider them simply as facts. Think about people with psychiatric diagnoses, for example. What assumptions do we make regarding the cause and treatment of their difficulties? Reflective use of self involves dissecting where our assumptions about people come from, even if (or especially if) our training has taught us to uncritically accept, for example, diagnostic assessments and/or clinical categorizations. Public discourses and law and order agendas encourage us to individualize and punish crime. Punishment is viewed as holding the perpetrator accountable. We are cautioned not to excuse actions by placing them within the context of such things as poverty and abuse. My own perspective upon meeting imprisoned women was oppositional to dominant discourses. I took sides. This was my political stance.

Personally, I related to some of the struggles articulated by the women, despite wide gulfs in experiences and social locations. Does the fact that I connected my own anger and losses to those of the women in P4W mean that I am plagued by countertransference? In my work with these women would I overidentify and project as traditional literature on use of self may suggest? Or might I draw on my own pain and experiences as motivation for advocacy, activism, or healing work? For sure, it can be, at best, risky and, at worst, detrimental and unethical if one's own needs, values, and experiences are (mis)used to direct social work intervention. Is it not possible, though, that with skill, supervision, and consciousness, we can "use" our selves as the impetus for progressive change and striving toward social justice? Perhaps part of the answer to these questions lies in our notions of what helping is about.

"Helping" is not in itself a neutral term. It is laden with moralistic and paternalistic overtones that often position the helper as imparting knowledge to one who is somehow helpless. Marginalized people may not want or need the kind of help (however well intentioned) offered in this spirit. As Lill Watson, an Aboriginal activist, states in her famous quote, "If you have come to help me, you are wasting your time. But if you have come because your liberation is tied up with mine, then let us work together." Perhaps social justice efforts—whether they are as an activist, advocate, and/or individual support—are bolstered by selves that connect through a shared identification and sense of anger at abuses of power and other injustices. There may be strength in identification and shared struggle, in choosing sides and admitting you are not neutral.

THE PRISON SETTING: PUNISHMENT AND CONTROL

Back to the story: In sharing with us some of the experiences that they had outside of prison, the women at P4W also told us about struggles inside the prison itself. In many ways, the racial, gender, sexual, and class oppression they experienced on the outside was replicated and amplified within the prison walls. They talked about being triggered by the sometimes arbitrary and inconsistent use of power and by the variety of humiliations they were often subjected to in prison. They told the group of us—first-year MSW students—that they wanted/needed caring and understanding counsellors to support them in dealing with their histories of trauma. Despite the challenges involved in trusting prison therapists, they wanted to be given the chance to deal with their experiences of abuse. I decided that day that I would do my MSW field practicum at P4W. Although P4W was not on the books as an available field practicum, I made it happen. In fact, I did both my required practicums at P4W—an eight-month stint— and then stayed for another four years as a therapist on contract with the Correctional Service of Canada.

As a therapist I conducted individual counselling sessions for childhood trauma, substance abuse, eating problems, self-injury, and other issues. There were many instances within the therapeutic relationship where women seemed to be feeling connected and comfortable enough to articulate previously unexplored experiences of abuse as well as the ways in which they themselves had been abusive or damaging to others. Women examined connections between their past and how these experiences of racialization, poverty, sexism, and/or abuse contributed to limited options for survival. Within this context, they often found a way of taking responsibility for the harm they had done others. Many also learned that they had done the best they could to survive unimaginable situations and began to see a pinpoint of light beyond their feelings of self-blame and self-hatred. I witnessed some remarkable women reclaiming long buried selves during these sessions.

There were also many times where the mandate of the prison contradicted therapeutic gains and processes. I quickly learned that my goal of "walking beside women" and fighting injustice was certainly a laudable ideal but really hard to actualize in the prison context. The prison is not a treatment setting. It is neither empowering nor healing. It is a place made of bars, buzzers, locked doors, handcuffs, and solitary confinement. The mandate of the prison is *punishment* and the mantra of the prison is *security*. Women's behaviour is not seen in the context of either their past experiences or their current living environment: "Bad" behaviour is punished. Sometimes I had to conduct counselling sessions in my office with women wearing handcuffs around their wrists and shackles around their ankles.

Consider this situation: Given the very minimal accessibility of health care in prisons, a woman is taken to an outside doctor for a gynecological exam. She is experiencing pain and bleeding. She has survived multiple rapes as a child and as an adult. The guards come; they handcuff her and take her to the truck, which drives her to the hospital where the White male doctor awaits her. Once in the doctor's office she asks to have the handcuffs removed since the guards will remain by her side during the exam. They refuse and she must lie on her back during the gynecological exam, hands cuffed. She submits and quietly endures the procedure. When it is over, she stands up, gets dressed, and the guards take her back in the truck. Once she is seated in the car, she begins yelling. Her wrists cuffed together, she is banging on the seat, on her legs. She bangs her head against the window. She is screaming, "Fuck off! Leave me alone! Get away from me!" Once at the prison, other guards come out and four of them tackle her to the ground. She is taken to the segregation cell where she is stripped of her clothes and her belongings and left in a cell for 23 hours a day for the next seven days.

As a prison therapist, you may get called to segregation to do a suicide assessment on this woman and to find out what happened. In all likelihood, you will be assessing and counselling her though a small rectangular hole in the cell door, since her status in segregation renders her too risky for you to sit in a room with her. You might find out that the doctor's appointment had felt like a violation and the handcuffs increased her feelings of powerlessness. She might tell you that she "freaked out" in the truck because of the flood of memories and sensations that came over her once she survived the exam. You believe her when she says she felt invaded and scared and that she imagined she was protecting herself by screaming and banging. You might also think that she should not be punished for this behaviour as you understand it to be a result of retraumatization; she needs counselling and support, not punishment and surveillance. You might communicate your assessment and recommendations to the prison administration. They may tell you that her case will be reviewed the following week.

There is an inherent contradiction between social work notions of care and the mandate of the correctional system to punish and control. Although various individuals within the prison system may attempt to support prisoners, they are doing so within a context of punishment where control and surveillance of prisoners takes precedence over care and support. While some women may be engaged in therapeutic work around trauma and/or addictions, much of the work as a therapist involves helping women deal with the effects of imprisonment. This can at times be challenging, as the options for both the prisoner and the therapist may be circumscribed by the parameters of the institution. As a way of coping and rationalizing your professional role, you may try to separate yourself from the system by saying, "I'm not like that, I'm an ally. I just work in a bad system, but I do good things here." Often, this stance feels true and at other times the falseness of the dichotomy is unmistakably stark. Many times you ask yourself if you are simply providing bandages and, in doing so, perpetuating the legitimacy of an unjust system. This contradiction is not lost on the women inside. One time, a woman I had been counselling for about four years was yelling in my office about the fact that the pass to her father's funeral was denied. (I had nothing to do with the denial of the pass and in fact had written a letter of support advocating that she be allowed to go.) After a while, I asked why she seemed to be directing her anger at me. She paused and after a couple of seconds said, "Because you are just as powerless as I am to change the situation. All you can help me do is find a way to cope with this injustice."

The reality of imprisonment is that every aspect of your life—your rights, your privileges, your basic needs—is dictated by those who run the prison. It can become overwhelming to a social worker/therapist who is also often without the authority to change circumstances (allowing my client to attend her father's funeral, for example). It is tempting to succumb to feelings of powerlessness and frustration and to become immobilized. Regardless of how ineffective one may feel in the face of a large institution, however, employees are nonetheless nowhere near as powerless as are prisoners. There are ways to use one's power as an advocate and a supporter that at the very least minimize the destructive impact of some prison practices and may actually advance policy and practice changes in the long run. In order to attempt to adhere to critical social work principles of working on behalf of oppressed people and of seeking social change, creative strategies for "using one's self" are often necessary. This creativity

sometimes challenges conventional ideas about boundaries and the client/
therapist relationship.

SEXUAL ABUSE AND STATE ABUSE

I look out my office window about 10 a.m. and see Sasha pacing
around the prison yard. Her long black hair is combed neatly down
her back. Her face is immobile, determined not to betray her feelings.
Each step she takes is an effort not to break. After a year in segregation, I'm not afraid *of* her as many are. But I'm afraid *for* her.
                                    —MSW field practicum journal, 1991

The majority of women prisoners have experienced childhood sexual
and/or physical abuse as well as sexual and physical assault in their
adult relationships with men (Dirks, 2004). The prison environment
is characterized by power, control, invasion, humiliation and shame,
victimization by staff and sometimes fellow prisoners. These are the
dynamics of the abuse that many prisoners have already experienced.
Heney and Kristiansen (1998) argue that the four main processes present
in childhood sexual abuse—traumatic sexualization, powerlessness,
betrayal, and stigmatization—are also salient dynamics of the prison.
Routine prison practices such as pat-downs, strip searches, violations of
personal space, and being handcuffed and isolated may trigger familiar
feelings of violation and abuse (Girshick, 2003). Women survivors of child
sexual abuse often experience prison dynamics as a replication of past
experiences and may respond by reactivating coping mechanisms—such
as self-harm, drug use, aggression, and dissociation—learned in childhood.
Prison staff sometimes do not understand these behaviours and respond
to them punitively. A significant component of a prison therapist's job can
be training and educating prison staff about the aspects of imprisonment
that replicate abusive dynamics and how women may respond to them.

In many institutions, prisoners are strip-searched after receiving a
visit from their family or after returning from a day pass. This correctional
practice stems from the need to ensure that contraband (e.g., drugs) is
not brought into the prison. Debbie Kilroy, a member of an Australian
women's prisoner support organization called Sisters Inside, argues
that such things as routine strip searches represent "state sexual abuse"
(Kilroy, 2005). For many women, the process of strip-searching feels like a
replication of the humiliation and degradation they experienced as a child

while being abused by an adult authority figure (Girshick, 2003). In order to see family, make release plans, attend a community program, and/ or visit their children, women must expect to end their day with a strip search. They have to weigh the benefits of this trade-off and some may choose to forego visits and community contact as the humiliation of being strip-searched afterwards is too much to handle.

I once counselled a woman who very much wanted to see her children for a supervised visit in the community. She was terrified of the strip search she would have to endure when returning to the prison because each time she had experienced this, she had terrible flashbacks of abuse. She was concerned that this would bring up too much anger and distress and that she might not be able to control herself, which would inevitably result in some form of further punishment. As a result, she asked me if I would be present for the strip search so that I could assist her if she became too distressed and so that there would be a witness should anything happen. (She had been incarcerated off and on since she was a teenager and had been abused by correctional workers in the past.) Her request that I be present during her strip search raised several important questions about therapist-client boundaries. Many social workers are quite comfortable with encouraging and supporting survivors of abuse to take measures to increase their emotional safety when they feel they are at risk of being retraumatized. It is less common, however, for a social worker to be intimately involved in supporting an individual who is enduring a process of state humiliation while naked. My client's request raised several complex dilemmas and issues that I needed to consider.

I had been working with this woman for a number of months, primarily concerning her history of childhood trauma, her dissociative responses, and anger management. Her concern about how she might react to the strip search was a legitimate one. One of the things she had discovered was that when she felt vulnerable, her first reaction was anger and aggression in order to get the person from whom she experienced the threat to move away. She had been working on identifying events that pushed her into vulnerable emotional states as well as on developing new self-protection strategies. Given the role of correctional officers in punishing and conducting strip searches and the fact that they were not subject to the same ethic of confidentiality as social workers and psychologists, this woman did not feel comfortable disclosing her concerns to them.

As her therapist, I needed to consider several issues. One concern related to how I positioned my self vis-à-vis the prison institution. In prisons, therapists are often asked to "mop up" after someone has perhaps been denied parole, received bad news from home, was not allowed a visit, and/or had an argument with a staff person. Being in this role allows the therapist to distance himself or herself from the events and to be in the role of supportive helper. For example, generally my colleagues and I would help women cope with the effects of a strip search *after it had happened*. This allowed us to distance ourselves from the retraumatizing event and remain in the role of supporter. We could tell ourselves: "It was the prison officers who did this and prison policy that mandates it. I have nothing to do with this."

However, being a witness to a strip search would make me in some way a part of the process and might render me complicit in the violation. I would not be able to remain at a distance from this routine prison practice. Perhaps my presence would signify either my own or the woman's perception that I was condoning the procedure. Not only did this pose a risk to my own identity as a therapist in a prison, but there was also a risk that in retrospect the client herself would feel that I had been a passive witness to her humiliation. I had to grapple with the prospect of both feeling and being perceived as complicit in the strip search.

The organizational context also needed to be taken into account. Witnessing the strip search would mean placing myself, at least symbolically, in opposition to those who were conducting the strip search. My presence could send a message that I do not trust the officers to conduct the search ethically and that I am watching to make sure they conduct themselves appropriately. Sending such a message would not be helpful in establishing or maintaining positive relationships with prison staff. Further, my presence could actually backfire on my client. In a climate in which prisoners are generally mistrusted, infantilized, and pathologized, having a therapist accompany a woman who was being strip searched could be interpreted as the woman being too "weak" to take the required consequences of having the "privilege" of a day pass. As a result, subsequent requests for day passes could be denied on the grounds that she was unable to handle the requirements. This is a common dilemma when working within this type of coercive and hostile environment. Inherent in correctional policy and practice is the notion, either implicit or explicit, that a prisoner deserves whatever form of (mis)treatment she receives. This is reflected in the common quip, "If you can't do the time, don't do the crime." "Doing time" in this context means acquiescing to assertions of power and control as resistance results in further punishment. There is, of course, a glaring contradiction in attempting to support a woman's healing process within such a disempowering and retraumatizing context. As an advocate, it is crucial to negotiate your support by thinking through the dominant constructions of criminalized women and how your support will be perceived by other personnel—not solely to protect your own position, but so that your "support" does not result in further punishment of the woman.

From the point of view of traditional notions of the therapist's use of self, one might argue that my presence during the strip search would transgress client/therapist boundaries because I would be seeing my client naked and being violated. It might also conceivably be argued that I was rescuing my client and fostering dependency, as perhaps the woman should gain skills to cope with this on her own.

After discussing all these issues with my client, I made the decision to do as she requested and be present when she was strip-searched. In thinking through the decision, it was necessary to contextualize the woman's concerns within the context of power and control in which she was living. Living in a prison renders prisoners powerless and subject to the potential of unregulated control by prison officials. Strategies for coping with retraumatizing events that are available to those living in the free world (such as calling a friend, taking a walk, exercising, seeing a counsellor, taking a bath, getting a massage, etc.) are denied to prisoners. My client would have to endure the strip search and any emotional memories and reactions by herself and then be locked in a cell. Eventually, my client had her visit with her kids and the strip search was conducted. Later, we debriefed about my role as a witness and the safety she felt knowing I was there. She indicated that having me there reassured her that the officers would do their job professionally, and not transgress the boundaries of the strip search. The strip search was a violation she was forced to endure as a consequence of being imprisoned and felt like a replication of the many other sexual and physical violations she had suffered. In these prior experiences, she was also in a position of needing to trust that people in authority (e.g., relatives, partners, correctional officers) would not harm her. That trust had been dramatically abused. Prisoners also have to trust that correctional officers will conduct a strip search "professionally"—that is, without sexually or physically harming the woman—and this was a difficult leap of faith for this woman. The fact that I was there helped her suffer through the experience with some reassurance that violations of the boundaries of the strip search would not occur. Rather than feeling like

I was fostering dependency or sending a message that she could not do this on her own, this woman felt that by expanding my own notions of what being a therapist means and what a therapist does, I was validating her past experiences of abuse and proactively acknowledging that abuses of power within prisons can occur. She felt, I think, that I put my money where my mouth was. I did not only empathize with the hardships of imprisonment and support her healing from other traumas, but I shifted out of conventional notions of clinical work and honoured her request.

On my end, with the woman's consent, I asked the correctional officers if I could stand outside the cell during the strip search. (They would not allow me inside the cell because they felt the woman might pose a danger to me. I did not in any way share this concern, but did as they wished.) I explained that because of past abuses the woman had experienced, she had a high level of anxiety about the search and requested my presence to help keep her calm. I emphasized the woman's personal "issues" rather than institutional practices as the reason for my presence. This was, of course, a compromise on my part (and one that I had discussed with my client prior to talking to the correctional officers), given my client's and my own analysis that both past and present abuses of power were contributing to the challenges of this situation. By framing my wish to accompany the woman as she went through the strip search as a result of her emotional/psychological needs, I was perpetuating a common pathologizing of trauma survivors. I normally challenge this type of pathologizing, but in this case my discursive framing was deliberate and strategic. The primary role of correctional officers is to enforce the security of the prison. They generally do not wish for any prisoner to get angry, aggressive, self-abusive, or suicidal. Thus, in this moment, our two agendas were compatible and they allowed me to be there while they conducted the search.

CONCLUDING THOUGHTS: HOPE HAS TWO BEAUTIFUL DAUGHTERS

In writing this chapter I have been thinking about the many criminalized women I have spoken with both inside and outside the prison context. I have been trying to figure out if and how our current approaches to teaching use of self in social work education are relevant to anti-oppressive practice with imprisoned women. In recent years, many schools of social work have incorporated anti-oppressive theory and practice into their curriculum. In these courses, students are generally taught to recognize their own privilege within the context of social work practice as well as to be aware of aspects of their social location and backgrounds that position them as privileged (race, heterosexual, class, gender, culture). They are encouraged to reflect upon their own values in terms of how they may facilitate and/or diminish their ability to support particular clients and to examine values/attitudes that may lead to oppressive practices (e.g., religious values that discriminate against gay/lesbian/bisexual/ transgendered peoples; ideas about White privilege; ethnocentrism). We also teach students about working with involuntary clients, such as people in detention centres, jails, and prisons and those who are mandated into treatment, such as drug/alcohol programs and anger management programs. In practice courses we may address these issues in terms of how to develop a rapport with people who have not come to see us of their own volition, but in fact are being legally forced to. We discuss therapist/social worker reactions that may arise such as frustration, anger, and feelings of helplessness in the face of what many term "resistant" or "difficult" clients; in other words, those who do not participate in the social work encounter in the way we want them to. We teach students strategies for building trust and for bridging the gap between "us" and "them." We assume there is an "us" and "them."

Somehow these strategies seem inadequate. Anti-oppressive frameworks often discuss social workers' identity and the power imbalances in the social work relationship. Yet they often stop just short of how to *use* the self for social justice purposes and how to politicize our practice, particularly in the current social climate of individualist market-driven services. How can we think about use of self as political; as being about making decisions to act in ways that reflect taking a position within contexts of power relations? Of not pretending to be neutral? Such a conceptualization need not replace intersubjective understandings of use of self, for they too have their utility. Yet individualistic analyses have limited conceptual space for guiding us toward critical practices that challenge, rather than reproduce, marginalizing practices. As such, politicizing the concept of use of self necessarily gives rise to issues of ethics and power. It forces a reformulation of how we understand our work within disempowering contexts (welfare offices, child protection, psychiatric facilities, detention centres) and how we forge connection (rapport) within these contexts. It makes us question what we mean by "us" and "them."

REFERENCES

Dirks, D. (2004). Sexual revictimization and retraumatization of women in prison. *Women's Studies Quarterly, 32*(3/4), 102–115.

Girshick, L. (2003). Abused women and incarceration. In B. Zaitzow & J. Thomas (Eds.), *Women in prison: Gender and social control* (pp. 95–118). London: L. Reinner.

Heney, J. & Kristiansen, C. (1998). An analysis of the impact of prison on women survivors of childhood sexual abuse. In J. Harden & M. Hill (Eds.), *Breaking the rules: Women in prison and feminist therapy* (pp. 29–44). New York: Harrington Park Press.

Kilroy, D. (2005). Sisters inside: Speaking out against criminal injustice. In J. Sudbury (Ed.), *Global lockdown: Race, gender, and the prison-industrial complex* (pp. 285–293). New York: Routledge.

CHAPTER 8

MANAGING PARADOX
IN THE USE OF SELF: THE CASE OF
FAMILY GROUP CONFERENCING

Jeanette Schmid

I have always equated *use of self* with things one does in relation to the service user, and now appreciate use of self more as a lens through which one examines and comes to understand interaction. The "conscious use of self" has less to do with technique than a framework for analyzing power in relationships. This is, though, clearly an ongoing exploration.

At a recent conference I attended, participants in one particular session were asked to share their heritage and social location when introducing themselves. All of them work as coordinators in family group conference (FGC) projects. A Mexican woman shared that she can trace her own family back 400 years. She observed that this awareness of her own rootedness was what brought her into conferencing. She wanted others to have a similar connection to a kinship group, and this was what motivated her to become a FGC coordinator. An American woman, who had been raised outside her family and had never had the opportunity to know them, was drawn to conferencing because she wanted to ensure that other children would have a family circle that they could belong to. Another participant, who had wanted to become a priest, saw conferencing as a vocation. The reasons that people are drawn into the role of FGC coordinator and the selves that they bring are certainly varied.

I carry with me a history of activism and social work in the South African context. I have been a FGC coordinator for seven years in the Toronto Family Group Conferencing Project. Prior to that, I was a frontline child welfare worker for two years. I experienced traditional child welfare practices as frequently oppressive and demeaning to families. For me, family group conferencing offered an alternative, socially just, and respectful way of engaging with family networks that were dealing with child welfare issues.

This chapter will explore the paradoxes that conference coordinators need to manage through the reflexive use of self. It will reflect the voices of other coordinators, as well as highlight some of the dilemmas I have personally needed to deal with in the role of coordination.

MY STRUGGLE WITH THE CONCEPT OF USE OF SELF

I need to note at the outset how challenging it has been for me to even attempt to describe how I have learned about use of self. I find it extremely difficult to adequately express the nuances, depth, and complexity of this struggle. The account below will offer the reader a glimpse of the developments in my thinking about use of self in my work.

My (very Anglo-American) social work training emphasized use of self as the professional, conscious use of one's "personality" and individual history within the dynamic of a counselling relationship. The notion of boundaries was a definitive component, and personality was not defined. We were exhorted to ensure that we did not disclose too much or inappropriately who we were, or what constituted our agendas. Further, we were to be careful about transference and countertransference in our dealings with clients. My student cohort was predominantly White and so were the faculty, and at the time that we were being trained (1977–1980), it was assumed that many of us would be working primarily with White families once we graduated. The issues of race, class, privilege, and oppression were never raised. This was a time of extreme repression in South Africa, and few were willing to risk their careers or their futures to discuss such controversial topics. Only one experienced community worker even remotely touched upon these issues by advising us, "Always drink the tea that you are offered. Never think you are too good for that."

My second- and fourth-year field placements took me to a disadvantaged "Coloured"[1] community. Later I found employment in this community, initially working at a centre for children and adults with developmental delays for six years, and then working for a year in a project that trained women with only secondary education to become preschool teachers and set up community schools. My first introduction to Eldorado Park was through a local principal who decided that it was important that as White students we had at least a beginning understanding of the conditions our prospective clients lived in and took us on a tour of the area. He both confronted us with the poverty and explained to us how these circumstances had been created through apartheid policies. This became a formative experience for me within a long and painful journey of *conscientization*.

I began to struggle then with what it meant to be a White social worker in that community, and the 12-mile trip to and fro between the White city and the Black township was always a period of questioning and reflection. I thought about the role of social work in communities defined by poverty: What could one do that was meaningful and effective? I would wonder if I could ever understand what my "clients" were experiencing, and if I needed to. I would be burdened by the privilege that I had and would consider whether as a White person I had a place at all in a "Coloured" community. I felt more and more that I was living in two very separate worlds. Except for a few politicized people, my White environment did not understand and did not care to know about the reality of oppressed people in South Africa. The issues in each locality were fundamentally different. What was difficult for me was that I now belonged in neither world, and did not always know how to negotiate that outsider status either personally or professionally.

The notion of "professional behaviour" and the accompanying discourse of "boundaries" felt increasingly irrelevant to me. In part this was because I worked in contexts that emphasized participatory, democratic teamwork regardless of professional qualifications. There was more to do than traditional social work, and one contributed where one was needed. Sometimes this meant helping with food preparation, rushing children to the clinic, or doing playground duty. The label of "professional" thus gradually lost meaning for me as I was repeatedly confronted with the fact that my education had not made me any wiser or more capable in life. I also found the concept of boundaries unworkable when culturally, the community I was engaged in had such a different sense of personal boundaries. The focus was collective, and even as a Whitey, I was invited into people's homes, their families, their friendships, their lives. Even so, I was confronted daily with the differences and boundaries that existed because I was not of the same cultural background, and because the colour of my skin entitled me to a lifestyle that my fellow South Africans were actively denied. It seemed to me that adhering to the professional idea of boundaries reinforced these distinctions and potentially allowed me to avoid fully exploring the broader socio-political frameworks I found myself in and my moral responsibilities within this context. In this space I found that I needed instead to search for and establish what commonalities did exist. The process of discovering the humanity in each other was profound, particularly as the dominant society continually reinforced how fundamentally different we were and that co-existence was impossible. While searching for sameness and a common humanity was important, I also always understood that I nevertheless carried certain privileges and thus particular types of power. These are some of the insights that accompanied me when trying to understand use of self when I eventually took on the role of an FGC coordinator.

THE CONTEXT OF FAMILY GROUP CONFERENCING

Family group conferencing is a process that privileges the voice of the family network in decision making within a child welfare context. It is currently used in a number of settings in various parts of the world. The family group is invited to present their recommendations regarding a plan for their child or children to the child welfare team. Coordinators are responsible for preparing family members and service providers for the conference and hosting the deliberations. At the conference the service providers present their views about strengths and concerns in the situation, after which the family group meets privately to develop their plan. In the final part of the family group conference, the family proposals are reviewed with the professionals. If the recommendations ensure the child's safety, the plan is accepted.

The approach arises out of the Maori struggle in New Zealand/ Aotearoa to formulate a child welfare system that is respectful of their culture, traditions, and priorities (Connolly, 1999). It is thus important to honour the origins of conferencing whenever the model is promoted by affirming its indigenous roots and abiding by the principles of conferencing. FGC is identified as a philosophy rather than a technique because its value base directs how a conference process should be conducted. Key values include acknowledging that the family group is the expert on their own child; that children require a sense of connection and belonging with their family network; and that family members need to be active participants in developing plans for their children (Burford & Hudson, 2000). "Family" includes the nuclear family, relatives, and anyone else the family group identifies as significant. The paradigm has a collective rather than an individual bias, and sees the child in the context of family and community. The power differential between the family circle and child welfare team or other service providers is recognized, with the conferencing intended as a means of empowering kith and kin in the decision-making process.

This reliance on values as opposed to techniques means that the discretionary space in which the coordinator functions is a broad one. The coordinator's own awareness of personal and professional power and one's ways of using these thus necessarily enters significantly into how one manages the conferencing process.

THE LITERATURE ON USE OF SELF IN FGC COORDINATION

The coordinator's role is central to the success of the conference (Merkel-Holguin, Nixon & Burford, 2003). The activities and skills of the coordinator are clearly described in the literature (Connolly, 1999; Sippert, Hudson & Unrau, 2000). Also, the values a competent coordinator should have are highlighted, especially as it is contended that a technocratic approach to conferencing undermines the process (Burford & Hudson, 2000; Kemp, Whittaker & Tracy, 2000; Marsh & Crow, 2000; Nixon, 1999). Coordinator independence and "neutrality" are strongly emphasized. The coordinator should position himself or herself between the child welfare team and the family, not becoming invested in influencing the outcome of the conference (Merkel-Holguin, 1998). It is important for the coordinator to maintain an independence from the child protection office so as to prevent an overidentification with the child welfare agenda at the cost of the family's voice (Hansen, 1999; Nixon, 1999) and allow family members to credit the coordinator's claims of impartiality (Nixon, 1999; Nixon, Merkel-Holguin, Sivak & Gunderson, 2000). There is a debate as to whether formal social service qualifications need to be part of the coordinator skill set, particularly as coordinators coming from outside the ranks of social services are less likely to become inducted into the child welfare agenda or take on the role of "professional expert" (Burford & Hudson, 2000; Connolly & McKenzie, 1999; Love, 2000; Nixon, Merkel-Holguin, Sivak & Gunderson, 2000). They may be more sensitive to issues of professional power precisely because they themselves are lay people.

Only Harrison and Quinett (n.d.) write about coordinators developing an awareness of his or her own beliefs, strengths, and weaknesses, and this impacting on the process. This is expressed in the language of transference and countertransference. Love (2000) offers a critical approach that calls for an analysis of oppression and the coordinator's potential implication in it. This perspective has a very different theoretical and value base from the transference/countertransference approach to self-awareness. Similarly, while cultural sensitivity and competence are identified as important attributes (Connolly & McKenzie, 1999), only a few writers such as Love (2000) suggest that internalized oppression and the complexity of cultural knowledge and systems must be acknowledged, and the appropriation or abuse of cultural processes avoided.

In all the descriptions of the coordination role, the issue of how the coordinator critically uses her or his behaviours, skills, values, beliefs, social location, and life experiences in the coordination role appears to be almost entirely overlooked. I have also not come across a single study that directly reflects the voices and experiences of coordinators. This is thus an unexplored area that needs to be understood better.

VOICES OF COORDINATORS

Given that no one had heard directly from the front-line practitioners, I conducted a study in which I held individual in-depth qualitative interviews with seven coordinators in Ontario to elicit how coordinators understood the use of self in their practice (Schmid, 2005). I suggested to the coordinators that use of self involved the ways in which coordinators have applied their social location, life experience, personality (as I then thought of it), values, and sensibilities in their role. Some had not heard the term "use of self" before, and I attempted to offer them a loose framework within which to work, based on my understanding of the concept.

I am including the views of other coordinators here in order to bring in the voices of those whose personal and work backgrounds and social identities are different from my own. Four of the coordinators are relatively new at conference coordination, with the other three having more substantial experience in the role. Three of the coordinators were born in Canada, the remaining having come from elsewhere to establish themselves here. Their origins are Middle Eastern, Caribbean, African, and Asian respectively. All the interviewees are female. The group includes Muslim, Hindu, humanist, agnostic, and Christian adherents. Barring one coordinator who is in her 30s, all are in their 40s and 50s.

The coordinators spoke about three areas that they thought were central. These included the ability to develop a profoundly non-judgmental attitude as a way of being able to maintain "neutrality" and independence, self-awareness around issues of social location and values, and an ability to connect with family members in a short period of time.

DEVELOPING A PROFOUNDLY NON-JUDGMENTAL ATTITUDE TO MANAGE NEUTRALITY

A major area suggested by coordinators regarding appropriate use of self was developing a profoundly non-judgmental attitude to manage neutrality. As elaborated below, this involves a critical, reflexive approach to the task of coordination.

It must be said in advance that I recognize that the term "neutrality" presents challenges, particularly in a postmodern world. No one is neutral, and everyone holds views and opinions that influence his or her responses to events. Neutrality is used in the FGC field to describe the coordinator's task of maintaining the space between child welfare and the family. Coordinators are charged with ensuring that they do not increase the sense of subjugation to authority that families may be experiencing while working within the context of dominant child welfare practice. Against this backdrop, the goal of coordination is to prepare family members and service providers to be able to participate in the conference and to facilitate the conference in a manner that acknowledges the expertise (and mandate) service providers bring while privileging the voice of the family. To do this the coordinator occupies the space between the family and the child welfare system by not being inducted into dominant child welfare thinking, nor taking sides with the family. The coordinator has to avoid being invested in a particular plan or choosing to support one plan above another. The accepted FGC language of "neutrality" and "independence" refers also to the facilitation of family leadership and ensuring that as coordinator, one limits one's involvement so as to never be central to the process. It is in this way that independence is different from the traditional understanding of boundaries in that in order to be "neutral," the coordinator needs to pay ongoing attention to issues of power.

Finding an alternative term to "neutrality" has been challenging. "Independence" might be a more appropriate concept in that the coordinator needs to avoid being aligned with any parties. "Impartial" or "unbiased" is correct in the sense that the coordinator does not advocate for any plan; however, coordinators are not in a position where they have to evaluate a plan, which the term suggests. "Objectivity" is not a useful label either as it implies assessment and the assumption of a positivist stance, none of which the coordinator is doing. "Detached" seems unsuitable as the coordinator does in fact become quite intimate with all parties. Thus, there seems to be no ideal phrase or concept that captures the essence of the mental framework with which the coordinator should approach his or her work. "Neutrality" continues to be the flawed shorthand.

The coordinators I interviewed collectively recognized that keeping a neutral position was important. "[The conference participants] can see it if you have an agenda" ... "I wouldn't be effective because I would transfer how I felt about it" ... "You jeopardize your role." However, coordinators are not expected to become empty vessels. Indeed, while the coordinator is expected to maintain this "in-between space," she is simultaneously expected to embrace the conferencing biases toward inclusion, participation, and recognition of family expertise. These values counter traditional child welfare practice, which tends in Anglo-American models to be individualistic, punitive, adversarial, and professionally driven. Thus, at the same time as coordinators need to keep in check their views and opinions about the child welfare position and potential plans, they are expected to actively ensure that the philosophy of conferencing is reflected in the practice; in this respect, coordinators are decidedly not neutral. The coordinator is expected to be invested in the process, so the role is not passive or distant. Coordinators must, therefore, align with family strengths, though not with particular family members; amplify the family's voice without becoming the voice for the family; ensure safety in conference without taking responsibility for the safety plan themselves; provide the family circle with all relevant information; and facilitate a widening of circle. As a result, coordinators find themselves managing paradox from the time they accept an FGC referral.

Coordinators spoke about the "constant challenge" of managing neutrality. "It's not very easy," "I slip back and forth," and "It is a strong struggle" are some of the comments made. They struggled in part because no one is truly neutral and "one never is a clean slate." One's personal values might contradict those held by a family member or service provider. It was also difficult because both family members and workers might want to "pull you to support their idea," and by not offering explicit affirmation, the party might have felt that the coordinator did not understand the situation.

The coordinators interviewed identified a number of strategies to maintain independence. The primary strategy was to step back through self-talk, "thinking about the situation," and "reminding yourself that the family has power." This implies to me a process of critical reflection on the ways in which aspects of who they are have influenced them. Interviewees all spoke about using supervision and peer/team supervision as a means of gaining perspective at these times. "Managing one's role so as not to be central" was another strategy identified. Coordinators were not always aware of how they might unintentionally invite family members and service providers to make them pivotal. This ability not to become central or to abuse one's power is a huge challenge for coordinators. Some coordinators stated their frustration with the role explicitly. "I wish I could help more" was a sentiment that was expressed. These coordinators wanted to rescue and intervene. They wanted to advocate for the families. The coordinators found themselves persistently questioning their prescribed role and attempting to find ways of going beyond it. This would shift the coordinators out of the "in-between" role to one where they would become workers for the family, though these coordinators had to struggle to recognize this dynamic.

While it would be easy to criticize these coordinators, I have found that all coordinators face situations where they compromise their "neutrality" and allow themselves to assume a role outside of the coordinator's domain. For example, I remember agreeing to drive a grandmother home if she felt unsafe at the conference, rather than helping the grandmother to consider which family member could potentially take on that role. A number of factors potentially influence coordinators usurping the control that should be left to the family members. As helpers we want to be able to make a difference for families. This has been reinforced by our training, which teaches us to take the lead in problem solving. Many of us, myself included, sought out social work specifically because we wanted to make a difference in this world and believed that our training would allow us to become catalysts for change. I have been caught in the "expertise" trap, feeling that I have knowledge that equips me better than lay people to know how and when to intervene appropriately. I have learned to equate competence with control. My own needs for affirmation may also lead me to want to be central in the process. External pressures to prove conferencing is effective (and, in the above example, safe) have also influenced me to take charge.

To be an effective coordinator, one has to identify one's own drivers toward control, and be willing to unpack an often contradictory process. I know that I am more likely to go outside the bounds of the conferencing role if I feel that there has been an inaccurate and unjust assessment by CAS because I believe in fairness. And yet, despite believing in equity, I have seen that I am more likely to "cheat" for families that, in my subjective view, are "worthy." I am not certain that I even know what that category involves, but it would include people who seem to me to be willing to change, who have insight, and whom I can see care for their children. This demonstrates to me that I am subject to biases and judgments despite my efforts not to be, and despite my passion for social justice. It also reflects that I have more of a "rescuer" in me than I usually care to admit. I have a strong need arising out of childhood to present as effective, efficient, and adequate, and it takes significant discipline to remind myself that being at the centre is a constraint rather than a help in the conferencing process. I find that sometimes there is a "disconnect" between holding the value that families can be trusted, and actually practising as if I knew it to be true. I have had to learn (and relearn) that I can allow families to direct the process. Where I am aware that my views are shaping my sympathies and alliances, I attempt to review why I have been touched by a particular situation. Understanding what has triggered my departure from neutrality may suggest a range of activities: I may need to share information about the system with the family group; I may need to have further clarifying conversations with CAS about what has informed their position; I may simply need to step back and let the family take control.

The use of self in terms of understanding how one may be pushed or pulled to use one's power as a coordinator rather than being "neutral" is thus key to conferencing. The next section on social location explores areas where power might be located and how this influences the relationships with conference participants, whether they are family members or service providers.

SELF-AWARENESS REGARDING ISSUES OF SOCIAL LOCATION

The coordinators who participated in my study addressed a number of aspects of social location. All the interviewees felt that their life experience had enriched their capacities in their role as coordinator. One said, "I have gone through the thick and thin of life…. I understand the pain in families." Another reported that, "I can feel that I am in their shoes … and it really allows me to forge that connection with people" when speaking of conference participants who shared with her a history of immigration. Having dealt with challenges gave coordinators a maturity as well as empathy for the diverse experiences of prospective conference participants. Age was an aspect of self that certain coordinators used in developing a relationship with family members. One interviewee said, "The approach is different when I am dealing with a teenage mom … or a grandmother." Age can reflect a dimension of power in the relationship. For example, one interviewee commented that, "I think it probably helps that I am not young. A lot of people say to me 'You are not a young CAS worker.' Parents often have difficulty with that." Her age was thus an advantage in this situation and offered her a particular status. For another coordinator, however, the fact that she was perceived as being young created "an ongoing struggle for credibility." This coordinator did observe that when working with teenagers, her age became an asset as the youth felt that she could relate to them.

The informants did not reflect a consciousness about gender in the interviews, and how being male, female, or transgendered might play itself out in the interaction. None spoke about sexual orientation. One coordinator did note that it was harder to develop a connection with male participants as they tended to resist the coordinator's neutrality more often. It is not clear to me why the coordinators overlooked gender as it is such a central feature of social relations, particularly when power is involved. The group of interviewees was exclusively female, but this does not reflect the reality of the broader conferencing field where a substantial number (though not the majority) of coordinators are men. I wonder—but am reluctant to speculate—about whether male coordinators would have identified the issue of gender as important.

Not being attuned to factors relating to gender and neutrality would mean that significant dynamics shaping the interaction are inevitably being overlooked. I have for a long time supported the notion that men and women need equally to be included in the conferencing process, while at the same time being very cognizant of the power issues related to gender. Perhaps this strong sense of inclusion is rooted in my experience of restorative justice, which emphasizes that while each of us needs to be accountable for how we harm others, there is also potential redemption and reintegration. For me, we all have a place in community. I also always want to be cautious that I do not confuse power dynamics with a reason to exclude or to turn the tables of discrimination. I have more recently deepened my understanding of how fathers tend to become invisible in child welfare practice. My sense of how I need to engage with men has thus been sharpened. I know also that I engage in relationships with men with less fear than some women do, and I carry a trust in the world around me that is perhaps unusual. I have learned to respect that others may need to create safety for themselves in a way that is fundamentally different from my approach.

Regarding gender, I also attempt to pay attention to what it means in each interaction that I come into the process as a woman without children. Many family members feel that their parenting has been judged by people who have no personal experience of raising children, and I am thus often asked if I have children. I was a child welfare worker for two years and hated being confronted with this question as I felt defensive and worried that I lacked legitimacy in the eyes of the client. Because the role of coordinator requires that I *not* judge anyone's parenting, I now feel free to simply answer or volunteer the information, and allow the family member to direct the discussion from there. Frequently I will affirm that I do not have personal experience, but that I can hear from the family member how this is affecting him or her.

The coordinators suggested that class was another aspect of social location that was present in their work. The majority of families served by child welfare tend to be poor, though in meeting members of the family circle, the coordinator is likely to encounter people of both middle and lower socio-economic status. Despite this, the coordinators' comments tended to focus on situations where there was a class difference. I assume that this is because we register difference, and do not reflect on the ease and common language we likely share with others from the same class background. In observing differences, one interviewee noted, "There are all sorts of indicators [of class] that you cannot ignore, like your use of language...." Another observed that it was challenging for her coming from a privileged, middle-class background as "It is truly hard to understand where a person is coming from if you haven't lived out that situation."

It seems to me, from their way of speaking or not speaking about it, that some of the coordinators did not have a sufficiently nuanced analysis of the impact of class in their relationships with conference participants. One coordinator—who had her roots in poverty—reported that families had commented on her ease in their homes. Two others came from middle-class backgrounds, but had had times in their lives when they had financial challenges or had not worked as professionals, and felt that this helped them bridge the gap. "It shows in the way I treat people." "It is not difficult for me to identify with families that are ... economically challenged." While it is likely that these coordinators have a greater sensitivity, there also needs to be the recognition that the middle-class position coordinators hold—by virtue of their education, work, economic status, or some combination thereof—is also part of the interaction. This inevitably brings a certain power differential into the room, which must be acknowledged by the coordinator. The class status may mean, for example, that family members will defer to the coordinator, consciously or unconsciously, simply because of his or her social standing. It also means that coordinators may not be able to fully appreciate challenges that families have because of the differences in class background. On the other hand, where the socio-economic status between the family and coordinator is similar, there is the danger that coordinators believe they understand the family's circumstances better than they actually may.

In reflecting on the issue of class, I am aware that I too have double standards, which become clear in the Canadian context. Where poverty is evident, for example, a number of people are living in one apartment, and the frustrations regarding the lack of housing are evident, it is not difficult for me to appreciate the systemic issues that have contributed to this situation. However, I find also that where families appear resourced (they have food, clothing, appliances, telephones, and TVs), I may not have empathy for the family's situation. In South Africa, poverty means not having one's basic needs met. Because I equate material goods with income and possibility, when people appear to have physical comforts, judgments begin to creep in about people's lack of motivation and reliance on a system that is there for those who are more vulnerable. The value that one "needs to work hard and be independent," inculcated as a result of my Calvinist upbringing, overshadows my understanding that systemic factors are at play. My complex and confused response signals that I have a set of values, grounded in my class and culture, about poverty. I would like briefly to reflect on language because, as noted by one coordinator earlier, it becomes a signifier of class. Professional jargon effectively creates distance and mystifies the client's lived reality, placing it often into a scientific realm. The deconstruction and reinterpretation process becomes very important in creating more of a level playing field for the conference. Thus when one coordinator suggested that, "Language is a tool.... One needs to deconstruct words ... like conference ... and coordinator," she is not only talking about making oneself understood, but about ensuring that the language is accessible across class and other differences. Coordinators thus need to pay attention to their own language usage so as to minimize differences. Also, coordinators play a key role in creating a bridge between the language of the professionals and that of clients. People's inability to speak the dominant language fluently is frequently inappropriately interpreted as a sign of general incompetence and is used as a means of exaggerating difference and relegating someone to a lower status. It is thus important to also be sensitive where English is the second language for families. One immigrant coordinator felt that she needed to pay particular attention to how she spoke English because she wanted to be perceived as professionally competent, illustrating how language is connected to power.

Coordinators were aware that families would ascribe to them particular power, especially if the coordinator was perceived as being aligned with CAS. "Family members may be afraid to ask questions." Coordinators would thus invest time in clarifying the differences between their own and the child welfare role, clarifying the tasks, but also being explicit about their position and power in the situation. What coordinators seemed to appreciate less was that the very role of coordinator and the associated identification as a professional create a power differential. The position itself allows one into the private space of family life. Home visits were used by early philanthropists and modern social workers alike to scrutinize and monitor how poor families lived under the "cover of kindness" (Margolin, 1997). Even though coordinators allow family members to choose where they will meet the coordinator, and most frequently are invited to the home, there is likely to be some mistrust. Coordinators are visiting families with a very different agenda from most professionals – an agenda for collaboration – but have to know that family members may remain suspicious, even if one is clear about one's role and location in the process.

Further, some coordinators inadvertently reinforce the family's mistrust by wanting to "elicit the family's story," a use of self of which Margolin (1997) is relentlessly critical. In fact, coordinators are not required to do this, though they do need to be open to what is presented to them. This misperception of what the coordinator's role is signifies how deeply ingrained the view is that the professional's role is to gain information. As a coordinator, I am thus very careful to restrict myself to information sharing about the process, finding out who the family group wants invited, and to preparing the individual for the conference. If I do ask a probing question, I attempt always to provide a context for why I am asking that information, so that the individual understands where I am coming from and does not feel obliged to respond. Transparency becomes the guiding principle. To adhere to it, I must at all times ask myself why I am requesting information and be clear about the legitimacy of the purpose.

Race and cultural differences were further aspects of social location that were discussed. The coordinators carried with them an awareness of their own race, religion, and ethnicity. For one coordinator, this entailed "vigilance": "I am a person of colour and I never forget that ... always really watching, taking care." They felt that families sometimes questioned whether they were "knowledgeable enough" about child welfare processes and family dynamics. One coordinator said that when one is meeting with a family from a similar background, there "often is a greater sense of comfort from both sides.... I experience being more accepted, and there isn't this sense of being checked out. There is less of that." Some coordinators said that they came from societies or from families where race and ethnicity were not issues in the same way as in the Canadian context, and thus they had to learn to pay attention to these factors in this context.

Some saw their heritage as being advantageous in other ways. "I think that when I deal with Natives [sic] I can identify with them because they have a tribal concept that I have from my background.... When I deal with Black people, I have this advantage again where they can relate to me and I can relate to them because I am Black...." The opposite also occurs, and one White coordinator knew that she was being "checked out": "They raise the old treaties and say, 'Why should we take your word on anything?'... Your reaction is important — different to CAS, who get ticked off and use their power."

All coordinators stressed that they attempted to move quickly from a position where they were aware of race or ethnicity as something that created difference, to a position where they were connecting with the individuals they were speaking to. "After all, we are all human." They tended not to raise the issue of race as problematic with the family member or service provider ("I ignore it") unless they could see that it was causing an issue for the family or where there was overt racism. "I will draw the family's attention to it.... There are lessons to be learned." This is an issue that I will return to later.

I would, though, like also to share some of my own experiences on this theme. The dilemmas regarding race and heritage have been at the forefront of my consciousness as a coordinator. In Canada I have a foreign accent. I am immediately identified as a newcomer. In my work I have noticed that I have a positive bias toward non-Canadians. I find it easy to connect with them, as frequently we have common experiences. I find the context and challenges the family is dealing with easy to understand. I sometimes find that I share a common language with people who were activists in their country of origin. I am, however, aware that even where there is commonality, I nevertheless cannot fully understand the other person's situation. The differences may be in racial, ethnic, geographic, or other kinds of origins. Many may have been forced to leave their homelands as refugees, whereas my move was not made under duress. Our social positions in our countries of origin may have been different, but even when similar, our respective abilities to be successful in Canada are impacted by issues of race, ethnicity, and language.

Two potential complications arise from this sense of understanding the family's reality as based on shared experience. First, because I think I understand some of their experience, I see that I sometimes — with the permission of the parties involved — take on the role of a cultural interpreter, offering a frame to CAS of what might inform particular behaviours on the part of the family and vice versa. For example, one couple was very distressed by the CAS worker's reaction when the parents called family members as soon as CAS came to apprehend their children. The worker felt intimidated, misunderstanding why the relatives had been called and insisted that the relatives leave. As a coordinator, I attempted to explain to each party the intentions of the other so as to create common ground. I do feel that there is value in reinterpreting behaviours in certain situations, the way a mediator might. There are also situations where it may be helpful to share information about systems that make larger processes more transparent. However, I need to be more cautious about taking on this role of interpreter as it potentially disempowers the family by appropriating their voice, perhaps even misrepresenting them. The second potential hazard of assuming knowledge of the family based on shared experience is the very assumption that the shared experience is anything but partial. Thus, coordinators need to be careful not to assume that one knows the reality of the other, and to listen carefully for differences. While finding common ground is useful in building relationships, the coordinator needs to go beyond an assumed commonality.

Families have talked to me, in my role as coordinator, about their experience of racism. Families have let me know that they believe the child welfare system or a particular worker is racist, or that they worry that the other side of the family is discriminating against them. In the latter case, I ask for permission to alert these relatives to their concerns. Having witnessed the most extreme forms of racial discrimination in South Africa, I am fearful about offending anyone, or about inadvertently increasing any individual's experience of oppression. However, in writing this, I realize that where the allegation is that a worker has been racist, I have listened empathetically, but not done anything that addresses the issue directly. Sometimes I have said something like, "And here you are dealing with a White South African, whom you maybe assume is racist," a comment that aims to name the issue of race between us, yet does not make room for further discussion, effectively foreclosing the subject at the very moment it is opened up. I find myself now reflecting critically on this way of dealing with the situation and realize how complex such a moment is. I struggle with how to label the concern in a way that allows the family to choose between discussing their concern further if they wish or moving the conversation on to something else if they prefer. Above all, I wish that they might genuinely experience the choice as their own. This confusion occurs at various levels or, to think of it another way, involves different identities. In my role as coordinator, I don't know how to hear the family's story without feeling that I ought to become an advocate. However, I also want to maintain the role between the family and child protection. My identity as a White person makes me wonder if there is any legitimacy in me opening up the subject; at the same time, I do not want my power as a White worker to allow me to silence the family's voice, thereby recapitulating their experiences of racism.

At a broader level, I have worried how the family is experiencing the process in situations where the family group is Black and the service providers and I are White. This has also been on the mind of another coordinator, who shared the family's racial and cultural background: "And you are talking about power differentials, of being White social workers with a family of colour. This puts them on a little lower rung of the ladder. On top of everything else, this is another issue to deal with." For the worker who is herself from a racialized group, identifying more directly with the family's experience of racism than I can as a White coordinator adds a whole new layer of complexity regarding questions of power, who has it, and how to use it in a just way.

The values that one identifies with and one's social location thus clearly influence the interaction one has with conference participants, whether members of the family or the professional group. It seems that all the coordinators had a certain sense of awareness about various aspects of their social location. In some cases, however, coordinators would demonstrate sensitivity to one dimension while overlooking another. Our histories—personally, professionally, and politically—shape what we are willing to consider and what we choose to overlook. Working with awareness requires courage and honesty because it needs us to expose ourselves. There clearly needs to be more of an all-round examination of the impact of one's power on interactions with family members and service providers. I will return to this at the end of the chapter.

ENGAGING FAMILY MEMBERS AND SERVICE PROVIDERS

The final area coordinators spoke about was the importance of engaging the family member or service provider immediately upon making contact. Coordinators usually have only one meeting with each invitee. The process "goes nowhere if you haven't forged a connection," one participant stated. Creating communication is about finding a path for collaboration within the context of differences. It becomes a means of signalling how one hopes to acknowledge the power differences that may exist through demonstrating respect for the family's unique experiences, traditions, and culture. In this way the coordinator is attempting to make visible the expertise and value the family group has. I would like to focus particularly on the value of disclosing personal stories as a means of making connection, and the importance of accepting the family's hospitality. Coordinators might share information about their own lives that they felt allowed for a connection. They might also accept beverages and meals offered by the family. "Inviting you means a lot to them," one coordinator stated. "It is a means of respecting another's culture." Coordinators stressed that these actions — which involve crossing the boundaries normally prescribed in social work — "allow you to connect as a human being." The coordinators' responses regarding both self-disclosure and the acceptance of hospitality resonated for me as they echoed my sentiments around the issue of boundaries. Allowing the family member to host you on their turf becomes more important than creating professional distance. Coordinators did caution that one needed to ensure that one was still occupying the middle space between the family group and CAS, but felt that one could accept hospitality, share of themselves, and yet remain "neutral."

REFLECTING ON MY OMISSIONS

In writing this chapter I realize that the issue of faith and spirituality was not specifically addressed in the research, though it was raised by two coordinators who were interviewed. One reflected that her faith helped her to calm and centre herself in her work, and thus was important to her practice. Another coordinator spoke about how she had an engaging discussion with a woman about faith without disclosing her own religion.

The family member, who was Christian, was surprised to find at the end of the conversation that someone from a Muslim background had a common spiritual perspective with her. Our faith and spirituality are aspects we clearly carry with us into the conferencing process. Indeed, as coordinators we attempt to make room for the family group to express their spirituality through the conference opening. Like race and ethnicity, religion can create commonalities and divisions. The coordinator again needs to be aware of how this dimension potentially impacts on the communication with family members and service providers invited to the conference.

The issue of disability was left out of the study. I did not raise it specifically as part of one's social location, and in hindsight, I am surprised; usually it is an issue I am quite aware of. None of the coordinators raised this as a topic of discussion either. It would be useful for us as a group to reflect on why this might have occurred. Certainly many of the family members attending conferences have had physical or mental disabilities. Indeed, some conferences have focused specifically on disability: either where the child has a disability that is challenging for the family to deal with, or where the parent or caregiver has a disability that is in some way affecting his or her ability to adequately look after the child or children. None of the coordinators interviewed has a disability, which might have been one factor that contributed to this issue becoming invisible in the interviews.

I asked the first three interviewees how they thought their coordination was different from anyone else's on the team arising out of who they inherently were. People would say, "Well, I can't compare 'cos I don't really know...." Basically, it seemed that people did not want to blow their own trumpet or unintentionally put down a colleague. I guess no one wants to say directly either, "Well these are the parts of me that get me into trouble with others." For myself, I know my impulsiveness is a serious impediment, and I try all sorts of techniques to mediate this. Sometimes I manage and sometimes I just blunder and am happy to share that, probably because of that very impulsiveness! At a gut level I believe that one's way of being is key in how we work. People have often commented that I have a calming presence (which is strange as my internal experience is very different) and that this has been helpful to them. Certainly another coordinator I know has also been told that her quiet, gentle manner has helped to reduce the tension in situations. Yet another coordinator has the quality of persistence, which allows her to get certain results, such as widening the circle, when others of us would have given up and lost the vision of possibilities in that situation. I think some coordinators communicate respect simply because of how they move about in the world, not because they are trying to be respectful. Of course, how we deal with power and our awareness of issues comes across as part of our persona, and shapes how we are perceived. Insofar as our behaviour is shaped by the responses of others, what we think of as personality is largely socially constructed. To this extent personality can be "taught." As noted above, I use a variety of strategies to manage my impulsiveness while trying to retain spontaneity. But I think we also carry inherent traits that make some things easier for us than others and, at the same time, create challenges for us where others have opportunities. There are aspects of ourselves that are almost beyond our control. People tell me that I have a nice smile and this puts them at ease. Well, I couldn't smile differently if I tried. It is not something that is conscious and I could not make it conscious. I'm just lucky that my smile engages people. I have also had comments that my voice (and here in Canada my accent) is attractive. What I have to be conscious of is that these unique characteristics can work in my favour, and to be aware of when I do indeed use these traits to gain advantage. I also have to understand how my impulsiveness creates impediments in my work.

MOVING BEYOND AWARENESS IN DEVELOPING A CRITICAL USE OF SELF

Having a rounded awareness of how one's values, social location, and strategies for connection direct the process is an important beginning in developing a critical use of self. However, it becomes apparent that a sense of awareness of the issues alone does not seem to be sufficient. Simply knowing that power differentials are woven into the interaction does not automatically shift our practice or the experience of family members. As coordinators we need to develop a critical understanding of how to respond in particular situations.

One of the barriers to developing appropriate responses appears to be our desire to focus on commonalities and what makes us collectively human. As noted earlier, discovering the depth of our shared humanity is fundamentally necessary as this is what informs empathy and collective action. However, believing that affirming what we share is sufficient renders our interactions superficial and potentially meaningless. If we are doing so at the expense of examining necessary differences, we are doing the families we work with an injustice. We need to explore further when silence is appropriate and when naming is needed. This applies not only to race, but to all dimensions of social location that create power differentials between the coordinator and conference participant. However we approach the issues, we should not further subjugate family members.

I am not sure how to always do this. For example, placing the issue on the table is not always useful as people may not feel they are in a position where they have enough power to risk responding. I am hoping that as a community of coordinators, we can explore this issue further together and find ways of being responsive to power dynamics. This discussion cannot be limited only to our communication with family members or service providers. Issues of power are reflected also among our colleagues. As a team of coordinators in the Toronto program, we have not talked about differences among ourselves. We are clear that a diverse team is important, but have never explored how it affects the ways in which we interact with each other, or whether some team members legitimately need greater support than others. Who should take responsibility for initiating this discussion? Does it matter if it is a White member or a Black member of the team? Should it be the program coordinator, regardless of race?

CONCLUSION

Conferencing is a complex task, and there are no recipes for a critical use of self. Clearly, however, coordinators need a fine-tuned sense of self-awareness. In addition, they need to be prepared to critically examine how they are doing their work. A reflexive approach to practice becomes the process through which coordinators can maintain awareness of and develop strategies to deal with the issue of power related to our role and who we are within that role. The Toronto Family Group Conferencing Project is built on a mental health-child welfare partnership. Our learning has been supported by having to develop a common vision and philosophy, which has allowed for significant examination and review of practice. It has been useful to have an "interrogative community" through supervision and peer supervision where one can investigate how one is doing the coordination.

Writing this chapter has therefore been one reflexive exercise within a series in terms of developing a more complex and multilayered understanding of use of self. I had begun with the traditional definition of *use of self*, which was challenged by my experiences and by critical thinking. However, over the last few months, another facet of use of self has become clearer to me. This has occurred through grappling with the concept in the study, and in attempting to teach the concept in three workshops.

I have always equated use of self with things one does in relation to the service user, and now appreciate use of self more as a lens through which one examines and comes to understand interaction. The "conscious use of self" has less to do with technique than a framework for analyzing power in relationships. This is, though, clearly an ongoing exploration.

NOTE

1. Under the apartheid dispensation, four racial groups were identified: African, Coloured, Indian, and White. These were artificial distinctions. Very broadly, then, the designation "Coloured" referred to people who were descendants of Malaysian and Indonesian slaves, or who were of mixed descent.

REFERENCES

Burford, G. & Hudson, J. (Eds.). (2000). *Family group conferencing: New directions in community-centered child & family practice.* New York: Aldine de Gruyter.

Connolly, M. (1999). *Effective participatory practice: Family group conferencing in child protection.* With M. McKenzie. New York: Aldine de Gruyter.

Hansen, M. (1999). The transatlantic exchange: Looking at family group conferencing practice in Hampshire, England, and Washington State. *Protecting Children, 16*(3), 66–71.

Harrison, R. & Quinett, L. (n.d.). *How to implement FGC and restorative justice programs in child abuse cases: Lessons learned in San Diego County.* Document produced by Rutgers University Forum for Policy Research and Public Service.

Kemp, S., Whittaker, K. & Tracy, E. (2000). Family group conferencing as person-environment practice. In G. Burford & J. Hudson (Eds.), *Family group conferencing: New directions in community-centered child & family practice* (pp. 72–85). New York: Aldine de Gruyter.

Love, C. (2000). Family group conferencing: Cultural origins, sharing, and appropriation—a Maori reflection. In G. Burford & J. Hudson (Eds.), *Family group conferencing: New directions in community-centered child & family practice* (pp. 15–30). New York: Aldine de Gruyter.

Margolin, L. (1997). *Under the cover of kindness: The invention of social work.* Charlottesville: University Press of Virginia.

Marsh, P. & Crow, G. (2000). Conferencing in England and Wales. In G. Burford & J. Hudson (Eds.), *Family group conferencing: New directions in community-centered child & family practice* (pp. 206–217). New York: Aldine de Gruyter.

Merkel-Holguin, L. (1998). Transferring FGC technology from New Zealand to USA. Paper presented at the 12th International Congress on Child Abuse and Neglect, September 6–9, Auckland, New Zealand.

Merkel-Holguin, L., Nixon, P. & Burford, G. (2003). Learning with families: A synopsis of FGDM research and evaluation in child welfare. Promising results, potential new directions: International FGDM research and evaluation in child welfare. *Protecting Children* 18(1–2), 2–11.

Nixon, P. (1999). *Family group conference connections.* Proceedings: Building Strong Partnerships for Restorative Practices, August 5–7, Burlington, Vermont.

Nixon, P., Merkel-Holguin, L., Sivak, P. & Gunderson, K. (2000). How can family group conferencing become family driven? Some dilemmas and possibilities. *Protecting Children, 16*(3), 22–33.

Schmid, J. (2005). The use of self in conference coordination. Unpublished manuscript.

Sippert, J., Hudson, J. & Unrau, Y. (2000). Family group conferencing in child welfare. *Families in Society: Journal of Contemporary Human Services, 81*(4), Swedish Association of Local Authorities Homepage. webbredaktionen@svekom.se. Retrieved on February 1, 2005.

CHAPTER 9

ON THE MERITS OF PSYCHOLOGICAL AUTOPSIES: WHY REFLEXIVE USE OF SELF IS IMPORTANT FOR COMMUNITY SOCIAL WORK PRACTITIONERS

Ginette Lafrenière

There's a reason why I chose not to be a clinical social worker. I simply don't do well with people who are needy—at least not on an individual level. My personal comfort zone is working within groups of people. I think that this might have something to do with my experience of "safety in numbers." That is, if one is engaged in collective action, the strength derived by being in a group is nurturing and, at least for me, creates a sense of security. Somehow my own "neediness" collapses with the neediness of others and, as a result, we derive strength in collective nurturing. This is why I have spent the past 17 years of my life working in various collective spaces on issues ranging from student rights, French language rights, affordable housing and daycare, equal pay for equal work, immigration and settlement issues, and a host of other social justice spheres.

As I get older, I feel increasingly comfortable in my role as a community practitioner and I have come to a reflective space whereby I have attempted to sporadically deconstruct my "use of self vis-à-vis the people with whom I have worked. Specifically, for the past six years I have worked on a project that at its core attempts to understand the experiences of women as organizers and activists in Northern Ontario. I have come to understand that their experiences are mine despite certain differences. My work on this topic has brought me to a space of humility and deep reflection on how my use of self is intimately intertwined with the work I have embraced over the past 20 years.

REFLECTION AND COMMUNITY ORGANIZING

I came to embrace this notion of "use of self" when I was required to write a paper on my experiences working with women within the context of a qualitative research seminar required as part of my doctoral program. For weeks I reflected on how my experience as an activist and community organizer paralleled my personal journey, which evolved from student activist to mothering activist, to paid community organizer, to peace activist. My identity as an organizer has shifted as I, too, have shifted in my personal and professional identity. As I write this, I am aware that my identity continues to shift and today, I would qualify that I am now a research activist and academic.

It had also occurred to me that my passion for community work had much to do with the feelings I associated with being an active participant within the community. It is in the community where I felt (and feel) nurtured and cared for, where I felt valued. My commitment to social justice led me to my activist husband, who has taught me much in terms of patience and diplomacy (I am painfully aware that I still need to learn much in these areas) and as a couple we have worked for 17 years together on issues relating to diversity and inclusion. His nurturing and the loving community that shaped him ultimately shaped me and over the years restored my faith in the power of collective action. The community was and is a space where I can channel my anger at injustice, use my energy to advocate, and work side by side with people who traditionally have not had a voice. It is an arena that is most enjoyable, fulfilling, and a natural crossroad to developing and sustaining friendships with an eclectic mix of people. It is a space that keeps one "real" no matter how many letters one has at the end of her name. For me, to be real is to come from a space of humility and profound respect for those in the community with whom we choose to align ourselves. To be real is to be able to open doors in the community.

We are taught that issues of transference and countertransference may enhance or impede the helping relationship. How, then, can we entertain the notion that we can possibly develop empathy and an understanding for the people with whom we work in the community if we do not look into ourselves? Somehow, not to engage in a reflexive use of self among community practitioners smacks of hypocrisy. At least that is what I have been thinking of late. Writing this chapter offers me a space to do this reflection on self in this way and consider how who I am relates to the work I do.

It feels natural to organize and be connected to something larger than my small, immediate reality. My trajectory as an organizer has ebbed and flowed over the years. I started out as a student activist and grew into various roles as a community organizer within the larger community. Nine years ago, something so life altering happened to me that a definite shift in my identity as a community organizer occurred. This shift made me realize that one must attempt to connect often to one's core in order to truly be an effective organizer. In 1996, I had a baby. So completely unprepared was I for the impact that this little boy would have in my life that I could not integrate intellectually or emotionally that my life had changed forever because of him. Needless to say, the first three months as a community organizer and activist were not easy. It was in the spring of 1997 that I decided my son would be, by extension, a community organizer (until he was old enough to decide for himself how he wanted to spend his free time); I was not going to end what I was doing, but I would simply do it differently. Once I got over the initial shock, my identity as an organizer shifted as a result of my mothering experiences. Issues regarding accessible francophone daycares, safe playgrounds, and after-school programs took on a different, highly personal meaning. The phenomenon of women leaving private spheres and entering public spheres regarding children's health issues became more understandable to me as a result of my own repositioning as an organizer and mother. It is precisely because I am a mother that I understand the rage and outcry of women who battle multinationals and municipalities concerning unsafe drinking water and neighbourhoods built on toxic waste dumps. While I had worked alongside these same women before I became "Issa's mom," since I've assumed that role, I feel that I am more in tune with the commitment and passion women feel when defending their families and particularly their children.

My identity as an organizer is fluid and textured, as is life. Now that my son is older (he has just turned nine years old as I write this) and is capable of clearly articulating that he does not share my enthusiasm for social action, my work as an activist and organizer is coloured by my role as an academic. Since 2002, I have been employed as a professor at Wilfrid Laurier University. Negotiating my identity as a community organizer and as an academic was initially tricky; over time, I discovered that the two identities were congruent and this has definitely influenced the nature and depth of my research. As evidenced by the title of this chapter, I will posit that community practitioners cannot and should not bask in a smug disconnect from themselves and the communities in which they choose to operate. To reflexively question the nature of one's community work is to quite simply be a "better" organizer, a more sensitive organizer, one who is more self-aware and therefore more responsive to the needs of the community in which one operates. In my own research I have qualified use of self within the context of reflexive ethnography, which draws upon a researcher's personal experience in order to illuminate fields of study (Ellis & Bochner, 2000).

REFLECTION AND RESEARCH

In my doctoral thesis I spent an inordinate amount of time illustrating the merits of reflexive ethnography as a legitimate qualitative research tool. My research created spaces for dialogue and reflection on the experiences of women as organizers. What follows is a snapshot on the essence of why reflexive ethnography is important and why it has applications for the argument that the use of self for the community practitioner is *essential* if one wants to work in community. Community practitioners must be aware of factors such as social location, class, race, and language in order to best serve those whom we choose to serve. Ellis and Bochner (2000) have credited David Hayano for the term "autoethnography" in discussing the way cultural anthropologists study their own people. In this context, the researcher truly is a full insider (Hayano, 1979). This particular genre of writing is somewhat problematic because of its subjective nature. Ellis and Bochner's own attempts at defining autoethnography speak to the challenges of such a genre in social science research:

> Autoethnography is an autobiographical genre of writing and research that displays multiple layers of consciousness, connecting the personal to the cultural.... Like many terms used by social scientists, the meanings and applications of autoethnography have evolved in a manner that makes precise definition and application difficult. (Ellis & Bochner, 2000, p. 739)

Ellis and Bochner illustrate a lengthy list of similarly situated terms in order to understand fully the enormous breadth and scope of autoethnographic research. Among others, they refer to narratives of the self (Richardson, 1994), personal experience narratives (Denzin, 1989), auto-observation (Adler & Adler, 1987), first-person accounts (Ellis, 1998), personal ethnography (Crawford, 1996), and critical autobiography

(Church, 1995). They credit feminism with contributing "significantly to legitimating the autobiographical voice associated with reflexive ethnography" (Ellis & Bochner, 2000, p. 740). The beliefs and behaviours of the researcher are considered by Sandra Harding (1987) to be part of the empirical evidence for (or against) the claims advanced in the results of the research. Doing reflexive autoethnography isn't always easy, though. Kay Redfield Jamison (1995) acknowledges the angst felt by certain feminist researchers when writing reflexive ethnography:

> It is an awful prospect giving up one's cloak of academic objectivity. But, of course, my work has been tremendously colored by my emotions and experiences. They have deeply affected my teaching, my advocacy work, my clinical practice, and what I have chosen to study. (p. 188)

It is important for the researcher to make her text interesting to the reader by drawing deeper connections between her personal experience and the subject under study (Behar, 1996). For Behar, writing vulnerably requires great courage and also needs to be useful and pertinent, a legitimate vehicle to get at the essence of the object of the author's research:

> … it does require a keen understanding of what aspects of the self are the most important filters through which one perceives the world and, more particularly, the topic being studied. Efforts at self-revelation flop not because the personal voice has been used, but because it has been poorly used, leaving unscrutinized the connection, intellectual and emotional, between the observer and the observed. Vulnerability doesn't mean that anything personal goes. The exposure of the self who is also a spectator has to take us somewhere we couldn't otherwise get to. It has to be essential to the argument, not a decorative flourish, not exposure for its own sake. (p. 14)

LOOKING BACK

Although not wanting to engage in a psychological autopsy on how I came to embrace the notion that reflexivity is a determining factor that contributes to an "enlightened" community organizer, it is important for me to briefly illustrate my personal trajectory as a community organizer and activist. My earliest experience as an organizer is etched in a memory of myself as an eight-year-old in grade three, organizing a fund drive in order to buy a gift for our beloved teacher, who was preparing for her maternity leave. Twenty-eight dollars and a car seat later, I remember feeling very proud and powerful that I was able to rally my classmates around a common goal. I believe that this was my first attempt at what would be a precursor to a lifetime of community organizing and activism.

Growing up in Northeastern Ontario, my father's activism influenced and shaped my perceptions of the importance of civic participation. My household environment informed my view on what community organizing meant through the experiences of my father. His commitment to community organizing within Franco-Ontarian organizations and the labour movement influenced my perception of how culture and politics can determine one's perception and commitment to community development.

My first attempt at reaching out and volunteering in the community came at a time when my parents' marriage was coming to an end. Encouraged by an American draft dodger who was my grade 12 English teacher, I joined a peace group in Sudbury in the early 1980s. Somehow, connecting with this wonderfully active, creative, and committed peace group eased in many ways the pain of my family's fragmented reality. Hence, during the course of my journey, this was my first attempt at connecting personal experience to desires for connecting in a meaningful way to community development. To understand on a deeper level my commitment to community was both liberating and empowering.

As an extension of my activism as a high school student, during my first undergraduate year at Laurentian University in 1983, I became active in francophone student politics. After a short time, my activism shifted to what was then qualified as "Third World issues." This was influenced by the fact that I was a student in Native Studies at the University of Sudbury. To be exposed to ideas regarding colonialism and different ways of "knowing" encouraged me to get involved in international issues. In 1983, I became involved in the movement to boycott South African products and organized through a theatrical medium an awareness of the atrocities of the apartheid political regime in South Africa.

Shortly after my graduation in 1990 from the Master's program in Co-operative Management from the Université de Sherbrooke, I returned to Sudbury to work at a co-operative housing resource group. My work in social housing taught me to appreciate and be sensitive to the relative nature of community development within urban, northern, and rural contexts and that as an organizer, I would have to develop a sort of community "radar" in order to capture the subtle and at times not-so-subtle nuances that characterized any community development initiative regardless of where it occurred. Through a series of exceptional circumstances, in mid-October of 1990, I found myself lecturing in courses on co-operative development and management within the School of Commerce at Laurentian University. While initially stimulating, after six years of trying to promote the co-operative model within the School of Commerce, I decided to leave. It was hard being a social cancer in a business school.

In 1995, I assumed a new job as a paid community organizer within a newly established francophone community health centre, and so began another important chapter in my community-organizing trajectory. It was 1996 and the Harris government was in full swing, enforcing the basic tenets of his Common Sense Revolution. As the first community organizer for the Centre de santé communautaire de Sudbury, my work was to assess minority francophones' needs regarding health care. My work was exciting and, given resources, flexible working hours, and a supportive executive director, I worked on dossiers that were important to me as a woman and a francophone. I lobbied for French language services and worked in the area of race relations between Franco-Ontarians and francophone Africans, who were increasing in numbers within our community.

During the five years I worked at the CHC, I undertook a second Master's degree, this time in Social Work. Harris's Revolution proved challenging and I needed to understand how to be a better organizer by acquiring social work skills. After my maternity leave, I resumed work once again in 1997. Shortly afterward, I became heavily involved in organizing a union within my workplace. After the union was voted in by an overwhelming 90 percent and given management's limited enthusiasm for my presence, my partner and I decided to fulfill a shared life goal: we each embarked on the journey toward a doctoral degree.

My first year at McGill was very rich and intense. It is also at this time that I was introduced to qualitative research and mothering literature. My reflections as a northern activist, community organizer, and mother seemed to gel for three hours weekly, over four months, within the qualitative research seminar the program required. This academic experience became the catalyst for the idea to write about my experience as a community organizer from Sudbury. At that point, I wanted to illustrate somehow through the voices of fellow female organizers as well as my own voice that our shifting identities as women reflected the shifting that we negotiated within our community organizing experiences.

The desire to value and research women's community organizing experiences is a direct result of my reactions to debates that we entertained within our Ph.D seminars. On more than one occasion, I would challenge a few of my professors because I did not often see my identity as a woman and an organizer reflected in the scholarship we were required to read. On more than one occasion, I had also observed that the circles in which some of my doctoral colleagues exercised their degree of activism or community organizing were drawn pretty clearly along racialized lines (Collins, 1986). I questioned, for example, why a certain anti-globalization resource group did not reflect much ethnic diversity. Were francophones and anglophones the only groups of people interested in anti-globalization issues in Montreal? What made certain types of people gravitate toward certain types of causes? Why was it that the Anarchist Weekend in Montreal, which included a book fair, seemed to be very "White" in its composition? Where were the Black anarchists in Montreal?

These questions incited much debate, sometimes heated, with regard to the gendered, racialized experiences in which we all engaged as community organizers. This period of questioning was an intensely stimulating time in my life when I was challenging every basic assumption I had ever held with regard to community organizing practices both in Montreal and in Sudbury. Through discussions with my colleagues, I learned to value and appreciate their experiences as organizers in Montreal. I came to learn much about the challenges of working in a large urban city. Through their work in social housing and through a community health clinic, I began to appreciate the enormity of the difficulties that they faced as organizers, if only in dealing with the sheer number of people needing assistance on a wide variety of issues. I began to appreciate the fact that in Montreal, things were not necessarily easier or better, just different. I also came to acknowledge the tensions with which some of my colleagues had to negotiate between different groups of people such as anglophone and francophone Quebecers and people from various ethno-cultural communities. Whereas in Sudbury, organizing was often done within relatively homogeneous circles, in Montreal much attention had to be paid to the numerous stakeholders within any given project.

During the course of my work as an organizer in Montreal, I noticed that my approaches to community organizing were sometimes out of step with the urban reality of Montreal. On one occasion I had naively suggested to a group of Black feminists that it might be feasible to organize a series of focus groups with Black women from various communities in

Côte-des-Neiges for a particular project. My suggestion was politely heard and then rejected. I was told that I was assuming the existence of alliances among the various Black women's groups and that there would not be enough trust among women to make such an endeavour possible. I was surprised. I had indeed assumed that with the significant number of Black women's formal and informal organizations in Montreal, surely it would be easy to organize a series of focus groups.

What challenged me immeasurably was my inability to diplomatically challenge the reasons why a focus group among Black women in Côte des Neiges was not possible. What if the reason of not knowing one another was simply not a good enough reason? How could I manage my Whiteness within this committed group of women without offending or stepping on some unarticulated boundary as a White ally? I had naively assumed that it would be easy and compared my organizing focus groups with different Black organizations in the Sudbury area. Given the relatively smaller number of members of the various Black communities in Sudbury, it was easy to pull together a group of people from Jamaica, Trinidad, Congo, Rwanda, and Mauritius. Visible minorities in Sudbury collided socially with one another frequently and certain alliances among people were naturally engaged. I thought that the same occurred in Montreal. According to the women with whom I worked, this was not the case. I learned that geography in an urban setting does not automatically translate to a level of ease for engaging in organizing processes.

Evidently, reflexive ethnography has prepared me for my present reflections on my use of self in my work as a community practitioner and educator precisely because I have found a certain resistance to it among some of my colleagues and students. For reasons that I ignore, I have found that some of the very people to whom I look up as model community practitioners sometimes shy away from or scoff at the notion that reflexive use of self is important. They seem to believe somehow that type of work doesn't apply to "us." I would argue that if we don't engage in reflexive practice, we are compromising our ability to truly understand some of the determining factors that have led us to the community in the first place.

There's a certain impatience or intolerance that I have often witnessed among some of my colleagues in community practice (a few years ago I would have put myself in the same ideological boat) whereby the need to argue, advocate, disrupt, and fight may be greater than the need to understand just why we are engaged in such work and whom, exactly, we are fighting. Sometimes I think we fight for the sake of fighting because that is what we are good at, without truly allowing ourselves to listen to all sides.

Clearly when I was in my late teens and early 20s, I would have fought for any cause if I felt it was the right thing to do. My social location as a Franco-Ontarian, I believe, predisposed me to understand certain nuances of oppression, power, and privilege that I encountered in my courses in Aboriginal culture. It is a most humbling experience to take a program of study with Aboriginal peoples who are learning with you, at the same time, elements of their history and culture, even language, which was almost completely obliterated through colonization. I believe that studying Aboriginal culture when I did prepared me for a lifetime of work in community organizing within various cultural spheres precisely because it taught me early on that are were many ways of viewing the world, and that my Franco-Ontarian, feminist lens was but one such way. Being encouraged to examine my own social location and being reflexive in unaccustomed ways, while uncomfortable at times, was invaluable to me not only on a personal but a professional level. Additionally, the harshest lesson I learned while studying Aboriginal culture was that Aboriginal peoples didn't seem to need me as much as I thought I needed them. When a Native professor gently challenged my desire to pursue a career as a constitutional lawyer, I realized that the lessons that I had learned from the Aboriginal community were also invaluable in helping me navigate social injustice everywhere, not just within the confines of Aboriginal spaces. Again, being encouraged to self-reflect brought me to spaces or levels of understanding of community that were rich and complex. To get to that space was and is gratifying. I now realize that the tension that my fellow social housing advocates and I enjoyed with decision makers in Ottawa and Toronto fuelled our righteous desires to be heard and seen. Being geographically marginalized rendered us effective and vocal advocates precisely because we were economically and politically marginalized. What a gift it is to hone such skills in a lifetime of social justice work.

My reflection on my own use of self allows me to gauge what is propelling me to help in certain arenas. I'm afraid that I am not always successful, however. It is difficult at times to make that link between what has shaped me, what is important to me, and why I think that others share and should share in my enthusiasm for what is important. For example, it is my intolerance of sexism, not my working conditions, that motivated me to organize a union in my workplace. The enormous power and control that men exercised around the board of directors of my workplace frightened me. A union, in my mind, would level the playing field in terms of power. And it did. But what was so terrifying about a group of presumably committed board volunteers in our community health centre? Their ignorance — the fact that they were completely unaware of the labour-intensive work that was demanded of us as health care and social service professionals. Perhaps my fear of feeling misunderstood or even suffocated by such ignorance propelled me in my activism. As mentioned earlier, I am not always successful in attempting to understand my organizing efforts; all I know is that I have come to the conclusion that it's important to allow myself to think about these things so that I can have the illusion of clarity of thought and mind while engaged in various community actions or work. I have come to realize that one doesn't always have to understand the motivation, but one ought to acknowledge that something is going on.

REFLECTION AND THE ACADEMY

Since coming to Southern Ontario I have been challenged once again by my students who are anglophone and who come, many of them, from faith communities. I struggle with the attention and tension paid to faith and social work practice, having aggressively denied in the past that religiosity and spirituality could occupy space within social work practice. Yet I am slowly and almost imperceptibly finding legitimacy in creating spaces for dialogue, debate, and even dissent regarding issues related to religiosity and social work practice. I believe I can do so because I have engaged the timid courage of self-reflection as someone shaped by faith. At present I am working on a research project on sensitive practice for health care and social service providers working with survivors of war, torture, and organized violence. What our research has uncovered is that survivors want to speak of religion and spirituality within the context of their helping relationships. As an educator and researcher, I need to think about this information, which honours, not diminishes, the voices that have informed this particular research project.

As a French Canadian brought up in the Catholic faith, how have I been shaped by religion? Why am I at times uncomfortable entertaining bridges between religiosity, spirituality, and social work practice? My research has pushed me to think about my social location as a French-Canadian Catholic. I struggle with my anger at the Catholic faith for the damage it has exercised against women and yet I am proud and honoured by some of the social justice actions and initiatives in which representatives of my faith have engaged. I struggle with my faith because it is not simple, but textured and irritating and nurturing all at once. Again, reflexivity is key in being able to shed light on these questions. Reflection on use of self enables us as practitioners to be real with ourselves and create spaces for discomfort and truth.

Finally, why is this topic important to me as an educator? Last spring I taught a course on reflexive use of self for community practitioners and it was, quite simply, rather difficult. The look of horror on my students' faces at the mere suggestion that they would be encouraged to look at their own social locations while working with economically marginalized communities was amusing. Why would they want to look at class issues while working with poor people? Why would they need to think of White privilege? Of gender? They simply wanted to help. Introspection was for their clinical colleagues, not them. I remember on one occasion inviting as a guest speaker a colleague who does much work in the area of bullying through drama. One visualization exercise invited the students to think of certain unpleasant or painful experiences. The next time we met as a group, a few students expressed mild irritation at having to participate in an exercise that tugged at their feelings. To this I replied with not-so-mild irritation that to "feel" — and to be reflexive with regard to those feelings — is fundamental for the community practitioner. I stated that one could not be cloaked in the safety of the role of community organizer and dispense with the responsibility of thinking of one's social location and privilege. Why should only the clinical social work students deconstruct their feelings relative to helping relationships? It took some time before the students opened up and saw the merits of reflexivity.

CONCLUDING REFLECTIONS

I agreed to write this chapter simply because I have been writing and thinking about my own angst as a community practitioner for a long time. If I chide myself with thoughts on how I could have intervened with my Black colleagues in Montreal six years after the fact or now with my community partners and students, it is because the experience of working within community and teaching about community has challenged my sense of self and has forced me on many levels to be better, stronger, more diplomatic, more courageous, more humble, yet not so humble as to eclipse my sense of self.

It is very difficult work to navigate among various groups of people without often second-guessing oneself. Conversely, after 17 years of community organizing, I believe that second-guessing oneself is key to being an effective organizer. Whether one understands reflection as "use of self" or "reflexivity," what is certain is that without some type of personal reflection, one cannot be truly effective and helpful within the community. Reflexivity enables me to develop strength and to ask tough questions of my colleagues and allies. Most of the time, my truth ignites legitimate debate and discussion; being aware of my social location at all times, while an enormous responsibility, enables me to open doors that may not otherwise have been opened for me or to me.

Reflexivity is much more than a simple act of intellectual navel-gazing; it is an important element of best practice for those of us who choose to be of service to others — even if, at times, it is uncomfortable.

REFERENCES

Adler, P.A. & Adler, P. (1987). *Membership roles in field research.* Newbury Park: Sage Publications.

Behar, R. (1996). *The vulnerable observer.* Boston: Beacon Press.

Church, K. (1995). Forbidden narratives: Critical autobiography as social science. Newark: Gordon and Breach.

Collins, P.H. (1986). Learning from the outsider within: The sociological significance of Black feminist thought. *Social Problems, 33*(6), 14–32.

Crawford, L. (1996). Personal ethnography. *Communication Monographs, 63,* 158–170.

Davies, L. & Krane, J. (1996). Shaking the legacy of mother blaming: No easy task for child welfare. *Journal of Progressive Human Services, 7*(2), 3–22.

Dennie, D. (1999). *Les Franco-Ontariens et le matérialisme historique.* Livre non-publié soumis à un éditeur pour fins de publication.

Denzin, N.K. (1989). *Interpretive biography.* Newbury Park: Sage Publishers.

Devereux, G. (1967). *From anxiety to method in behavioral sciences.* New York and The Hague: Mouton.

Ellis, C. (1998). Exploring loss through autoethnographic inquiry: Autoethnographic stories, co-constructed narratives, and interactive interviews. In J.H. Harvey (Ed.), *Perspectives on loss: A sourcebook* (pp. 49–61). Philadelphia: Taylor and Francis.

Ellis, C. & Bochner, A. (2000). Autoethnography, personal narrative, reflexivity: Research as subject. In N. Denzin & Y. Lincoln (Eds.), *Handbook of qualitative research* (2nd ed.) (pp. 733–768). Newbury Park: Sage Publications.

Geertz, C. (1995). *After the fact: Two countries, four decades, one anthropologist.*

Cambridge: Harvard University Press.

Harding, S. (1987). *Feminism and methodology*. Bloomington: Indiana University Press.

Hayano, D. (1979). Auto-ethnography: Paradigms, problems, and prospects. *Human Organization, 38,* 113–120.

Juteau-Lee, D. (1982). The Franco-Ontarian Collectivity: Material and symbolic dimensions of its minority status. In R. Breton & P. Savard (Eds.), *The Quebec and Acadian diaspora in North America* (pp. 167–182). Toronto: The Multicultural Society of Ontario.

Redfield Jamison, K. (1995). *An unquiet mind.* New York: Random House.

Reitsma-Street, M. & Rogerson, P. (1999). Implementing principles: An alternative community organization for children. In K. Blackford, M.L. Garceau & S. Kirby (Eds.), *Feminist success stories* (pp. 289–306). Ottawa: University of Ottawa Press.

Richardson, L. (1994). Nine poems: Marriage and the family. *Journal of Contemporary Ethhnography, 23,* 3–13.

CHAPTER 10

"IN AND AGAINST" THE COMMUNITY: USE OF SELF IN COMMUNITY ORGANIZING

Eric Shragge

INTRODUCTION

The teaching of community organizing practice within schools of social work has a strong tradition and has gone through periods in which it had greater and lesser importance in the development of professional curriculum and education. During the 1970s, in the United States and Canada, community organizing took big steps in becoming part of social work training. Professors were hired, texts written, and courses and field placements developed. It was in that context that I was hired at McGill University's School of Social Work. My tasks were to locate and develop field placements in community organizations and work with and supervise students in their daily work in these placements. In order to do so, I was able to participate actively in the organizing work. This was my beginning in combining organizing and teaching. I have persisted since then in teaching and involving myself in many community organizations and related projects.

The practice in the community has changed in many important ways since that period. The image of a community organizer, when I began, was a tough, action-oriented doer. In a profession largely dominated by women, there were a disproportionately high number of male students who chose to be organizers. Many argued that the real work of social change could happen only through organizing and that other methods, particularly casework, maintain the status quo and keep the poor subservient. As a group, "C-O" students saw other forms of intervention as too focused on the individual; organizing, on the other hand, was the way to begin to collectivize social problems, fight inequality, and help the poor and other oppressed groups gain power and address their problems through action. C-Os were the last ones to worry about the use of self. Many were influenced by New Left and/or Marxist ideology and were involved, they believed, in a movement for fundamental change. The processes of self-critical reflection on the use of self would slow down the process and lead to mainstreaming organizers and co-optation of their practice by a hidden force of clinicians.

This is a parody of the reality, which was more complex and nuanced. However, there is an element of truth even in this exaggerated presentation. The split in social work education between community organizers and the rest was real enough and remained for many years despite attempts to dilute community organizing and its radical content of practice through integrating it into different forms of "generic" practice. In the 26 years that I worked in the School of Social Work, there was always a handful of students who rejected either clinical or generic practice and found ways to engage in and learn about community organizing. However, in all of this time, the area of discussion that was rarely broached was the use of self. Social and political analysis, strategy, and tactics dominated the agenda. The use of self was secondary, if at all, and certainly never as such. However, this has changed because "the revolution" was not around the corner and a longer-term approach was needed. In addition, contributions from both feminist activists and scholars and the emergence of "presenting of self" as part of newer social science approaches influenced by feminism and autoethnography opened new possibilities for a critical reflection on the use of self in organizing and wider political and social movements.

I have structured the chapter with the underlying idea that the use of self in community organizing is shaped by three interrelated and interacting factors. The first is who one is, including one's own values, politics, and reasons for participating in organizing. This is central because we all bring our own personal histories and perspectives into this work. The second is the role we play in the organizing process. In this chapter, I identify organizer, activist, and ally as three possible and at times overlapping roles. They each structure how one works and therefore how one uses self. Finally, the context is a key element that defines the traditions of practice, its relationship with a variety of bodies, and the changes in the wider community sector that influence practice. It is shaped by a combination of external factors that are very powerful, including the wider political economy, relations of class and other forms of power, and the specific traditions of community organizations and the relations that they have with the bodies that fund them.

The use of self in community organizing is constructed by the interaction of one's own politics, the related vision, and the role one plays within the particular context in which community organizing takes place. Engagement in everyday practices challenges individual stances and forces an ongoing tension between what one would like and what is. It is within this tension that one discovers how to use oneself. I will refer to myself as a teacher and practitioner throughout the chapter; it is therefore important to understand a little about me. I would describe myself as being clearly and unambiguously on the left, influenced by Marxist analysis of capitalism and, more importantly, by the political traditions of anarchism and the impulse for direct democracy and control of everyday life by collectivities of people. However, the revolution is not around the corner. In the meantime, I try to work with and contribute to those community organizations that reflect both a critical analysis of the larger system — capitalism, shaped by patriarchy, racism, and other forms of domination — and engage in different ways to oppose it. There are many ways to build this opposition ranging from local mobilization to creating places of opposition culture and popular education. I believe that this has to be done in a way that is self-conscious and at the same time responds to the needs and problems that people face while building on their strengths so that they can speak on their own behalf. This, to me, remains the key element in why one acts as an organizer and in a fundamental way shapes how I believe community organizing should work.

I have divided the chapter into four sections. In the first, I will present some of the literature that has contributed to an understanding of the use of self in organizing; as well, other literatures that clarify roles and practices in organizing will be introduced to form a base for an analysis of the self in practice. The second section will argue that the use of self is interrelated with context, and that changes over the past 30 years have had a major impact on the use of self in community organizing and community work in general. Finally, I will present my own experiences and personal reflection on the use of self. I will conclude with a reflection on the current conjuncture and the challenges for how one can engage in social change practice in an era in which that agenda is rarely present in schools of social work or in the wider community sector.

LITERATURE AND USE OF SELF

The literature on the use of self in community organizing is limited. A
beginning point is to acknowledge that there is such a role. The role and
position of a community organizer shapes the possibilities for how one can
use oneself. There have always been people who played a leadership role in
the process of organizing their communities, whether to challenge power
or to develop relations of solidarity, services, or programs. However, the
role is not often named. Perhaps the person to develop and name the role
of a community organizer was Saul Alinsky. He believed that organizers
were the driving force behind an organization and they provide both
vision and technical knowledge (Alinsky, 1971; Mondros & Wilson, 1994).
This role has become recognized and accepted as a legitimate one with
visibility in and accountability to local organizations. At times, the role
is there, but it is named differently; it can be a community developer or a
variety of staff positions. In practice this position consists of many roles
and, as I will develop, ideal characteristics are contested. To examine these
debates, I will start with Alinsky, then look at some feminist alternatives
that provide a contrast.

Alinsky begins with the assumption that organizations are created in
large part by organizers, and asks what creates an organizer. He states
that specific organizing skills can be taught, but that there are several
important personal characteristics that are necessary for success. These
include curiosity, irreverence, imagination, a sense of humour, "a bit of
a blurred vision of a better world," an organized personality, "a well-
integrated political schizoid" (p. 78), a strong ego, a free and open mind
and political relativity, and, finally, the ability to create the new out of
the old. These character traits describe a lot of people. Despite these,
and perhaps more important, the role of the organizer is central in an
organization and often with a larger-than-life persona, as was the case with
Alinsky himself. Burghardt (1982) provides words of caution. Alinsky and
others, usually men, create what he describes as "The Great Organizer
Theory of Organizing" (p. 52), which states that every organizer should
be able to perform well within all important strategic situations such as
running an office to organizing a demonstration. The possibility of their
doing organizing work, particularly through that model, is questioned. A
more realistic examination of the self and organizing is required in order
to pursue a more inclusive possibility.

Burghardt (1982) is one of the few writers who have analyzed the complex roles that organizers play and the way that individual traits contri-

bute to successful accomplishment of the demands of the job. Awareness of how personal effectiveness varies from situation to situation is a starting point in understanding the strengths and weaknesses that each person brings to the organizing role. He argues that community organizers tend to be task-oriented rather than process-oriented personalities, but many situations require process, interpersonal, and intuitive characteristics. It therefore becomes important for organizers to identify the situations in which they may or may not be comfortable and find ways to work on those areas of weakness with modesty in setting goals and using strengths to work on areas of difficulty (p. 61). A challenge for community organizers is to become self-conscious about the roles they play and this is the first step in effective use of self. Mondros and Wilson (1994) identify the central skill sets as technical and interaction or expressive. Technical skills include those related to efficacy on issues and those contributing to organizational health and effectiveness while interactional or expressive skills include the ability to work in various ways with individuals and groups. The latter is key when the objectives are to build leadership and processes of collective power. Through these processes, organizers and their organizations engage citizens directly and build participation. These elements are key because they demonstrate the complex demands made on those working in the community. The tension between process and outcome is central in organizing. As I will argue later, with the transformation of the role of the community, the pressures on outcome far outweigh the processes. As a consequence, the direct organizing and citizen participation diminish.

Up to this point, I have referred to literature that presents an organizer as the key player in the organizing process. In addition, this role is usually a paid one, and the individual is the staff person within the organization and can carry out a number of functions from direct organizing to administration, publicity, fundraising, etc. As work in the community has developed over the past 30 years, these roles have changed, but it implies that there is a relationship between employee and organization. Often the employee is not necessarily part of the group that is being organized or to whom service or programs are directed. The criteria for credibility for this position are based on capacity and skills and not necessarily on who the person is. In the tradition of Alinsky and related perspectives, a good organizer often has to cross lines and work with people different from himself or herself. The skills brought by the organizer and the loyalty and commitment to the cause are the basis of his or her acceptance and legitimacy for his or her presence and central role. The growing influence of feminism and anti-racism frameworks challenges a simple acceptance of this position. I will explore other ways to conceptualize organizing, based on the use of self that are in synch with these latter perspectives. They challenge the centrality and the power of a community organizer as an outsider that are inherent in the older model.

The feminist movement raises an implicit challenge to the role of the outside organizer and a model of organizing that focuses only on limited concrete victories. The personal dimension and the way that issues touch daily life are central. Adamson et al. (1988) discuss aspects of feminist organizing and argue:

> One obvious factor was the ability of "the personal is political" and CR (consciousness raising) to link the individual experiences of each woman's life to the wider political context, and thus make sense of them. This link was essential because it provided women with a sense of the direction they needed to take and thus made it possible for them to act together to create change; ... the success of these ideas is a reminder that visions of change need to be rooted in the reality of personal experience. (p. 206)

There is an important shift that occurs with the emergence of a feminist perspective. The organizer as an outsider is implicitly challenged; instead, shared experience is the basis for organizing. The process itself becomes broadened and the goal becomes not only immediate gains but also personal transformation through collective action and CR. The role of the organizer disappears from this discussion and the role of the self becomes that of an insider who shares in experiencing conditions of patriarchy.

Drawing on feminist traditions is the question of standpoint theory and positionality (Naples, 1998). Rather than focusing on an organizer, this literature begins with women as activists working on issues that directly touch their own lives and often this engagement has an impact on their self-definition and identity. Their role is as insider activists, working on their own behalf, self-interest, and, at the same time, possibly transforming themselves through the work. Personal transformation is a key consequence of community organizing and activism. It can include learning about issues and processes of social change and, more importantly, about the way individuals learn how to act differently, to build a sense of confidence, to redefine themselves from passive to active, to build solidarity and break isolation and become public actors (Church et al.,

2000; Foley, 2001). These transformations can be encouraged by organizers and activists being aware of the importance of the potential of community organizations as political activity centres (Barker, 1999) in which the day-to-day learning and transformations can be encouraged and supported. These processes can be lost if organizers become overly concerned with concrete and specific results and not the processes and their impact on individual participants.

Organizers play a key role here, supporting the development and the transformation of individuals, particularly how they see themselves in the organizing processes. The relationships between activism and identity are complex and involve shifting political and social relations in the process. As Naples (1998) explains:

> Women are politicized and drawn into local battles in a myriad of ways that reflect a wide diversity of personal and political concerns as well as varying constructions of community and social identities. Regional political economy and cultural practices woven in and through racial-ethnic and class formation also structure how women engage in community activism and what successes they achieve. Explorations of how women from different ... backgrounds confront different constellations of power that differentially shapes their political consciousness and oppositional political practice.... (p. 344)

With this perspective, the use of self in community is far more complex than the organizer who comes from the outside. The role of local activist is affirmed with all of the complexities of identity and the forces that shape local conditions and how "insiders" act in working for social justice. Coming from within immediately lends itself to personal legitimacy as an actor working with those sharing a common social position. Identity-based organizing and related projects become framed as activists. The difference between activist and organizer becomes blurred, with those working locally playing overlapping roles with the primary and most important one as those directly affected by an issue and acting on their own behalf. There are those in activist work who play the role of organizers, but this is often shared and implicit rather than professionalized and explicit.

It is important, however, not to lose the role of an organizer. In the discussion of activism cited above, the specific roles played by organizers, paid or unpaid, tend to disappear. Organizations usually include people who play that role, who facilitate, plan, and provide vision and direction.

Acknowledging these roles then allows a more specific understanding of organizational dynamics and processes, regardless of whether the organizer is an insider or an outsider. To understand the process of how people can grow into the organizer role and take their place in these processes, we turn to the example of Linda Stout (1996). She describes her evolution from a girl growing up in poverty in Appalachia to an organizer building an organization for peace and social justice in a poor rural community. She talks about her success with others as follows:

> When I talk to people who are struggling to develop their own leadership, I tell about my own struggle to believe that I could be a leader. People see me now as a leader, though I keep reminding them that I am no different than other people in our community. I do not pretend that I have always had the skills that I have now. This is important to communicate to people who are beginning to develop their own leadership skills. (p. 153)

One of the important contributions she makes is to demystify who can be a community organizer and what this role entails. For students, particularly women, Stout's personal account, in contrast to the "great man," encourages them to believe that they are able to take on this kind of work. The insider, as discussed in the feminist literature above, is usually an activist. Stout's perspective opens the possibility of an insider organizer, who plays a particular role in the organization and brings useful skills to it. The reality of a lot of local work is that there are many people who emerge as organizers from within oppressed populations and play central organizing and leadership roles, but they are not acknowledged. Similarly, in social movements such as the ecology or peace movements, organizing is played out but not acknowledged as defined professional activities. These are usually referred to as staff positions, taken over by activists from those movements, acknowledging the organizing roles even as insiders.

Another dimension to this question is: How can outsiders act in a way that supports but does not displace insiders as the leaders and without taking on the central role of the organizer? Anne Bishop (1994) discusses the role of ally. She begins with an analysis of the different and divisive forms of oppression and argues that these are all part of a "single complex interrelated self-perpetuating system" (p. 10). Allies, according to Bishop, are those who give up privilege to join the struggle for social change. In contrast to the characteristics of an organizer described above, she presents those of allies. These include

... their sense of connection with other people ... their grasp of the concept of collectivity and collective responsibility; their lack of an individualistic stance and ego ... their sense of process and change; their understanding of their own process and learning; their realistic sense of their power ... their grasp of "power-with" as an alternative to "power-over" ... their acceptance of struggle.... (p. 95)

The role is different from both an organizer and an activist because the leadership rests with those who are members of an oppressed group and it is their leadership that counts. This is particularly important for social workers and community workers: to learn to find an appropriate place and relationship with an organization or group in which they can offer skills and resources but be in the background, accountable to members. It is easier in theory than in practice. More realistically, it is important to see these relationships in a tension between those who bring organizing skills and experience and those who are part of an oppressed group. Acknowledging the tension and the roles is a first step, but it does not cause them to disappear.

Kruzynski's (2005) research illustrates this tension. She interviewed women who were active in the working-class community of Pointe St-Charles in Montreal for more than 25 years. For many of them, there was an "outside agitator," who raised questions and issues and was the first to organize them and encourage their participation and leadership. The women discussed the ambiguities of this relationship and the conflicting feelings about these outsiders. On the one hand, they saw their power through the politics, skills, and knowledge that they brought and how these opened possibilities for local residents. On the other, they saw these relations as controlling and not allowing local people to be in real leadership positions. In contrast, Church's (1995) experience with the psychiatric survivor movement shows how the leaders of an oppressed group can take real control and then see allies as useful, as long as the allies do not bring their own agenda and analysis. On the ground, the relationships between allies and oppressed groups is complex and it is important to underestimate neither the importance of the skills and knowledge of outsiders nor the relations of power that can be part of it.

In selecting this literature, I have examined roles and attributes of organizers. The tradition that comes from and follows Alinsky names the position and focuses on the role and characteristics. The organizer is pivotal in the organization and even with the democratic structures and citizen participation he or she remains central. There is a continuity with some modifications to account for gender and ethnic, or other minorities, through contemporary organizations like ACORN (see www.ACORN.org) and many of the recent writing in the field (Sen, 2003; Staples, 2004). The importance of this tradition is that it acknowledges and describes the role of an organizer. It is explicit, and there are skills and analysis that go with it. Further, there is an organizational context and accountability to that organization. However, in the Alinsky tradition, the power of this role is often underestimated. There needs to be an analysis of who the organizer is and what role he or she plays in relation to the people being organized and how much control people have over that person. With the introduction of activist and ally, the centrality of the people directly affected by the issue becomes clarified. The "people" rather than the organizer are the central actors. The implicit and often hidden power of the outside organizer is challenged. This lesson helps to put in the centre the goal of organizing; that is, increasing people's power in their everyday lives, and respecting the real difficulties inherent in their finding ways to organize collectively and build an independent voice. However, even with this lesson, in both the activist and ally literature, the discussion of organizer roles is usually absent. All community organizations have this role. It can be concentrated in one or two key, paid people, or be more diffuse and shared. However, in order to build democratic processes, the role and related tasks have to be transparent and acknowledged, otherwise they become hidden and problems of accountability result. The organizer, paid or unpaid, insider or outsider, plays a central role. Those working in that role have to begin with an understanding of how they are part of a process and understand their relationship to those with whom they are working.

TRANSFORMATION IN COMMUNITY AND USE OF SELF IN PRACTICE

In the previous section, I have discussed the role of community organizers, activists, and allies. All these share the goal of progressive social change, what I describe as "oppositional" (Shragge, 2003). However, at the same time, community organizing and related development and local service provision can contribute to the integration of individuals into the system without challenging it in any way. With the restructuring of the relationship between the state and community organizations, more services are provided by the latter to compensate for cutbacks by the former and the growing poverty and unemployment beginning in the late 1970s. Perhaps the most striking example of this was the growth in food banks. Many community organizations have become new forms of charity acting in solidarity with community members facing hard times. There has also been a growth in entrepreneurial practices such as community economic development (Shragge, 1997), which used strategies of job development and training to integrate the unemployed into the labour market. These can be contradictory and create political spaces (Church, 1995), but this is not the dominant practice. These changes have had a major impact for the use of self in practice. I will briefly trace the evolution of the community sector in Quebec and examine the implication for the use of self in practice.

The community sector in Quebec has gone through significant transitions over the past 40 years, which are similar to the evolution elsewhere (Fisher & Shragge, 2000; Hasson & Ley, 1994). I will draw on Quebec for the purposes of illustrating this discussion. In the 1960s and 1970s, we witnessed a renewal in community practice that was connected to urban movements (Hamel, 1991; Shragge, 2003). Much of this work, whether it was grassroots organizing or service provision, created new democratic practices based on direct participation of citizens. By the late 1970s, the capacity of local organizations to mobilize citizens diminished and many organizations became primarily points of local service provision. The shift was led by service professionals who were able to secure government funds and, over the years, greater recognition from the state. These services, although often innovative, redefined the relationship between these organizations and those they served, who were treated primarily as clients rather than active political and social actors. Their growing professionalism and knowledge of local problems, combined with their ability to use innovative strategies, have contributed to the expertise of community organizations to intervene on a variety of social problems and issues. Often these practices began with grassroots initiatives that then became recognized, supported, and regularized as part of state-community policy. This implies a shift from a conflict-based approach to a collaborative one (Hamel et al., 2000). These organizations have created relationships with each other, and different tiers of government and other funding bodies in order to obtain resources, to initiate local interventions, and coordinate activities. Thus, over the past 20 years the relationship between the community sector and the provincial government has gradually become formalized. The highly structured system of representation through "regroupements," or coalitions based on local or sector of service, form the context of the way that community organizations are able to influence and shape government policies. The formalization of the community sector's representation allows organizations to defend their self-interest and influence policy on funding and conditions for it. The push back from the government is to define with increasing force a subcontractual relationship between community organizations and various ministries, particularly those involved in the health social services and regional development as the provincial government has downloaded specific functions to community organizations. For the community sector this recognition of its professionalism promises greater stability, but narrows its functions and reduces its autonomy. Parazelli and Tardif (1998) contrast what they describe as autonomous community action based on people in a community defining their own needs, strategies, and priorities with "communautique" in which the community sector becomes linked to the technocratic apparatus of the state. The clash between this "evolution" and the older democratic traditions creates the central tension in the community sector, with some organizations still protecting their radical origins against the pressures to comply with the new way.

These tensions and changes have profound consequences for the use of self in community work. The use of self cannot be separated from the larger context that structures the direction of and the nature of the work and the roles played by organizers. The growing professionalism and the increasingly complex organizational environment require new technical skills and practices. In the 1970s, among others, the skills an organizer required were interpersonal. Direct contact through outreach and face-to-face discussion was required in order to recruit and work with leaders and members, and help them build their capacities. Building organizations and other related activities was from the bottom up and the first priority was direct involvement of citizens. Group skills were important for facilitating meetings and groups. How one presented oneself, building trust with another (usually from a different background), and engaging in a discussion about local conditions or personal situations all demanded that organizers should work well with local people at the individual level. One had to be open, but at the same time clear about why one was there. The only means organizers had at that point was how they were able to present themselves, convey possibility, and support leadership development. The work was at a grassroots level and the processes were dynamic; success was measured by the participation and degree of activism of citizens. The organizer had to have credibility in proposing a path that, for many who were poor and had never been active before, was hard to fathom. The outside organizer had to help people build the confidence and the belief that collectively they could have some impact. Further, as Kruzynski so vividly describes in her thesis, political education came after their trust and relationships had been established, even with outsiders, particularly among women. The organizer's use of self was key in moving from agitator to teacher, to supporter, to ally and always building relationships on the way.

The changes in the community sector described above resulted in the displacement of engaged citizens to the status of clients receiving local services. This does not imply that these organizations do not remain active on social and political issues. However, it is the professionals/staff of the organizations who act as spokespeople on issues, representing the interest and needs of the group they are serving. There have been changes in the organizational level as well. They are larger, usually governed by an elected board with a limited and relatively inactive membership. Managing day-to-day operations, and fundraising become complex and demanding tasks. With the growth of the social economy and community economic development (Shragge & Toye, 2006), expertise in writing business plans and loan applications is required. All of these tasks are challenging and are time consuming, particularly when there are only a few staff members, and the core functions of the organization are not stable or well supported. Community workers have to devote more of their time to organizational management and fundraising, plus report writing to funding bodies that require results or outcome evaluations. The use of self becomes defined by the role and skill set required to work in community; these have changed from an organizer to a manager, a fundraiser, with increased similarities to working in the private sector. The growth of the community sector has spawned many training and capacity-building programs that contribute to preparing practitioners for this environment. This change has been frustrating for those who believe that the community sector should be about the building of grassroots power for social justice and using conflict strategies to get there (Fisher & Shragge, 2000). The building of a broad social consensus through community organizations based on a service agenda has resulted in a depoliticized context in which the use of self is increasingly based on professional managerial capacities. The growing importance of community organizations in the context of neo-liberal transformation (Jessop, 2001, 2002) reflects the evolution of these organizations from "oppositional" to playing a "responsible" social role, even with the tensions in these changes. Community organizations have moved from marginal and oppositional (with their legitimacy based on their capacities to mobilize and organize) to central and recognized components of social services and development (with their legitimacy based on formality of organizations and professionalization of their employees).

As I turn now to a personal reflection, I think it is important to see what follows *not* as a wish to return to the good old days, but much more as a critical perspective and the need to support the politicized work that still goes on in community organizations.

SITUATING SELF

This section will develop my understanding of how I use myself in the different dimensions of my work. I have discussed my own evolution as a teacher and active participant in community organizations at length elsewhere (Shragge, 2003) and will not repeat it here, except to state where I am currently situated. After working at the School of Social Work, McGill University, for 26 years, where I taught community organizing and social policy, I moved to a small interdisciplinary department, the School of Community and Public Affairs (SCPA) at Concordia University. I was hired to direct a new Graduate Diploma Program in Community Economic Development. I had many reasons for leaving, but perhaps the central one for this chapter was the marginalization of community organizing within social work education. At the SCPA, I was hired precisely because community development and organizing are valued both in the graduate program and at the undergraduate level.

My "use of self" comes at three levels: as a teacher, as a researcher, and as someone engaging with community organizations. I will explore each of these and their interconnections.

The Graduate Diploma Program in CED is structured to accommodate practitioners working full- or part-time in community organizations. I teach two courses in the program: One focuses on basic concepts in community development and organizing, and another is related to on-going field projects that the participants undertake over two semesters. The initial challenge for me was how to teach people who brought extensive experience to the class. I had to create a place in which experienced practitioners could share with and learn from each other, and at the same time deepen their own understanding. With some groups my role was not to teach "how to" but to facilitate critical reflection on practice and in the process introduce new ideas and perspectives. The pedagogy that I use begins with the assumption that everyone, including the teachers themselves, is both a teacher and a learner. Thus, shared experience is highly valued and the exchanges between program participants are a key element. Starting with these premises, my role then is to encourage and to support interaction in the class and, at the same time, to introduce concepts, analysis, and my own experiences to illustrate practice issues and encourage discussion. A challenge is to balance free-flowing discussion with a focus on theory and readings. One of my early observations in practice teaching is that there is an anti-intellectual culture among practitioners in their pursuit of relevance. My goal in teaching is to make sure that three elements are present—analysis, intervention, and critical reflection on practice.

The analysis begins with the impact of social, political, and economic dimensions on different levels in the society ranging from the international to the local and their interconnections. There are both benefits and problems with this. The benefits are that it introduces a critical perspective on the forces that shape the specific social problems in a community. The nature of globalized capitalism and neo-liberal social and economic policies shape much of daily life as well as the specific manifestations of gender and racial oppression that continue. Community practitioners require this kind of critical analysis to understand what they are up against and the necessity of long-term fundamental change, connecting what can be gained in the short term and what its longer-term implications might be. On the negative side, however, it is also discouraging and can lead to despair because of the huge challenges facing practitioners. Often in the literature the social analysis presented is too simple and within a "liberal" framework and, as a consequence, the possibilities of practice are overly optimistic (Alinsky, 1971).

The personal challenge is how to have a critical analysis and understand that, even though this shapes the limits of practice possibilities, it does not necessarily lead to a sense that the opposition is too powerful to challenge. In the period of transition to neo-liberalism, and as we watch massive ecological catastrophes, it is easy to give up and many I know have. One way for me to understand what I do and stick to it is to think in terms of opposition and trying to limit the gains on the other side. It is for that reason that building opposition is so important; it is understanding that society is based on an ongoing relationship of conflict and power. The second dimension is more personal; it is about whom I find with me. The networks and colleagues who work in opposition are an unusual group of people who stand outside the mainstream, usually with humour and shared values and vision. These are invaluable in sustaining the work.

The second dimension is direct intervention itself—what people do in the day-to-day world of practice. There is a wide range of skills that can be taught, such as how to work with individuals and groups, strategies and tactics, organization development and maintenance, fundraising, planning, etc.

This brings us to the third dimension—critical reflection, a dimension that post-acceptance interviews with incoming students have indicated is highly valued by those with considerable community experience. The interaction between context and practice needs to be critically evaluated as practice processes evolve. We need to step back and see what is being gained and the effectiveness of the work, but with which guiding principles? Political and value frameworks that guide interventions have to be made explicit for this to happen. Critical reflection is required to understand the complexities. However, it is important to recognize that community work starts with individuals and their reasons for building projects. A beginning point is to name our own experience and how this influences what we do and why. Therefore, I assign to the class an exercise as a means of introduction and as a way of understanding their own politics and values. I ask students to write a "political autobiography" in which they discuss their own evolution, the factors, events, and people that influenced them. The underlying idea is to begin to articulate one's politics and values, but within a personal historical context. This exercise provides a beginning point for moving toward an understanding of one's vision for community organization practice, a vision that can help to sustain workers in the difficult conditions of community work. Through this exercise two results emerge. The first is that most of the students, despite a high level of diversity, share many values; and, second, these put them in opposition to the dominant social values. An explicit discussion of these conflicts contributes to insight and understanding about what is at stake and how one can sustain one's contribution to longer-term social change. Without this reflection, it is easy to get caught up in whatever the latest grant or project is about and become led by government or foundation programs. A sharp, critical social analysis and personal critical reflection then become the compass to maintain a sense of social and political direction. Discussion of practice is inextricably linked to an analysis of the context and influences it. At the same time, reflection on practice needs to be introduced at every step. In order to teach community organizing and development effectively, it is important that I have direct involvement in local organizations. As an academic, I have the privilege of choosing to be a "volunteer" in them and therefore have the flexibility to define both where and how much I can be involved. Over the last five years, I have been on the boards of directors of three organizations — The Immigrant Workers Centre (IWC), L'Action Communiterre, and Centre for Community Organizations (COCo). All three of these organizations stand outside of the mainstream of the highly structured community sector in Quebec. They share a critical analysis and their commitment to social justice and progressive social change is explicit. Being on the boards of all three organizations requires work between meetings, including planning and fundraising. With the IWC, because of the lack of any substantial funding, there is a blurring of roles between staff and board members and, as a consequence, much of the day-to-day operation of the organization is shared. I bring experience and contacts to the organizations, but also an analysis and a critical perspective on the community sector, which contributes to an analysis about how to work both inside and outside of the mainstream community sector.

Because of the nature of these organizations — their critical politics, their being relatively new, small and innovative, on the margins of the community sector — they always face challenges, such as funding. These challenges provide important examples to bring to class. My own learning comes through working to resolve issues, how to maintain vision and pragmatic engagement, how organizations survive in a hostile environment. The way I work in a group depends on the group itself, who is there, and the issues. If the members of the group are the people facing an issue, e.g., welfare recipients, I tend to play the role of supporter and facilitator. Helping to build their leadership is the key challenge. In other places, like COCo, my role is to try to keep the critical dimension present in the various decisions that are made. These diverse experiences challenge, make the teaching and research real, and ensure that there is something at stake for me. There are no formulas, but the examples and lessons allow for continual growth both in my own understanding and analysis of practice and in what I bring to the classroom.

As an academic, one engages in research and writing. One of the major changes in academic culture since I began my career is how this is understood. One of the main underlying expectations that govern university research is that the academic is a research entrepreneur. The challenge that I face is how to do funded research *with* community organizations that contributes to their agendas, and is accountable to their leadership and members. In addition, is it possible for community organizations to benefit financially from research monies? Within the granting structure, I have had success with projects that allow some control to community organizations and have contributed to their work. Still, it can be a messy process. Accountability is to two very different sets of values. Academic traditions demand numbers of interviews; use of the literature; rigorous analysis; and fixed, predictable, and planned methodology. Some of these traditions are useful to community organizations, but secondary to why they might want research done. The differences in culture and expectations are difficult to bridge. It is important to remember that despite the power differentials, the partnership with community organizations provides a level of legitimacy for the research project, which can give the community organization some room to negotiate their agenda. I am sometimes able to use both my position in the university and the connections that it brings and my direct relationship with a given organization. It is important to understand what the opportunities are that come with a university position and to figure out how these can be advantageous to the community organization, to engage in discussion with the group, and not compromise the goals of the project by falling into the academic detachment and traditional definitions of knowledge.

Returning to the question of use of self, one important lesson is that use of self begins with where one is positioned and the wider context. For me this has meant learning to be in the university, teach, involve myself in practice, and do research in a way that is connected and contributes to community organizations and organizing. Drawing on the distinctions made above between organizer, activist, and ally, I have to understand which role I play in different circumstances. There is, however, a boundary that has to be crossed from the university to be seen as someone who can contribute to the community. It has not always been clear to me how I was able to do this. It took many years of being active in organizations and being willing to do day-to-day work and put in time. Another part of it is learning when to speak. The social authority of being a White, educated male with a position in a university leads others to perceive you as an expert on any number of issues and questions. Academics are paid to talk and write for a living and these abilities, although valuable, can silence others. One has to be discriminating and understand that contributions can be made through supporting leadership of people associated more directly with the issues involved. It is important not to speak on their behalf and make sure that participants do not become silenced because of the expertise that is supposedly present because of education and position.

It is also important to recognize the contributions that one can make. The university itself offers many resources, including students and their time. One of the roles I play is to make sure these resources are available and I have worked to supervise and teach social work students. These relationships have been key for me both in helping to mentor their organizing and activism and in their contribution to my own intergenerational learning. This has been one of the pleasures and privileges of my work—engaging with new generations of activists and organizers, sharing their work and challenges, and working alongside them on projects such as the IWC. My work is primarily that of an ally when I am working there. My intention is to keep a low profile and play a support role, using my skills and finding resources for the work. As I said earlier in the chapter, the goal of organizing is to help people build power and have a voice of their own. Many organizations these days feel it is okay to speak on behalf of a particular group or clientele. I reject this. If progressive social change is going to happen, it will be because of large numbers of people acting on their own behalf for this change, not a bunch of old White guys monopolizing the podiums. My role is that of both an ally and an organizer. There is an overlap with an organizing role and at times I work directly on committees and campaigns and do outreach. This is important to me as it keeps me in touch with the direct work of the centre and the people with whom we work. In both of these roles there is accountability to the organization and to a process of ongoing discussion of direction and priorities. As a board member of other organizations, I bring in my own positions and act as an activist. At times the role I play is to be "in and against" (London-Edinburgh Weekend Return Group, 1980) the dominant direction of the community sector. To do this, I use my "credibility" as a researcher, teacher, and a community practitioner to challenge some of what is, in my analysis, the mainstreaming of community organizations. This stance also comes into my teaching, research, and writing. It is here that I define my own activism. With the shifts in the community sector, the goals of progressive social change are easily lost as service replaces mobilization and organizing. I recognize the difficulty of the latter, but nonetheless it is key not to lose sight of its necessity if community organizations are to contribute to social change. Encouraging critical reflection on practice is a prerequisite for changing it. I am able to contribute to that through my teaching.

Even with the opportunities to do teaching practice and research, and the autonomy to define my involvement, I find that my position is increasingly outside the mainstream in the community sector both in Quebec and nationally. The push for technocratic solutions and highly formalized organizational forms, drawn from the private sector, imposes a new order on local work, channelling it into state structures and priorities. These models can produce "local colonization" (Halperin, 1998, p. 253). Further, following the insights of Smith (1999), the growing emphasis on measurable outcomes, written products, and other manifestations of Western social science as definers and indicators of successful practice leads to a growing homogenization of practice. The struggle for opposition and real local culture and democracy disappears with this process. Putting a redefinition of a vision of community on the map would feel like a daunting task, except for the presence of some allies and a younger generation of activists and radical who are also willing to be "in and against" the community.

REFERENCES

Adamson, N., Briskin, L. & McPhail, M. (1988). *Feminist organizing for change: The contemporary women's movement in Canada.* Don Mills: Oxford University Press.

Alinsky, S.D. (1971). *Rules for radicals: A pragmatic primer for realistic radicals.* New York: Vintage.

Barker, J. (1999). *Street-level democracy: Political settings at the margins of global power.* Toronto: Between the Lines.

Bishop, A. (1994). *Becoming an ally: Breaking the cycle of oppression.* Halifax: Fernwood.

Burghardt, S. (1982). *The other side of organizing: Resolving the personal dilemmas and political demands of daily practice.* Cambridge: Schenkman.

Church, K. (1995). *Forbidden narratives: Critical autobiography as social science.* New York: Gordon & Breach. (Reprinted Routledge, 2004).

Church, K., Fontan, J.-M., Ng, R. & Shragge, E. (2000). *Social learning among people who are excluded from the labour market – Part one: Context and case Studies.* New Approaches to Lifelong Learning (NALL), Ontario Institute for Studies in Education, University of Toronto. www.nall.ca/res/11sociallearning.htm.

Fisher, R. & Shragge, E. (2000). Challenging community organizing: Facing the 21st century. *Journal of Community Practice, 8*(3), 1–20.

Foley, G. (2001). Emancipatory organisational learning: Context and method. In *Conference proceedings from the Second International Conference on Researching Work and Learning* (pp. 278–284). Calgary: Faculty of Continuing Education, University of Alberta.

Halperin, R.H. (1998). *Practicing community: Class culture and power in an urban neighborhood.* Austin: University of Texas Press.

Hamel, P. (1991). *Action collective et démocratie locale: des mouvements sociaux urbains montréalai.* Montréal: Presses de l'Université de Montréal.

Hamel, P., Lustiger-Thaler, H. & Mayer, M. (2000). Urban social movements – Local thematics, global spaces. In P. Hamel, H. Lustiger-Thaler & M. Mayer (Eds.), *Urban movements in a globalizing world* (pp. 1–22). London: Routledge.

Hasson, S. & Ley, D. (1994). *Neighbourhood organizations and the welfare state.* Toronto: University of Toronto Press.

London-Edinburgh Weekend Return Group. (1980). *In and against the state.* London: Pluto Press.

Jessop, B. (2001). Institutional re(turns) and the strategic-relational approach. *Environmental Planning, 33,* 1213–1235.

Jessop, B. (2002). Liberalism, neoliberalism, and urban governance: A state-theoretical Perspective. In N. Brenner & N. Theodore (Eds.), *Spaces of neoliberalism – Urban restructuring in North America and Western Europe* (pp. 105–125). London: Blackwell.

Kruzynski, A.K. (2004). Du silence à l'affirmation: Women making history in Point St. Charles. Thèse de doctorat, McGill University, Montréal.

Mondros, J.B. & Wilson, S. (1994). *Organizing for power and empowerment.* New York: Columbia.

Naples, N. (Ed.). (1998). *Community activism and feminist politics: Organizing across race, class, and gender.* New York: Routledge.

Panet-Raymond, J. & Mayer, R. (1997). The history of community development in Quebec. In B. Wharf & M. Clague (Eds.), *Community organizing: Canadian experience* (pp. 29–61). Toronto: Oxford University Press.

Parazelli, M. & Tardif, G. (1998). Le mirage démocratique de l'économie sociale. In L. Boivin & M. Fortier (Eds.), *L'économie sociale: L'avenir d'une illusion* (pp. 55–99). Montreal: Fides.

Sen, R. (2003). *Stir it up: Lessons in community organizing and advocacy.* San Francisco: Chardon Press Series, Jossey Bass.

Shragge, E. (Ed.). (1997). *Community economic development: In search of empowerment.* Montreal: Black Rose Books.

Shragge, E. (2003). *Activism and social change: Lessons for community and local organizing.* Guelph: Broadview Press.

Shragge, E. & Toye, M. (Eds.). (2006). *Community economic development: Building for social change.* Sydney, NS: Cape Breton University Press.

Smith, L.T. (1999). *Decolonizing methodologies: Research and indigenous peoples.* London: Zed.

Staples, L. (2004). *Roots to power: A manual for grassroots organizing* (2nd ed.). Westport: Praeger.

Stout, L. (1996). *Bridging the class divide and other lessons for grassroots organizing.* Boston: Beacon

CHAPTER 11

ACCOMPLISHING

PROFESSIONAL SELF

Gerald de Montigny

This text employs common transcription symbols of conversation analysis (Psathas, 1995). Round brackets indicate descriptions of the talk or other directions; square brackets indicate overlapping talk; the equal sign indicates latching of turns; two backslashes indicates interruption; up or down arrows indicates rising or falling intonation.

197[1]	E	I was dead fer two minutes.
198	G	What↑
199	E	Yep, I hawa, I was eight years old, went down a foot ravine, on a bike, BMX.
200	G	Yah.
201	E	There was a sharp turn, I made that turn, and there was a big bouwlder there.
202	G	Oh lord=
203	E	I was going fast enough that I hit that bouwlder dead on=
204	G	Yah.
205	E	It made me go inta the air about 10 feet across, I was bein skidded on my back, I was still
206		being skid fe about 5 feet, hit anothew big bouwlder with my head, and tuwn my body
207		vewtical-cal, then I was on my stomach. And I was dead fer two minutes wight then, and
208		getting back, and I woke up in a house, it was my fwiends house.
209	G	Jeeze=

210 E   And I said wow.

211 G   That's pretty scary.

212 E   And yecan, outta body expewience.

213 G   Didja, you really did?

214 E   Yah.

215 G   An outta body experience. Yah, well that's pretty awesome.

216 E   But it's jist.

217 G   Yah, yah.

218 E   Strange.

219 G   Huh.

220 E   Because I was, my body was dead but not me.

221 G   Didja see yerself?

222 E   I was walkin around.

223 G   No.

224 E   But when I came to I was in a house.

225 G   Heh, that's amazing.

226 E   I din thought I got myself hurt, but when I=

227 G   Yah=

228 E   Stood up, I walked, an forgot about the bike.

229 G   Didja hafta go to the hospital?

230 E   Yah, I spent about two months, them picking at my back gettin all the rwocks out.

231 G   Was there any concussion?

232 E   Mm uh.

233 G   No, eh?

234 E   My head wasss like a rwock.

235 G   Yah.

236 E   Like all I got when I hit those rwocks with my head, all I got was a big like, big goose egg.

237 G   Yah.

238 E   What covered right there. My head wasn't split open or anything, even though I hit that

239   rock.

COMPLEXITIES OF PROFESSIONAL USE OF SELF

What does it mean to speak of the professional use of self? How might one begin, given the enormous range and depth of the analytic fields suggested by the conjoining of the domains of profession and self? To speak of a profession invokes attention to dense and complicated sedimentations of practice and analysis of practices that have over time congealed into a corpus and a congregation of participants. To understand professions today demands examination of broad social locations and functions, e.g., to be an "intellectual" within modern or industrial society (Gramsci, 1971); to occupy class positions, and positions of privilege, power, and authority (Freidson, 1986; Larson, 1977). It is by virtue of formal, institutionalized education, credentialing, employment, and performance of work, repeated day after day by cadres of similarly organized others, that professional identifications and bodies arise.

To speak of self evokes philosophical debates about core constitutive features of identity and personhood, which raise, in turn, debates about rationality and agency, morality and ethics, memory and subjectivity. While for psychologists self raises complex debates about the functioning of individual ego, cognitive development, and personality, for sociologists attention to self demands a focus on social interaction (Mead, 1934) and language. When considering writing a chapter about such matters I could not help but feel daunted by both the enormous scope and complexity of the issues woven into the apparently simple expression, professional use of self.[2] To manage such complexities, I pursue a modest course by examining transcribed interview segments taken from an interview I conducted with Ed, a 17-year-old First Nations youth. The interview was completed as part of an ethnographic research project that explored the stories of youth in care, focusing on their experiences of entering care and living in care.

INTERVIEW FORMS AND RELEVANCE FOR USE OF SELF

Clearly the question arises as to whether or not an interview produced for research can tell us anything about professional use of self. I think it can. First, although the interview was produced for a research project rather than in a social worker-client relationship, its accomplishment articulates not only my use of social work skills but Ed's knowledge of how to participate in an interview and, accordingly, our conjoint orientation to interactional forms that replicate social work in general. Our meeting, our talk, our orientations to topical coherence, and the structured nature of our interaction — use of questions, responses, turns, length of turns, use of acknowledgement tokens, and so forth — expressed our mutual orientation to work rather than play, friendship, or informal street meetings. As the interviewer, my orientation was to elicit relevant details of Ed's life story, while Ed's orientation was to provide, within the boundaries of his own levels of comfort and ability, responses to my questions, which cumulatively would stand as his story. The patent asymmetries in our participation within the interview articulated our orientation to forms of interaction, expressing issues of leadership, authority, power, deference, and so forth, which correspond to professional forms of interaction generally.

Further, my work with Ed was structured by a series of organizationally relevant antecedent or structural conditions. First, Ed came to the interview having been referred by his social worker. A core criterion for referral was the requirement that social workers assess that the youth might benefit from talking about their experiences in care. More will be said on this below. Second, I conducted all interviews with an appreciation not only of my requirement to act in accordance with child protection legislation, but to act in accordance with social work ethics and standards of professional conduct. Third, the simple fact that the interview with Ed was conducted in the child protection offices of his community meant that, at least for him, there was familiarity and association or correspondence between our interview and other interviews he had had in these same offices with his social worker in the past. Similarly for me, doing an interview in a local child protection office was a familiar, if not a nostalgic, event. Of course as Ed and I met, we could hear the movements of social workers, and their clients passing in and out of rooms, the ring of telephones, talking on phones, and so forth, which combined to continually remind us of our physical location inside the office.

I argue that this interview and accordingly these segments can be treated as relevant to and representative of professional use of self in social work by virtue of the fact that I designed the research project and the interviews to correspond, as closely as possible, to social work purposes and functions. My objective was not only to provide youth with an opportunity to speak about their lives but, whenever possible, to help them develop some new insights, syntheses, and understandings. During the course of interviews I never pretended to be "objective." Rather, I interacted with youth as I would have had I been their social worker. Indeed, precisely because I have been a child protection social worker, and because I had worked with children in care over several years, I felt deeply committed when doing the interviews to not only protecting the youth I met but advocating and supporting their right to lives without abuse, neglect, or deprivation. Even though I conducted only one interview with each youth, I felt impelled nevertheless to ensure that our time together would be helpful and constructive. I believed that it would be irresponsible of me to simply elicit youth's stories without attempting whenever possible to give them something back, thus to try to help them to identify and address – though not necessarily work through or resolve – core issues, which they could then take up with their social workers. Finally, when meeting with youth in care, I could not help but be reminded of my own children, who at the time were all teenagers, and their friends, and the many talks that we had had over the years about life's difficulties.

ANALYZING INTERVIEWS USING CONVERSATION ANALYSIS

Through close scrutiny of segments taken from my interview with Ed I demonstrate how I struggled to accomplish a professional use of self on this specific occasion. By turning to ethnomethodology (EM) and conversation analysis (CA), I seek to explicate professional use of self as an accomplished interactive production that comes to be effected time after time through such practical engagement in socially organized relations.[3]

It must be noted that although the use of CA as a tool in social work may seem new, the importance of close attention to actual or performed talk has long been recognized as a valuable tool for counsellors. Perhaps on this matter we would do well to recall Carl Rogers's advice provided more than half a century ago:

> Only by a careful study of the recorded interview – preferably with both the sound recording and transcribed typescript available – is it possible to determine what purpose or purposes are actually being implemented in the interview. "Am I actually doing what I think I am doing? Am I operationally carrying out the purposes which I verbalize?" These are questions which every counselor must continually be asking himself.... Only an objective analysis of words, voice and inflection can adequately determine the real purpose the therapist is pursuing. (1951, p. 25)

Further, even though EM and CA may be largely alien to most social workers, the abiding attention with the everyday, the practical, and the mundane (Garfinkel, 1967, 2002; Heritage, 1984; Mehan & Wood, 1975) resonates with social workers' own day-to-day preoccupations with people's struggles, troubles, and travails. The scope of the attention for those doing EM and CA is purposefully modest, in that these are methods driven by a fascination with the accomplished nature of "the social" in the most apparently taken-for-granted and unremarkable instances from the life that surrounds us.

In CA, by beginning with such seemingly trivial matters as response tokens (yah, mmhum) (Gardner, 2001), pauses or silence (Jefferson, 1989), overlapping talk (Schegloff, 2000a), repairs and repair positioning (self-initiated, other initiated repairs/corrections) (Schegloff, 1992a, 2000b), or laughter (Glenn, 2003; Jefferson, 1984), the fundamental sociability of interaction unfolds. Through similar foci of attention social workers can better come to understand not only the mechanics of interactions in interviews, but the art by which we concretely practise in forms that reflexively constitute both moments of social work and correspondingly ourselves as accountably social work professionals. By adopting EM and CA we can examine professional use of self as a "potters object" (Garfinkel, Lynch & Livingston, 1981)—that is, as accomplished and as made accountable through socially organized practices for articulating here-and-now interactions to professional forms.

By avoiding the lofty winds of philosophy and ethics, and swimming in the powerful currents and dark swirling waters of human practice, my aim is to show how I did professional use of self on one occasion, and thus how it might be done multiplicatively and replicatively. As such, analysis of an interview occasion provides a window into the essential reflexivity[4] of practice (de Montigny, 2005; Mehan & Wood, 1975). Attention to the essential reflexivity of practice enables us to recognize that common or taken-for-granted social work phenomena, interviews, clients, assess-ments, diagnoses, and so on are not only brought into being through practice, but in their form are very expressive of those practices. Through such a simple focus on practice we may begin to discover how social work comes to be done on multiple, repeated, and iterative occasions, so that social work becomes visible and is recognized as an artifact of socially organized and practically effected mundane forms of interaction. Indeed, it is from out of such sedimentations and aggregations of practice that the bright lights of our profession are able to pronounce, in journals of ethics, practice, and theory, that this and not that is what social work looks like, should look like, and must look like. It is in the disjunction between the doing of such things as talking with a young man in care, performed as an interview, and their reportage in properly warranted form, i.e., as an interview, that we can begin to grasp the practical accomplishment of those domains that we readily identify as professional.

TURNING TO INTERVIEW MATERIALS

As noted above, the preceding segment is from an interview I (G) conducted with Ed (E), a young man in care. In the interview Ed related a story about a bicycle accident that was both extraordinary and fantastic. He claimed that he had been dead for two minutes (line 197), that he hit a boulder with his head (line 206), that he had an out-of-body experience (lines 212, 220, 222), and that despite such obvious trauma, he did not suffer a concussion (line 232) because, as he explained, "my head wasss like a rwock" (line 234). Just as fascinating as his story, however, is my response as the interviewer. First, given the fantastic nature of Ed's claims, it seems remarkable that I do not argue with or contradict him. The closest I come to challenging Ed's claim to having had an out-of-body experience is when I ask, "Didja, you really did" (line 213), though it must be conceded that the tone of my enquiry was more properly indicative of an encourager, speaking to collusion and agreement with the cogency of his experience. What was going on? What sort of work was I doing with Ed? How did I receive the story and what work did I do with Ed's story?

While it is easy enough to imagine an acquaintance, friend, or family member treating Ed's claims with dismissal, my reticence at this moment to confront Ed spoke both to a commitment to listen and to understand. At that moment I wanted to elicit his story without providing critical comment (Rogers, 1951; Shulman, 2006). Although we can easily imagine a listener who might debate and argue against the possibility of out-of-body experiences, in doing an interview my orientation was to understand Ed's world, not to enter into philosophical debates about the nature of reality. By not contradicting or disagreeing, and by listening, I appear to accept Ed's story, and in so doing I aim to win his trust and co-operation to the extent that he will provide me with voluntarily produced stories from his life.

The structure of this interview paralleled the first meeting in any helping process. Ed and I were strangers to each other, and as such we needed to work through the sorts of issues Shulman (2006) identifies, i.e., can I trust this person, what does he or she want of me, and can we work together? While fantastic stories and claims might be noted as material to be explored in subsequent meetings, in a first meeting I and, I suspect, other social workers, may let them pass, with minimal interrogation or challenge. That fantastic stories are not initially challenged does not mean that they are any less remarkable, but only that for the social worker the time is not yet right. Further, even if a story is fantastic, challenge may be warranted only if the fantasy is patently self-destructive or harmful. For Ed the story of coming back to life from death functions positively as a sign of his strength, tenacity, and will to live, and as such has a positive rather than negative function. Furthermore, such stories resonate with powerful spiritual currents expressed by many people in our society, and as such fall within a spectrum of "normal" understanding.

This segment demonstrates that what is said, turn by turn, is shaped by strategic concerns. My next turns are shaped to perform certain types of work, quite apart from explicit or overt content. Such strategic attention points through content to what social workers have historically identified as the "emotional transfer" (Taft, 1924), or "rapport" (Robinson, 1939), "the relationship process" (Smalley, 1967), or "the casework process" (Perlman, 1957). Such concepts point to the emotional energy transfers that occur between social workers and the people with whom they work. Attention to emotional processes demands a sculpting of interaction in which oneself and one's own emotional reactions are continually subject to internal and external scrutiny and regulation. The result is that the emotional persona I present to Ed is one structured by a fundamental effected control, regulation, and reflexive monitoring. Thus, how I aim to be interactively present for Ed, and how I experience my own presence, is as a dialectical synthesis of an unfolding, present, and here-and-now, which is continually and unceasingly subject to mediation through reference to memory, recollection, and recall of idealized, universal, and abstract professional forms. In a word, my interaction with Ed is controlled.

My face-to-face social work emerges in an unbroken reflexivity that articulates the press of a here-and-now mediated by professional and organizational forms of knowledge and codes. In my here-and-now activities I anticipate future review, either effected internally – "I think that session went well" – or externally, "We received a complaint about your work with X." My recognition of the ongoing accountability of my actions has as its effect the displacement, or sublimation, of immediate responses in favour of controlled and sculpted action that are warrantable as properly professional.

The work I perform as an interviewer and as a social worker are designed to communicate to Ed not only that I am listening, e.g., (line 200) "Yah," but that I was prepared to enter into the emotional tone of his story and experience, e.g., "Oh lord" (line 202); "Jeeze" (209); "That's pretty scary" (211). Though such simple ejaculations communicated an interest and a solidarity with the emotional tone of his story, they lacked emotional depth, such as might be expressed by Ed's parents, who might recall this episode as a time when their child just about died. My entry into the emotional tone of Ed's story is limited and conditioned by my ability to maintain a professional constitution of self in interaction.

Carl Rogers advises that, "it is the counselor's function to assume... the internal frame of reference of the client, to perceive the world as the client sees it, to perceive the client himself as he is seen by himself, to lay aside all perceptions from the external frame of reference while doing so, and to communicate something of this empathic understanding to the client" (1965, p. 29). Yet how is this done? Of course, for each of us the mechanisms for entry into a client's world are effected with greater or lesser ease and greater or lesser depth. Just how social workers form an emotional connection with a client is a complex matter. When engaging Ed or any other client, I attempt to focus on their expression of mood through continuous study of their face and body comportment and gestures. Indeed, it is through a concentrated focus on face, body, and the physicality of tone of voice that I struggle to effect an entry into the emotional bond with a client. As Ed spoke, I could easily imagine myself careening down a hill, out of control, recognizing the impending collision, and feeling fear, terror, and panic. Although Miehls and Moffatt argue that, "The displacement or the disassembly of the self is essential to engaging responsibly with the other"[5] (2000, p. 344), I side with Winnicott, who insists that empathy consists of "the ability of one individual to enter imaginatively and yet accurately into the thoughts and feelings and hopes and fears of another person" (1986, p. 117). It is by virtue of drawing on core aspects of self, in memory, and our capacity to creatively manipulate memories into imaginative resources and recreations that we engage with others' stories.

Yet beyond the individual reliance on memory as a resource of self my ability to achieve an empathic response is not idiosyncratic. Rather, empathy articulates my location, my history, and my emergence through social interaction into forms of being whereby certain dispositions, attitudes, or ethics condition the composite of my desires to act "virtuously" and to be "virtuous" (McBeath & Webb, 2002). Further, empathy evokes a professional discourse of considerable duration in which social workers such as Biestek (1957) advised social workers to ensure "purposeful expression of feelings" (p. 35) and "controlled emotional involvement" (p. 50), thereby underscoring the centrality of conscious purpose, self-regulation, and self-direction. Indeed, the historicity and sociability of such dispositions are reflected in the ubiquity of the development of so-called helping professions across Western nations, which in turn express the deepest sedimentations constructing the moral and ethical dimensions of personhood (Rhodes, 1986).

The accomplishment of "good" social work, or virtuous action, articulates a reflexive accomplishment of self in a hermeneutics of socially organized practices and interpretations (McBeath & Webb, 2002). What comes to count as good or virtuous action might be better grasped as an articulation of a process of the internalization of professional discipline by which certain virtues come to be replicated in and through practice. McBeath and Webb outline, "The practice of virtue developed through experience, reflection and circumspection — is the very stuff of good social work" (2002, p. 1020). Although I might respond to a good friend or family member who might tell such a story by exclaiming "BS," laughing, or with sarcasm, such rejoinders are not desirable or permissible within an interview context. In an interview the orientation to work must be paramount. The way that I am, myself-in-interactions, is governed by different sets of rules.

TROUBLING PROFESSIONALISM

I want to shift ground away from this segment to focus on troubles that arose in the course of this interview. From the start I found this interview to be difficult. Ed entered the office by seating himself in the chair beside the desk, and skidding backwards across the floor to the furthest point against the wall, announcing, "I need my space, man." Further, in the initial phase of the interview I seemed to miscue and misunderstand him, not just once but repeatedly. At times I feared that Ed would get up and leave, or that he would get angry with me and create an unpleasant scene. I feared the embarrassment of failure. From the beginning I wondered how I might move Ed past his need for a space, particularly as it seemed to foreclose the mutual development of trust and rapport. I wondered how to create an interview with Ed that was not marked by hostility, impatience, and tacit threats, but was friendly, comfortable, and open. Though I felt that by the end of the interview we had moved into a better space, getting there seemed to have been a struggle. This was an interview where I felt as though I was walking on eggshells.

By addressing such troubles I must confess to feeling vulnerable. Might the troubles be a sign of my deficiencies, lack of skills, or a reflection of my unsuitability to do social work (Lafrance, Gray & Herbert, 2004)? Might they reveal certain dysfunctional patterns or tendencies in my own practice? Indeed, the fear of such evaluations are not only an anxiety for social work students and new practitioners, but express the deepest fears of failure even for those more experienced. Troubles in interviews with clients, while unsettling, do compel us to search for an explanation and sense, and thereby to craft our practice and interactions differently. Put simply, we can learn from troubles.

I recognize that in these moments of professional work Ed was responding to me not simply as I was, but as he perceived me to be, perhaps drawing on his understandings of past encounters with middle-aged White men. We were shaping each other's next turns (Malone, 1997) as we were present for each other, and as we idealized or imagined each other to be present. Although I recognized, as did Ed, that we had come together from across divides of age, race, geography, and life opportunities (Kohler Riessman, 1993), and while I felt compelled to bridge these by creating some sense of rapport, dialogue, and trust, I could not be sure that Ed shared my objectives. While I wanted to create a commonality and shared purpose in dialogue, I also feared that Ed might find my project problematic and difficult. I recognized that Ed must be uncertain of what to expect from me. Accordingly, I struggled to craft a presence and shape my responses to win his trust.

ENTERING THE INTERVIEW

For any social worker interviews with clients are fraught with potential difficulties. In particular, a first interview is an occasion in which two strangers come together. Pawson observes that, "subjects ponder (mostly in silence)—'who is this person?,' 'what is she after?,' 'why am I being asked?,' 'what have others said?,' 'what should I be saying?'" (1996, p. 306). The meeting of strangers creates not only anxieties but significant practical difficulties. Just as I enter the office with my agenda, so too does the interviewee. Just as I wonder who this person is and how he or she will affect me, so too do they wonder about me.

As noted, Ed's preliminary announcement of his need for space acted to warn and test me. Would I respect his space or would I violate it? Would I earn his disapproval, displeasure, and dismissal as yet another person in authority? Although I did not explicitly address his demand for space as a shot across my bow, he must certainly have been monitoring me to see how I would respond. While Ed's identification of space cautioned me to avoid seeming intrusive, rather paradoxically it increased my curiosity. It made me want to understand why space was so important for Ed. The puzzle I faced was figuring out how to move into territory that I had been warned to avoid entering.

Beyond curiosity I recognized that Ed, as with any interviewee or client, was an enigma. In doing an interview I recognize that I do not know what a client really means when he or she speaks (Anderson & Goolishian, 1992). I recognize that there is a fundamental "uncertainty" in interaction that demands being awake to a discovery of ambiguity (Parton, 1998). An approach that embraces not knowing unsettles and disturbs, what Garfinkel has called, "the sanctioned properties of common discourse" by which people in everyday interaction pretend to understand each other by relying on et cetera and let it pass devices (Garfinkel, 1967, p. 3). In ordinary talk ambiguous statements are allowed to stand without question, probes, or challenge as communicating a good enough sense for practical purposes. Yet an interview is not an instance of ordinary talk as seemingly sensible claims become subject to questions and requests for further elaboration. An interview and, accordingly, social work demand unsettling everyday conversational routines by which communicative sense is achieved. When working with people I rather consistently treat ordinary claims such as "he abused me," "we fight all the time," or "we don't get along" as problematic ciphers. It is in the press for details, organized by an acute sensitivity to "uncertainty" and "ambiguity" (Parton, 2003) or "not knowing" (Anderson & Goolishian, 1988), that enables me to begin to understand their "experience."

TROUBLES FROM THE START

I turn to look at a segment taken from the beginning of the interview, lines 7 to 11.

7	G	Wh what's cha been up to today?
8	E	Out walkin around being tirwed.
9	G	Yah, late night↑

10   E   Naw, went to bed early, woke up too early.
11   G   Mmhuh.

My question would normally stand as a rather standard opener. It has a familiar though formulaic colloquial quality, such as might characterize a greeting in ordinary conversation. When asked, "Wh what's cha been up to today?" Ed responds that he has been "Out walkin around being tirwed." My response could have taken any number of possible directions. I could have asked: "Where were you walking?"; "Are you tired because you walked a long way?"; or, "What made you tired?" Yet, I did not respond by asking another question. In part my response is shaped by a recognition that asking questions may itself create problems. Questions may make me seem inquisitorial and invasive,[6] which particularly, given Ed's demand for "space," might have proven problematic. Rather than respond by using an overt series of questions, I provided a possible explanation, although as shaped with a rising tone at the end, nevertheless functioned as a question, "Yah, late night↑." Ed not only provided a "repair" but an explanation: "Naw, went to bed early, woke up too early." By rejecting my interpretation, to instead offer his own, Ed risked possible trouble as he was indicating that I had not correctly understood him.

My offer of "late night↑" drew on my own personal life experiences as a teenager, and as a father of teenagers, as well as the familiar commonsense understandings about teens in our society. "Late night↑" draws on the stock-in-trade of parental complaints about all-night teen parties, drinking, and hanging out with friends. Further, as a volunteer with a Children's Aid Society Teen Group over several years, I was able to draw on the stories of many teens who complained about "being up all night" and "being tired in the morning." Yet despite my reliance on such "inference rich devices" (Sacks, 1995, p. 41), Ed was able to reject my explanation as incorrect. While I recognized that Ed's rejection of my interpretation might have been because it was not correct, I also recognized that he might have rejected it simply because I had offered it.

In the next segment we see what appears to be a simple confusion.

32   E   Because when I woke I jist, I have a window right in front of me.
33   G   A what? A window, ooh, what win?//
34   E   I noticed when I woke up it was 6:00, but it was bwight, bwight, like this.

35	G	What do ya look onto?
36	E	What do I look onto?
37	G	Yah, what does yer window look on to?
38	E	Oh, ah, it not my window, it was my fwends, I was up at his place last night.
39	G	Oh yah, do, ah sleep over.
40	E	Mmmhuh, yah.

Ed explains that he awoke at "6:00" because "it was bwight, bwight" (line 34). My ability to understand his claim depends on our shared context in Northern Canada, and the fact that it was conducted on June 17 just before the summer solstice, the longest day of the year. This is a time when there is continual light through the night. Rather than address the problem of bright light at 6 a.m., I formulated a next turn by assuming that he was speaking about awaking in his own room. My question, "What do ya look onto?" while perhaps appearing to be off topic, was an attempt to direct Ed to describe his current living arrangements. Unfortunately, my move to redirect failed. Ed countered that he had awoken in a friend's room.

Only slightly later as I returned to explore Ed's living arrangements in more detail, and his connection with family, did the following exchange occur.

41	G	Where're ya livin these days?
42	E	Forest Glen.
43	G	Forest Glen, with who?
44	E	Mmhum, my dad, and my bwother, and thwee of my cousins, and my aunty.
45	G	What's yer dad's name?
46	E	I'm named after my dad.
47	G	Oh yer dad's Ed too.
48	E	But his Smith, in his last name.
49	G	Smith.
50	E	Yah.
51	G	So who's name is Jones [Ed's last name]?
52	E	It's my mom.
53	G	Uh huh, and who's yer mo, and you live with yer dad and your brother.
54	E	Yes, but I ain't gonna say all their names.

| 55 | G | Well, just so I can, just when you, cause later you'll mention their names. How, okay, older brother, younger... younger brother? |
| 56 | E | Older. |

The preceding segment begins with a simple question to determine where Ed is living. He responds by stating with "my dad, and my bwother, and thwee of my cousins, and my aunty." In response I ask for his dad's name, and trouble once again occurs. Ed outlines that though he shares his dad's first name, he does not share his dad's last name, Smith. Rather, Ed has taken his mother's surname, Jones, as his own. Having survived this confusion, I begin by asking, "who's yer mo," but effect a repair, interrupting myself, to state, "and you live with yer dad and your brother." Ed counters, "Yes, but I ain't gonna say all their names."

Ed's response marks both real and potential trouble. As the interviewer, I feared that Ed's refusal to provide names might be a sign of growing frustration, hostility, and anger toward me. I wondered if he would become increasingly secretive and guarded. Would he refuse to continue with the interview? Should I voice my growing fears, or would confronting Ed only worsen the situation? Although I recognized signals of trouble, I was unsure how to respond. My dilemma was not just moral — e.g., speak the truth, speak what you perceive — but tactical. In retrospect, when doing the analysis I realized that I might have said, "When you say you don't want to provide the names of your brothers and sisters I wonder, do you find my questions too prying?"[7] This direction might have created an opening for Ed to respond, "You're right," but it might also have led him to add, "Let's end it now."

So why didn't I explore the troubles at this point? Was it a tactical decision to not name troubles? Was it fear of conflict? As the interviewer I had to decide whether to ignore troubles or to react to them. I felt confused. Should I have followed Shulman and addressed what he calls "the authority theme" openly? Or, by ignoring the authority theme, was I able to negotiate past immediate difficulties to build a good enough relationship? While I recognize that troubles that are ignored, whether in a dysfunctional family or an interview, do not cease to exist as they become part of what we should not or cannot talk about, thereby leading people to pretend to get along, I also believe that tactically at certain times some things are best left unsaid as making them explicit will only increase conflict and tension. Indeed, by "disattending" conflict,[8] I believe that people can still manage to look past mutual dislikes to do good work. As a pragmatic principle I understand that from time to time an orientation to task rather than to the dynamics of relationship may be tactically and strategically preferred in order to move work forward.[9] Further, I hoped that by disattending troubles at this point and continuing to work together Ed and I might move on to get the work done. I worried that by addressing troubles at a point when our relationship was new and volatile, I might only unleash an escalating spiral of confrontation. Further, I not only recognized that securing his siblings' names was not consequential for the overall integrity of the project, but that sidestepping the issue of this point would not prevent Ed from revealing their names as he told the story of his life.

Beyond the troubles signalled by Ed's refusal, fortunately I recognized his need to assert some autonomy and control over the interview process. His refusal marked off his personal territory and established the nature of his contribution to our interaction. I recognized that such needs had to be respected. In the next segment Ed uses correction and disagreement to assert his independence and to effect control.

70	G	... So right now are you, are you in care, are you?
71	E	Yah, I'm in care of this place.
72	G	But you're livin with yer dad.
73	E	Yah.
74	G	Okay, what's that about?
75	E	It's what my court order said.
76	G	That you hafta live with your dad.
77	E	No. I don't hafta live with my dad if I don't want to. I'm capable of living wherever I
78		want. I can live on my land.
79	G	Yah.
80	E	If I wanted to.
81	G	Yah. Do you do that?
82	E	If I wan to, but which I don't have it staked out yet.
83	G	You don't, eh?
84	E	Uh uh.

When I asked Ed "are you in care" (70), I referenced a legal status by which children and youth come to be either through court order or voluntary agreement with their parent(s) a temporary or permanent ward of a child protection office. Being in care meant that control over his life was exercised through government offices – indeed, those offices where the interview was conducted. He responded, "I'm in care of this place" (71). I expressed my confusion by observing, "But you're livin with yer dad" (72). Again, Ed managed to put me off balance. I understood that normally a youth in care does not live with their parent(s), yet Ed claimed to do so. I asked, "Okay, what's that about?" Ed replied, "It's what my court order said." I focused on the concept of a court order to offer, "That you hafta live with your dad." Ed disagreed, "No. I don't hafta live with my dad if I don't want to. I'm capable of living wherever I want. I can live on my land."

What is going on? First, Ed makes it very clear that regardless of what any court might order, he is master of his own life. He asserts that he can determine with whom and where he lives. To underscore his independence, he suggests, "I can live on my land" even though later he concedes that, "I don't have it staked out yet" (line 82). The promise and allure of a future in which he is free to live on his own land is powerful indeed. Ed drew on a deep iconographic frontier and northern fantasy, which he could hardly guess that I shared, just as my father and his father before had. This is why I so eagerly ask, "Yah. Do you do that?" (line 81). Curiously, Ed's expression of mastery coincides with my own desires for escape into the north. Sadly, in the next turn we confront the realities of our lives in a denouement of subdued resignation: "G You don't, eh?" to which Ed replies, "Uh uh."

While Ed's responses to my questions initially left me feeling confused and off balance, I struggled to see beyond their immediate form to appreciate them as signs of his independence and strength. Ed seemed to use puzzles, contradictions, and paradoxes to assert his control over the process. Fortunately, I had enough presence of mind not to resist his need to maintain control.

CONSTRUCTING GENDER?[10]

Throughout the interview Ed produced stories that relayed a preferred version of himself as a moral actor and I actively colluded with and supported him in this enterprise. In the following two segments we can see the ways that Ed and I join to affirm a common view of virtue and moral action. The first was in response to my attempts to determine his family composition. Ed addressed his parents' relationship:

171	E	Then they brwoke up, and went their own ways, and sheee kinda went and got, her
172		actually was goin out with my, ah, foster dad.
173	G	Yah, yah.
174	E	I jist call him call him foster dad=
175	G	Yah, yah.
176	E	Because he was there more years than my real dad was=
177	G	Yah.
178	E	So, and he had, ah, three other kids, and two of them died.
179	G	Oh.
180	E	Two of my baby sisters.
181	G	How did that happen?
182	E	Wahhaw, they was jist babies, this one had a breathing pwoblem, and one had a heart
183		pwoblem. Mmm so, I don't worry about that, I jist jist natural te me.
184	G	Yes.
185	E	I don't worry about, you know, one dies, lives.
186	G	Yah.
187	E	To me it's jist the way the wowld works.
188	G	Yah.

Along with reference to the specific deaths of two siblings, Ed makes a claim about how he manages death and loss generally: "I don't worry about that, I jist jist natural te me" (183), and in an elaborating move he repeats, "I don't worry about, you know, one dies, lives" (185). While the details of the hardship are unsettling, again it is important to ask how his claims operate to present a view of himself to me. Goffman notes that such instances of "impression management" allow us to understand how people co-operatively produce what he calls a "social establishment" as a "place surrounded by fixed barriers to perception" (1959, p. 238). In this sense Ed and I collude to effect barriers or preferred versions of what it is to be a person or, as I would prefer to express it, what it is to "be a man." For Ed to be Ed — that is, to recognize himself as a person with integrity — demands being strong, brave, and courageous.[11] Perhaps not surprisingly I consistently accept these implicit frameworks. I do not challenge his preferred presentations of self. I do not suggest that perhaps it might have been better, in the face of his siblings' deaths, to have responded by becoming distraught, crying, depressed, or anguished. Ed and I both deploy barriers against weakness by relying on implicit codes for proper masculinity.

Ed claims that he deals with and manages extremely difficult and traumatic life events as he does not "worry about that." He is able to push concerns about life and death out of his mind. He is not only fearless but pragmatically fatalistic. Ed recognizes "it's jist the way the wowld works." As a man he gets on with his life and courageously accepts the travails of misfortune. As a male interviewer I share Ed's view of life. Ed does not need to explicitly claim that he is brave, that he has courage, or that he is a survivor. He trusts that I will know this by listening to him and that I will respect him for his strength. In this sense he is quite correct.

I neither question nor challenge the apparent good sense of Ed's self-presentation. Further, through the repeated use of acknowledgement tokens, "yes" and "yah," (184, 186, 188), I indicate that his account not only makes sense, but that I agree with his interpretations. In such moments we can begin to glimpse the differential intersection of such issues of gender with professional practice as I clearly draw on the resource of an identified male stoicism and emotional rectitude as a preferred form of action for managing difficult situations. In this moment we seem to be colluding as co-participants in the erection of a preferred, perhaps distinctly, male approach to managing troubles.

The next segment began with my question about why Ed no longer lived with his mother.

420	G	So what was goin on with her that you're not livin with her, and you kept comin inta
421		care?
422	E	Nahh, I didn' wanna live with them. Jist didn' wan to. Got too tiwred.
423	G	How?
424	E	Nothin, te do, the same thin' over and over=
425	G	Yah=
426	E	Arguments=
427	G	Yah=
428	E	Te me, my bwother, my kid sister-[ster]
429	G	[Yah]
430	E	-ster, P would fweek out, and end up tryin te frow at knife at us or somethin.

431	G	Who's P?

431 G   Who's P?
432 E   My kid sister. The one who got the singing job.
433 G   Is that right? Tryin te throw a knife at you?
434 E   Yah.
435 G   So a lotta fightin goin on in the home.
436 E   Yah, and afta she did that, Mom jist said, "You wanna do that, P, listen I won't care if you
437   got beat up by them." An I jist said, "Heh, I ain' goin te beat her up."
438 G   Yah=
439 E   Maybe I might defend myself, but I ain' goin' te beat her up.
440 G   So, but you were in and out of care, though, before 11. You knew foster homes,
441   receiving homes//

Ed follows up his claim that he left his home because he "Got too tiwred," and explaining with a single word: "arguments." Ed then claims that his sister P threw a knife at him, the details of which Ed did not provide, nor for which I pressed. However, what is remarkable is that in the next segment Ed claims that his mother gave him and his brother permission to beat up their sister. Ed describes his response: "An I jist said, "Heh, I ain' goin te beat her up.""... "Maybe I might defend myself, but I ain' goin' beat her up." In this passage Ed is plainly communicating a picture of the sort of person (man) he is.[12] He is a person (man) who would not beat his sister, a girl/woman, even when provoked. He is a person (man) who will not use violence against his sister, and we might, by extension, presume a person (man) who will not use violence against those weaker than himself. He is not a bully. He is a person (man) able to exercise restraint even in the face of provocation. Again, as a (male) interviewer, I do not challenge but rather collude and agree with Ed's version of proper action through the acknowledgement token "Yah."

In this passage Ed presents himself to me as a young person (man) who inhabits a moral universe marked by some sense of respect for those weaker than himself, even when they threaten his safety. We also see that Ed sets the limits to his behaviour. He demonstrates that he is an autonomous actor who, despite seeming to have been given permission by his mother to beat P, will set his own moral compass and the course of his own actions. I, in response to Ed, accept his self-presentation as unproblematic, signalled through the response token "yah," and the fact that I shift the subject in my next turn.

SPACE AND SAFETY

When I attempted to explore why Ed had been placed in a facility for young offenders, he provided the following explanation.

288	E	Cause I was, it was in fronta J's office, but she was in J's office, cause, I was standin at the
289		door, and she kept on invading my space, and tellin me te get out an everything, but I
290		said no, "I wanna say my piece," you deserve fwhat you get.
291	G	Mmhuh.
292	E	And the next thing she push, and I said, whoa, what didja do that for, and she did that two
293		oth, two other times before that, one in frwont of a long flight of stairws, which was
294		leavin downstairs, and I got lucky there, and then there's another time, this was another
295		flight of stairws.

Ed explains that troubles arose because a staff person was "invading my space"(289) and refusing to allow him to "say my piece" (290). Ed's demand, "I wanna say my piece," not only functioned as a story about the past, but served to mark his expectations in the present and in this interview. J's refusal to let Ed say his piece not only was an affront, he perceived her action as a violation of his space. The theme of space arises not only in relationships of confrontation, but as a key to respect, hence to respect Ed is to respect his person, his right to speak, the integrity of his words, and his space.

451	E	-n't, but my real dad, I don't know, don't care. He does what he wants, I do what I want.
452	G	Yah.
453	E	Nn, an I don' interfere with his business, and he doesn' interfere with mine.
454	G	He doesn't?

455	E	He rwespects my space and everything, an so.
456	G	Yah. You need te ha, you need te have yer space.
457	E	Mmhuh, my dad respects that=

Ed is intent on asserting his independence. For Ed the proper way of being
(a man) is to be autonomous and to have his space respected. I join Ed by
agreeing, "You need te ha, you need te have yer space."

Yet, as the interview progressed I became increasingly aware of the
need to explicate space and its importance for Ed. I suspected that its
significance was rooted in a traumatic violation of Ed's space in the past,
whether as physical or sexual abuse. Clearly space functioned to mark
boundaries against being approached or touched by others on terms he did
not accept. Again, later in the interview Ed revisited the theme of space,
and the ways that troubles arose when others violated it.

589	E	It takes three, three cops te pin me down. An took them a good bout
590		twenty minutes=
591	G	Iz that right? (softly)
592	E	For I went went down.
593	G	Iz that right?
594	E	And the only reason that is 'cuz one got on my back and I smashed him
595		against the wall.
596	G	Mmuh.
597	E	And everything-thing, friggin, and I was'nt doin nothin-thin, and I jist said
598		"Shoot me-me-me" an I don't achtully mean shoot, me-me, what I'm tryin
599		te mean, is like knock me out man, like shit, like, but when he grwabbed
600		me wrist te handcuff me, I said, okay man, don't mess around, you're in
601		my space, and if you do that again, I'm gonna, and he didn' get out, so I
602		did what I hadta do, an...
603	G	Mmhuh.
604	E	Mm I don't care if it's the cops or anything, like, they're invading my

605		space=
606	G	Yah=
607	E	I will get them outta my space=
608	G	Yah=
609	E	=Neither way I can=
610	G	Yah=
611	E	=Like, n'aw was even a hundrwed percent, and I was alwready thrwashing
612		thrwee cops-s, and that was only as 50 percent.
613	G	Yah.
614	E	If I was at a hundrwed, it would take bout five coawps then.
615	G	So what's this space. How much space?
616	E	I have an arm's-length space.
617	G	Yah.
618	E	So if anyone's in my space of an arm's length, I'm not gonna be too
619		nice.
620	G	Wh what makes yer space important for ya? When did that become
621		important for ya?
622	E	That came important te me when I was a little baby=
623	G	Yah=
624	E	When I's a baby about five years.
625	G	Yah, tell me bout that.
626	E	I don't want to.
627	G	No.
628	E	Mm uh. It's done an over with he's go' his punishment, it's over.
629	G	Oh somebody hurt you.
630	E	No. Not me, my little sister-ter.
631	G	Yah=
632	E	But, I didn' wan te see it, but I woke up at that time.
633	G	I see, an, so she was being sexually abused=
634	E	Yes=
635	G	And you saw that. Did that happen to you?
636	E	Noo:if ee, after I woke up, I' kinda faked slep, and when he came try doin

637   thin'k te me, like, put the diaper over me-m', b' that's all he
               did with me,
638   an=
639   G   Yah=

Quite apart from a theme of male braggadocio connected to his physical
prowess, Ed again returns to mark off space and to warn others,
including me, of what happens when his space is violated. By this point
in the interview I recognized that the task of building trust demanded
communicating respect for Ed's boundaries, yet, at the same time, pressing
into his discomfort to allow him to articulate the trauma that produced in
him a strategy for safety articulated through the structures of space. The
puzzle I faced was to figure out how to open up the issue of space without
seeming to invade his space.

Once Ed had disclosed sexual abuse, I faced a problem. Such disclosure,
quite apart from being a taboo subject (Shulman, 1999), almost invariably
awakens painful and traumatic experiences rooted in memory or experience
structure. While invoking such materials may be therapeutically justified,
for the purpose of this interview it was not justified. For this interview, I
only needed to know that a sexual abuse violation had occurred in Ed's
past, and that it had had definite effects on his presentation of self and on
the practical techniques he used to manage social situations with others,
and that these had proven to be problematic over time. What did matter
was that I respected Ed's need for space to earn his respect.

Although I met with Ed as an interviewer, I was acutely aware of my
obligations to engage in good practice as a social worker. I could not open
up trauma without ensuring some means for follow-up and ongoing care.
At the same time I felt that it was important to make explicit the connection
between Ed's experience of sexual abuse and his sometimes violent
concern to protect his space. I worried that Ed's efforts to protect his space
had resulted in criminal charges and violent confrontations with people
in authority and power. In my orientation to being a social worker, above
and beyond doing the interview, I felt obligated to help him disentangle
past hurt from present situations, and to use less confrontational and more
appropriate strategies to protect himself.

In the next segment Ed outlined that the man who sexually abused
him had been "locked up." Ed noted:

640   E   But's that's what's done an over with.//

641	G	But, no, but you see, it's not done and over with, because you see you need yer space.
642	E	See, I need my space, you wanna know why?
643	G	Yah.
644	E	Because I respect=
645	G	Yah=
646	E	=Other people's space=
647	G	=Yah=
648	E	=So, also=
649	G	=Yah, cause.//=
650	E	=An I, I like te be at arm's length, either way=
651	G	Ah yes, I, yes, I [underst]and that.
652	E	[Iz' not], iz not always b'cause that but=
653	G	Yah=
654	E	I don't think of that like, as like why'm I respect my own space-s, and
655		respect other's [people's space].
656	G	[absolutely right] (space)
657	E	It's just like, I count fer that wa=
658	G	Good fer y'=
659	E	Like if anyone came up an wreally touched me, like, go like that, an I did'n wan it.
660	G	Yah=
661	E	And tell im, w'd please don touch me.
662	G	Don't do that.
663	E	Mm.
664	G	Good fer you=
665	E	Like, I don' wan te be touched, when I want te be touched I'll=
666	G	You'll let im know.
667	E	Yah=
668	G	Right on E=
669	E	Like=
670	G	Right on. Now is that a problem a school that peop, people'll...
671	E	No, it's not a problem at school, like not much kid'zll go up an go// "hey."
672	G	"Hey man, how's it goin?"

673	E	Like when I'm at school, like I really won't care like if anyone touched
674		me, cause they're all my frwends=
675	G	Yah, I see,
676	E	At school. Like...
677	G	Okay, so one of the ways that you kinda deal with that kinda threat is say
678		look, this is my space, you don't invade it.
679	E	Yah, like I only do that to people-ple-ple that I don' like that much=
680	G	Yah.
681	E	Like frwends and all that=
682	G	Mmuuhh.
683	E	It's totally diffewent.
684	G	Good. No, that's cool. It's cool.

Although Ed insists that the matter is done and over with, I do not accept this version. I openly disagree. I note, "But, no, but you see, it's not done and over with, because you see you need yer space." Ed recognizes the challenge, and responds, "See, I need my space, you wanna know why? (G Yah) Because I respect= (G Yah=) =other's people's space= (G =Yah) =so, also= (G =Yah, cause//) =an I, I like te be at arm's length, either way." Ed's response is fascinating and characteristic. He insists that it was not what others have done to him that makes him value space, but rather that it is the choices he has made, what he values, what he respects, that make him demand his own space and "other's people's space." Equally fascinating is my close use of responses, encouraging and supporting him as he seeks to find coherence in his talk. Ed struggles to outline that, unlike others who violated his space, he respects others' space. He is not like his abusers and tormentors who do not respect the space and integrity of others, and I signal my clear agreement.

CONCLUSION

By taking up face-to-face interview work I have tried to explicate an instance in which I have struggled to accomplish a professional self. In an examination of my face-to-face practice I recognize that being a social worker, or accomplishing myself as a social worker, is rife with potential conflict, awkwardness, and dis-ease. Yet it is only in such in vivo moments that we manage to bridge a dialectic between the universalized and ideal forms of professional identity—lodged in memory as education, past work, friendships, and associations—and the contingent, confusing, and ineffable unfolding of here-and-now interaction.

The here-and-now pressure of practice demanded that I weigh sanctioned forms of practice against strategic and local considerations. For instance, I faced the problem of figuring out how far and how hard to push Ed for details, how to ensure the coherence of whatever stories we produced together, how to ensure some semblance of practically effected ethical practice, and, of course, how to ensure that our talk corresponded to the interview purposes. To accomplish this range of objectives I needed to bridge his insistence on a space of distance and separation to secure intimate and personal details of his life.

In this sense achievement of oneself as professional may be thought of as a sedimented series of rituals involving multiple participants. First, Ed and I were obviously present for each other. Second, behind the moment of our work together was the work of the social worker and team leaders who had not only referred Ed, but 30 other youth in care to our project. Third, even as Ed and I met I was continually aware of my requirements under child protection legislation. Similarly I recognized that our meeting presupposes the operation and categorization of Ed as a "child in care" as a result of complex work processes of child protection and court work. Fourth, further back in the shadows of the moment of our work were those at my university who had reviewed the design of my research to ensure compliance with Social Sciences and Humanities Research Council ethical guidelines. Fifth, yet more distant were the phantom voices of teachers, supervisors, and co-workers with whom I had chattered away over the years about doing good practice. Finally, in the interstices of memory and desire was that core of self, which struggled toward virtue in this moment, this here-and-now, as ceaselessly impelled but never completely realized.

In the preceding pages we saw how both Ed and I struggled to craft representations of self for each other. We pursued this work turn by turn and as expressed in the most mundane forms of utterance and responsive positioning. Ed's responses must be read not only as communicating the events of his life, but as displaying and affirming for me, as the listener, his moral orientation to the world, just as mine do for him. While Ed invites me to inhabit his preferences, actions, understandings, and virtues, so too do I invite him to inhabit my own. Ours are both moral orientations that shape our views of self and others. It is essential that social workers recognize that it is not only themselves as professionals bound to codes of ethics and professional values, but their clients who interact and work from out of such complex moral universes.

What then can we say about professional use of self, having journeyed through these pages? First, I have provided only the thinnest slice or skeletal view of one moment of practice. While some contours have emerged there is much that has escaped attention. While I have focused on my struggles to bridge the disjunctions between the contingent here-and-now with the overarching dysbound temporality of professional and organizational realities (Kovel, 1981), much more could and should be said about the dialectical flux of identity and change, context and transcendence, than has been addressed in these pages. However, if by developing an analysis using transcribed segments from talk-in-interaction, I am able to encourage social workers to consider this most material of resources to address such complex matters as "professional use of self," then my more modest objectives are met.

NOTES

1. Line numbering throughout this chapter represents placement in the context of the entire transcription of the interview, which was 790 lines.
2. Malone observes that, "from 1974 to 1995, 19,341 social science books and articles have had 'self' in their titles or abstracts or as key words (Sociofile, 1/74–4/95)" (Malone, 1997, p. ix).
3. Gramsci addressed the distinction between the functions of the intellectuals, what we might call professionals, from that of other "social groupings," to observe: "The most widespread error of method seems to me that of having looked for this criterion of distinction in the intrinsic nature of intellectual activities, rather than in the ensemble of the system of relations in which these activities (and therefore the intellectual groups who personify them) have their place within the general complex of social relations" (1971, p. 8). Gramsci's redirection of enquiry to an examination of activities as fundamentally socially organized resonates with the ethnomethodological redirection.
4. That reflexivity is described as essential is distinctive to an ethnomethodo-logical approach, in contrast to "idealist" approaches where reflexivity is treated as volitional or intentional. Hence Miehls and Moffatt suggest, "Reflexivity can be accomplished through careful consideration of the self" (2000, p. 343). In contrast I argue that reflexivity is always, everywhere, and continuously accomplished by virtue of an interweaving ontological structure, thus that which "is," through the effects of everyday practical activities.

5. It is critically important to recognize that that with which I engaged was not "the other" but "this other," this person, that is, Ed. He and I inhabit a world populated by real, not abstract, others. Benhabib expressed a similar argument against Habermas's discourse or communicative ethics, as she critiqued his (male) reliance on the philosophical "generalized other," proffering instead the importance of addressing a "concrete other" who, "like ourselves, is a being who has concrete needs, desires and affects" (1992, p. 159). Indeed, it is in the encounter with a concrete other, another living person, that we experience the reflective mystery of the ineffable plenitude of our mutual existence.

6. Buttny found that, "some therapists ask few direct questions, but instead attempt to elicit information from the clients by 'telling them something about themselves'" (1996, p. 128).

7. My avoidance of trouble, hence my decision to avoid naming Ed's refusal, points to my own need to be liked and to be successful. While such desires may have the negative effect of producing a *folie à deux* or what Shulman calls the illusion of work (2006), on the positive side such desires as expressed lead to mutuality, trust, and care for others. Shulman convincingly argues that addressing the authority theme can provide important inroads for developing honest and open dialogue. However, at this point in the interview I chose to avoid explicitly naming the authority theme as I hoped to establish rapport by continuing to work together.

8. Michael Polanyi (1966) modified Austin Farrar's notion of "disattending from certain things" and "attending to others" to outline that "in an act of tacit knowing we attend from something for attending to something else." That which is attended from he calls the "proximal" and that which is attended to is "distal." In the interview the proximal tension is disattended in order to attend to the distal objective. This way of thinking about conflict allows us to grasp the dynamic nature of shaping interaction, in a way that the simple notion of ignoring conflict does not.

9. I hesitate to note it; however, my commonsense understanding or, as others might put it, prejudice is that many men, when faced with interpersonal conflict, focus on tasks rather than on the relationship as a means for surviving the work. Fortunately, I can find some support for understanding in Gilligan (1982), and in particular Lever (1976), whom Gilligan quotes. Lever watched boys at play in games. She noted, "boys were seen quarrelling all the time, but not once was game terminated because of a quarrel and no game was interrupted for more than seven minutes" (1982, p. 9). Boys got on with play by recourse to the rules of the game. Similarly, I have survived conflict in workplaces by disattending conflict, and by attending to doing the work. By focusing on the job at hand, I am able to continue to work with people whom I may not like. To return to the interview, we recognize that my responses to Ed are informed by implict or tacit reliance on not only this prejudice, but a series of unspoken and often unexamined internally held understandings.

10. The question mark signifies an anxiety and perhaps a sense of my bad faith. Although I have identified the connective theme in what follows as being a man or doing masculinity, at no point in these segments is this made explicit by either Ed or me. My guilt is raised as Schegloff insists that conversation analysis be ordered by the criteria of "relevance" and "procedural consequentiality." Simply, he argues that rather than understanding instances of talk as organized by "gender," "masculinity," or any other such sociological category, the analyst is obligated to demonstrate how such categories were "relevant" for the participants or how the categories were "procedurally consequential" for participants as revealed in "the details of the talk or other conduct in the materials" (1992b, p. 110).

11. At this point Schegloff's demand for procedural consequentiality seems to be met. A formulation of simple "being" does not seem to provide an adequate resource to explain what is going on for Ed and me. Rather, Ed not only relies on a preferred form of being for himself, but, by extension, invites me into accepting the good sense of this form. Together we accomplish the good sense of an unnamed preferred form. Further, we orient ourselves to the implicit good sense of this form. Our mutual acceptance of this structured form of "being," while not explicitly named as "male," nevertheless draws on and becomes sensible only by recourse to "male" as a socially relevant resource.

12. Indeed, the good sense of Ed's narrative draws on a familiar recognition that men, in general, tend to be larger, stronger, and more able to use physical force to control others than are women.

REFERENCES

Anderson, H. & Goolishian, H. (1992). The client is the expert: A not-knowing approach to therapy. In Sheila McNamee & Kenneth J. Gergen (Ed.), *Therapy as social construction* (pp. 25–39). London: Sage.

Benhabib, S. (1992). *Situating the self: Gender, community, and postmodernism in contemporary ethics.* New York: Routledge.

Biestek, F. (1957). *The casework relationship.* Chicago: Loyola.

Buttny, R. (1996). Clients' and therapists' joint construction of the clients' problems. *Research on Language and Social Interaction, 29*(2), 125–153.

de Montigny, G. (2005). A reflexive materialist analysis. In Steven Hick, Jan Fook & Richard Pozzuto (Eds.), *Social work a critical turn* (pp. 121–136). Toronto: Thompson Educational Publishing.

Ferguson, K.E. (1984). *The feminist case against bureaucracy.* Philadelphia: Temple University Press.

Freidson, E. (1986). *Professional powers: A study of the institutionalization of formal knowledge.* Chicago: University of Chicago Press.

Gardner, R. (2001). *When listeners talk: Response tokens and listener stance.* Philadelphia: John Benjamins.

Garfinkel, H. (1967). *Studies in ethnomethodology*. Englewood Cliffs: Prentice-Hall.

Garfinkel, H. (2002). *Ethnomethodology's program: Working out Durkheim's aphorism*. Lantham: Rowman & Littlefield.

Garfinkel, H., Lynch, M. & Livingston, E. (1981). The work of a discovering science construed with materials from the optically discovered pulsar. *Philosophy of the Social Sciences, 11*, 131–158.

Gilligan, C. (1982). *In a different voice: Psychological theory and women's development*. Cambridge, MA: Harvard University Press.

Glenn, P. (2003). *Laughter in interaction*. Cambridge: Cambridge University Press.

Goffman, E. (1959). *The presentation of self in everyday life*. Garden City: Doubleday Anchor Books.

Gramsci, A. (1971). The intellectuals. In Q. Hoare (Ed.), *Selections from the prison notebooks of Antonio Gramsci* (pp. 5–23). Translated by G.N. Smith. New York: International Publishers.

Heritage, J. (1984). *Garfinkel and ethnomethodology*. Cambridge: Polity.

Jefferson, G. (1984). On the organization of laughter in talk about troubles. In J.M. Atkinson & J. Heritage (Eds.), *Structures of social action: Studies in conversation analysis* (pp. 346–369). Cambridge: Cambridge University Press.

Jefferson, G. (1989). Preliminary notes on a possible metric which provides for a "standard maximum" silence of approximately one second in conversation. In D. Roger & P. Bull (Eds.), *Conversation: An interdisciplinary perspective* (pp. 166–196). Clevedon Hall: Multilingual Matters.

Kohler Riessman, C. (1993). *Narrative analysis*. Newbury Park: Sage.

Kovel, J. (1981). *The age of desire: Reflections of a radical psychoanalyst*. New York: Pantheon.

Lafrance, J, Gray, E. & Herbert, M. (2004). Gatekeeping for professional social work practice. *Social Work Education, 23*(93), 325–340.

Larson, M.S. (1977). *The rise of professionalism: A sociological analysis*. Berkeley: University of California Press.

Lever, J. (1976). Sex differences in the games children play. *Social Problems, 23*(4), 478–487.

Malone, M. (1997). *Worlds of talk: The presentation of self in everyday conversation*. Cambridge: Polity.

McBeath, G. & Webb, S. (2002). Virtue ethics and social work: Being lucky, realistic, and not doing one's duty. *British Journal of Social Work, 32*, 1015–1036.

Mead, G.H. (1934). *Mind, self & society: From the standpoint of a social behaviourist*. Edited by C.W. Morris. Chicago: University of Chicago Press.

Mehan, H. & Wood, H. (1975). *The reality of ethnomethodology*. Malabar: Robert E. Krieger Publishing.

Miehls, D. & Moffatt, K. (2000). Constructing social work identity based on the reflexive self. *British Journal of Social Work, 30*, 339–348.

Parton, N. (1998). Risk, advanced liberalism and child welfare: The need to rediscover uncertainty and ambiguity. *British Journal of Social Work, 28*, 5–27.

Parton, N. (2003). Rethinking professional practice: The contributions of social constructionism and the feminist "ethics of care." *British Journal of Social Work, 33*, 1–16.

Pawson, R. (1996). Theorizing the interview. *The British Journal of Sociology, 47*(2), 295–314.

Perlman, H.H. (1957). *Social casework: A problem-solving process.* Chicago: University of Chicago Press.

Polanyi, M. (1966). *The tacit dimension.* Garden City: Anchor Books.

Psathas, G. (1995). *Conversation analysis: The study of talk-in-interaction.* Thousand Oaks, CA: Sage.

Rhodes, Margaret L. (1986). *Ethical dilemmas in social work practice.* Milwaukee: Family Service America.

Robinson, V.P. (1939). *A changing psychology in social work.* Chapel Hill: The University of North Carolina Press.

Rogers, C.R. (1951). *Client-centered therapy.* Boston: Houghton Mifflin.

Rogers, C.R. (1965). *Client-centered therapy: Its current practice, implications, and theory.* New York, NY: Houghton Mifflin.

Sacks, H. (1995). *Lectures on conversation* (Vols. I & II). Edited by Gail Jefferson. Oxford: Blackwell.

Schegloff, E.A. (1992a). Repair after next turn: The last structurally provided defense of intersubjectivity in conversation. *American Journal of Sociology, 97*(5), 1295–1345.

Schegloff, E.A. (1992b). On talk and its institutional occasions. In P. Drew & J. Heritage (Eds.), *Talk at work: Interaction in institutional settings* (pp. 101–134). New York: Cambridge University Press.

Schegloff, E.A. (2000a). Overlapping talk and the organization of turn-taking for conversation. *Language in Society, 29*, 1–63.

Schegloff, E.A. (2000b). When "others" initiate repair. *Applied Linguistics, 21*(2), 205–243.

Shulman, L. (1999). *The skills of helping individuals, families, groups, and communities.* Itasca, IL: F.E. Peacock.

Shulman, L. (2006). *The skills of helping individuals, families, groups, and communities* (5th ed). Toronto: Thomson, Brooks Cole.

Smalley, R. (1967). *Theory for social work practice.* New York: Columbia University Press.

Taft, J. (1924). The use of the transfer within the limits of the office interview. *The Family, 5*(6), 143–146.

Winnicott, D.W. (1986). *Home is where we start from.* Harmondsworth: Penguin.

CHAPTER 12

ETHICAL USE OF THE SELF: THE COMPLEXITY OF MULTIPLE SELVES IN CLINICAL PRACTICE

Merlinda Weinberg

INTRODUCTION

Research has indicated that how a practitioner uses herself[1] plays a key role in the therapeutic process (Baldwin, 2000). But the "use of self" is one of the thornier and more elusive concepts in practice, often undertheorized and assumed. There are multiple aspects to the use of self — intrapsychic, intersubjective, cultural, institutional, and professional — and these facets may offer inconsistent and even contradictory options for the clinician about what concrete action is the best for practice. In this chapter, these different registers of the use of self will be illustrated and examined.

Additionally, the "use of self" can be an instrument to move toward ethical relations in practice. By an ethical relation, I am referring to "a nonviolative relationship to the Other... that assumes responsibility to guard the Other against the appropriation that would deny her difference and singularity" (Orlie, 1997, p. 62). But being non-violative by guarding a client's distinct individuality is difficult given the paradoxes that are rife in practice. For example, since practitioners' actions often have an impact on more than one individual (for example, different members in a family or diverse residents in group settings), actions that are taken to support the needs and rights of one may conflict with those of another. Thus, the question of how one should use the self ethically in a therapeutic relationship in not easily answered.

One response seems to lie in recuperating and expanding the concept of the "use of self." I contend that it can be a tool in ethical helping relationships. In this chapter, I will explore one worker's uses of herself to investigate the impediments to and complexities in achieving a non-violative relationship with a client. I have selected a case vignette from a series of interviews I conducted with Charlotte,[2] a middle manager in a maternity home in Ontario, Canada. This material is extracted from a broader qualitative research study on ethics in clinical practice. At the point of our contacts, Charlotte was about 40 years old, a White, married woman with children. She was working with Isobel, a pregnant, 19-year-old client of a White mother and an Ecuadorian father who had come into the maternity home at a point of crisis. I have chosen this case example because Charlotte openly questioned and struggled with her relationship to Isobel, offering rich material to examine the concept of an ethical use of self. This case example also provides a window into the paradoxical nature of clinical practice.

I offer new analytical devices of the "preferred self" and "actualized self" as tools that can be utilized to broaden an understanding of "the use of self" for ethics. I have also argued the need to recognize structural dimensions, both institutional factors and categories such as race, class and gender, for "use of self" to be a valuable tool in theorizing practice. Through these refinements and emendations, I believe the concept of the "use of self" can be applied to move toward more effective and ethical practice.

CHARLOTTE'S CONFLICT

Let us look at the conflicts that arose from discrepancies in Charlotte's uses of herself internally, as well as interpersonally between Charlotte and Isobel. Charlotte articulated that Isobel "challenge[d] [Charlotte's] whole concept of doing social work." She went on to explain, "She's bucking me … she wants a different sort of way for me to work with her."

There was a specific incident in which they had "butted heads." Charlotte portrayed the episode this way:

I got into it with a girl [Isobel] yesterday because she said, "I'm not going to say anything to you" and "you'll do nothing about it [the way the residence was operating]" and she had told me the day before that she was annoyed with me because I presumed something … and I said, "I have to go drop something off and do you want to come in the car with me, we'll spend some time together?" and she said, "Why?" and I said, "Well, I'm just noticing there are some changes going on for you and I'm wanting to give you the opportunity [to talk about these]." And she said, "Don't presume. I absolutely hate it when people presume." And I went back to her later and I said, "I'm really sorry if you felt that I presumed. I didn't mean to. I had seen some differences [in the way Isobel was functioning] but that's just my perception.... I'm sorry."

In addition to "presuming," Isobel's other major complaint was that Charlotte would "do nothing" regarding residents' grievances about the way the maternity home was operating.

PREFERRED AND ACTUALIZED SUBJECT POSITIONS/ INTRAPSYCHIC SUBJECT POSITIONS

Why was this situation challenging for Charlotte? One factor relates to Charlotte's "preferred self." What do I mean by "preferred self"? In post-structural, feminist theory, the humanist, Enlightenment idea of a unified, fixed, and coherent self is disputed. An alternate notion is put forward, that of "subjectivity," namely, the "conscious and unconscious thoughts and emotions of the individual, her sense of herself and her ways of understanding her relation to her world" (Weedon, 1997, p. 32), which lead to differing subject positions or "ways of being an individual" (Weedon, p. 3). These ways of being in the world are constantly shifting each time an individual speaks or thinks, leading to an infinite range of possible contradictory subject positions. In this chapter, I am looking at subject positions as a means to explore a worker's use of self. I find "subject positions" a valuable way of thinking about the self, for "subject positions" recognizes the lack of coherence in the self, permitting an investigation of the vicissitudes of Charlotte's responses to Isobel. From this array of subject positions, at any moment in time, an individual takes up or actualizes a particular subject position from an infinite range of possibilities that are "highly occasioned and situated" (Wetherell, 1998, p. 394). The "use of self" then is really an unlimited operationalization of uses of selves or subject positions.

Some subject positions are a better internal "fit" for the worker and are the positions I am referring to as "preferred." At the intrapsychic level of the self, there is an internalized ideal of the self (Benjamin, 1995, p. 20), which is the aspect that I am referring to as the "preferred" self or selves. By intrapsychic, I am referring to internal processes that are both conscious and unconscious that occur within the mind of an individual, rather than between a person and her environment (Sidran Foundation, 2005). I think that when a worker is able to "actualize" a favoured subject position, there will be little, if any, sense of conflict. But whether a particular favoured position is actualized is influenced by myriad micro and macro factors. When workers enact subject positions that are ego-dystonic, justifications and/or reservations may be articulated or felt. Ego-dystonic refers to aspects of people's behaviour, thoughts, and attitudes that they view as "repugnant or inconsistent" with their view of themselves (Abess, n.d., Section E). I am suggesting that workers have conflictual feelings when the subject positions they enact are not consistent with that "preferred" sense of self. The terms "preferred" and "actualized" positions are analytical devices that can be used to explain the emotional reactions that accompany the adoption of certain subject positions. They also provide a means to explore what might arise as an ethical dilemma because an individual enacts one subject position from a multiplicity of potential divergent subject positions.

But how can there be an internalized coherent view of the self when I have suggested that the self is really a performance of multiple subject positions? Liberal humanist thinking, the dominant discourse in the modern era, conceptualizes the self in a healthy individual as an integrated whole, possessing "a unique essence" (Weedon, 1997, p. 77) that makes a person who she or he is. This is the singularity we hope to guard in ethical practice (Orlie, 1997). There is also a conceptualization of the unity and continuity of the self: what is meant by an identity (Baumeister, 1986). As part of that identity, individuals have a desired, idealized internal notion of their "true" self. Davies (2000) explains that it is through these desires that we know ourselves. Desires are more than physiological responses; they are psychic qualities as well. She clarifies, "Although those desires are demonstrably discursively produced and thus collective in nature, they are 'taken on' by each individual as their inner core" (Davies, 2000, p. 75). While I do not believe individuals *have* a stable coherent self because that is the dominant discourse, I think most people *perceive* themselves as having a core or stable sense of their identity. How we behave and what we understand about how we behave are not one and the same. I would speculate that most people believe in a coherent identity. One aspect of that identity is an idealized image of themselves. Individuals have a desire to see themselves acting in a way that is consistent with their idealized version of themselves and when their behaviour does not match that portrait, anxiety, tension, or distress may follow.

At a conscious level, Charlotte's preferred sense of herself included thinking of herself as respectful and affirming. She stated, "Respecting is what I do" and "I have a gift … [of providing] affirmation, positive affirmation." This was one of the "preferred subject positions" that Charlotte wished to enact and wished for others to see as representing part of the "true core" of her self. However, according to Charlotte, Isobel neither perceived Charlotte as affirming nor respectful. Not being perceived of as helpful conflicted with a preferred subject position for Charlotte. Nor did Isobel recognize Charlotte as functioning in this preferred way. Charlotte acknowledged, "I was feeling uncomfortable. Why am I feeling uncomfortable with her? … It may be … a personality [issue], like we can be sandpaper with people." The use of the metaphor "sandpaper" suggests that their two personalities rubbed up against each other and that Charlotte viewed herself as being an abrasive presence for Isobel, certainly not the affirming subject position Charlotte wished to actualize. Charlotte took responsibility for this conflict, suggesting that she did not think "it [was] her [Isobel]." Charlotte feared she was not providing what Isobel needed. She explained that "the sense of needing to be respected [was] very important" to Isobel. And Charlotte preferred to operate and think of herself as the type of person that a young woman could come to and say, "'I value that you're somebody safe enough that I can talk [to] about this." However, Isobel had been overt about stating that she would not talk to Charlotte about what was bothering her.

The conflict with Isobel was intensified due to Charlotte's feelings about Isobel. Charlotte perceived Isobel as "very, very bright," "very insightful," and "very much a leader" in the maternity home. Charlotte stated that when Isobel was being "disrespected or not … listened to or … dishonoured," she could "challenge" those whom she perceived of as responsible for those breaches. Charlotte was one of the people whom Isobel challenged.

Charlotte's questions about why she was feeling uncomfortable provided an opportunity for her to explore the intrapsychic dimensions of the social work relationship. Freud, the originator of the idea of the unconscious, fashioned the term "transference," referring to the client's unresolved unconscious fixations rooted in childhood development, which are part of the intrapsychic level of the self. The companion concept in Freudian theory is that of "countertransference," referring to the therapist's unconscious reactions to a client that arise from the worker's own unresolved neurotic conflicts, activated by the material in the therapeutic relationship (Cooper-

White, 2001). In traditional psychotherapy, a component of the use of self for the practitioner is to monitor countertransference reactions and to work to surmount them when necessary. In my interviews with Charlotte, she had spoken about her relationship with her family and having to "contend" with siblings with whom she could not compete. She said they were "very, very bright." Historically, Charlotte believed that she was "just different from them" and "that [she] wasn't as smart." Consequently, in her youth, her behaviour was out of control for a period of time. In thinking back to that phase of her life, Charlotte described herself as "such a screw-up." Working with a client whom Charlotte perceived of as "very, very bright" might have activated countertransference issues for her. She felt inadequate as a child and young adult, and Isobel had the potential to make her feel like a "screw-up" again. Additionally, Charlotte explained that Isobel attempted to relate to her as "if she's my peer as opposed to her being a client." I would speculate that potential issues of rivalry with Charlotte's siblings might have been re-enacted by having a client who wanted a more egalitarian relationship and who was "very bright." More than intrapsychic dimensions of sibling rivalry are involved here in a use of self. Issues of power and the social inequality of the therapeutic relationship are being challenged by Isobel. Later in this chapter, I will directly address the power differential in the helping relationship and how this was resolved for Charlotte in her work with Isobel but at this juncture I would like to focus on the intrapsychic dimensions.

One of the reasons that the term "use of self" has been widely disputed by critical thinkers is the emphasis on this intrapsychic level of interaction. When the weight in clinical practice is on transference issues of clients' histories of parental failure, current structural and environmental causes of difficulties can be ignored. This traditional approach has been attacked as being misogynistic and racist, blaming the victims by perceiving all therapeutic work as stemming from internal conflicts, individualizing clients' struggles, and ignoring multiple layers of systemic injustice and oppression that may contribute to a clients' concerns and distress. The silence about other levels in which the self is operating for both the client and the worker has significant implications for the construction of truth and the evaluation of an individual's functioning. The emphasis on the intrapsychic can lead to pathologizing the individual, blaming the victim, and maintaining a silence about structural barriers that should be addressed.

The other reason that use of self has been critiqued is that in traditional notions of the use of the self, the practitioner is framed as "possessor of a more informed, knowable, objectively determined reality" (Hanna, 1993, p. 54) than that of the client without recognizing the social construction of that knowledge and the vested interests of the practitioners in constituting certain definitions of truth. Feminist post-structural theorists see knowledge as socially constituted through discourse. Rather than being transparent or objective, it is "contradictory and subject to change," based on the meaning attributed by those in a position to promote certain views of reality (Weedon, 1997, p. 74). Practitioners, more often than their clients, are those with the political power to determine what constitutes "truth." I wonder whether Isobel's demand for a more egalitarian relationship, in part, stemmed from a wish to alter the balance of whose "truth" would be accepted about the terms of the relationship and the assessment of her own functioning.

INTERSUBJECTIVE SUBJECT POSITIONS

In addition to the difficulties listed above, traditional psychoanalytic theory has been negatively appraised because it does not recognize the conscious "real" relationship between worker and client. Consequently, a "relational" perspective in psychoanalytic thinking has emerged in which analysis of the treatment process includes both intrapsychic and intersubjective levels. The therapeutic interaction is viewed as "operating in a two-person rather than a one-person field, so that two subjectivities, each with its own set of internal relations, begin to create something new between them" (Benjamin, 1995, p. 3). Benjamin hypothesizes that each individual experiences the Other as both part of the self and discrete (Benjamin, 1995, pp. 6–7). Utilizing relational theory in examining the relationship between Charlotte and Isobel, a distinction would be made between the "outside other," the phenomenological "real" Isobel, and the intrapsychic object, "the Other within" — that is, the selves that Isobel invokes of Charlotte that Charlotte may or may not prefer to acknowledge and accept about herself (Benjamin, 1995, note, p. 87). In relational theory, it is speculated that for the worker, the inner representation of the other can either represent an ideal for the self (a preferred self) or a disowned part of the self, which can be viewed as a "monster, the Other within" (Benjamin, 1998, p. 86). In order to achieve a relationship to an outside other without assimilating or being assimilated by that other, an individual must recognize the other as an "independent center of self without threatening or feeling threatened by that other" (Nissim-Sabat, 2003, p. 270). It is in this manner that a worker is able to guard the singularity of the other against appropriation (Orlie, 1997). For this to be accomplished, Charlotte had to recognize and confront her monster, the Other within, of "screw-up" or "inadequate sibling," without making Isobel the problematic client to ward against this threat. Reaching this form of recognition is both a developmental (Benjamin, 1998; Nissim-Sabat, 2003) and an ethical achievement, and I believe a goal in the use of self in the therapeutic process. Without an examination of countertransference, workers risk being punitive or castigatory because they do not recognize that the monster, the Other within, has been activated. They may put their discomfort back on the client as the client's inadequacy or dysfunction. As we shall see in the next section, Charlotte's aggression was stimulated by Isobel, leading Charlotte at times to see herself and Isobel negatively.

Charlotte explored neither the transferential nor the countertransferential aspect of the interaction in the quote. Instead, in response to Isobel's statement that Charlotte reminded her of her mother (an indicator of transference), Charlotte replied,

> I'm sorry, that's not the role that I want to take, but if I'm drifting into that for whatever reason ... let me know ... so that I know that that's what [is] happening and I will be very aware of that working with you because I am not your mother at all.

This response was on the intersubjective level of the relationship, the real interpersonal level that develops along with the transferential relationship of psychoanalytic theory yet is distinct from it (Greenspan, 1983). Charlotte was concerned about the "role" she was taking with Isobel and how Isobel understood and interpreted that role. She missed an opportunity to explore the transference that she had stirred up for Isobel. More importantly in terms of use of self, Charlotte did not explore the countertransference issues that were evoked for her. Her emotional responses to Isobel might have been better managed had she been able to recognize – through reflection or supervision – that perhaps clever, feisty Isobel symbolically represented the siblings with whom Charlotte had felt unable to compete in her youth.

Professional Subject Positions

On the intersubjective level, recognition of the other carries with it a "clash of two wills which is inherent in relationships" (Benjamin, 1995, p. 45).

There is a danger of being angry and retaliatory toward the client when the monster, the Other within, has been activated. Charlotte was very distressed by the relational charges levelled by Isobel. Since to be a helper is the fundamental subject position for a professional, the possibility of not being recognized as helpful would be highly problematic for any clinician. Charlotte described the follow-up to the incident when she and Isobel "butted heads":

> So she [Isobel] came to my office wanting to speak to [the clinical director]. [The clinical director] was too busy ... one of the [other] girls came in and start[ed] telling me what the situation was and she [Isobel] stood there and she was kind of cocky and just kinda said, "I'm not going to say anything to you 'cus I've heard someone else say something about this situation and I know what your answer is." And *I said, "Don't presume."[Laughter]* (Italics added)

Charlotte described that she "bit" and used Isobel's words against her by responding with "Don't presume," just as Isobel had said to Charlotte. Being in the world exposes us to different others who reflect our lack of control and who also evoke in us aspects of the self we wish to repudiate, as Isobel did with Charlotte (Benjamin, 1998, p. 95). In an exploration of the uses of selves for ethical practice, the advantage of examining the intrapsychic component of the relationship is to prevent the monster, the Other within the worker, from being externalized as the problematic client. Using the term "bit" implies that Charlotte had been provoked to use Isobel's own words against her, perhaps to upend the equality Isobel wanted and to unbalance Isobel. Charlotte went on to explain, "I turned around and said exactly what she said to me." Charlotte felt conflicted about her actualized subject position, illustrated by her laughter and by her saying "I wasn't professional in that or maybe I was just being real." She acknowledged, "Maybe I was personalizing things too much ... and that wasn't fair [to] her...." Furthermore, Charlotte referred to Isobel as "cocky." I think this designation was derogatory and suggested that Charlotte was engaged in a power struggle, or clash of wills, with Isobel. To reach an ethical stance required a recognition of Isobel being outside of Charlotte's control but also non-threatening (Benjamin, 1998) to Charlotte's preferred view of herself as respectful and affirming. Later in this chapter I investigate Charlotte's attempts to reconcile her actions with her preferred self.

Up until this point, I have not examined Isobel's charge of Charlotte "presuming." Let us look at this whole concept of presumptions. I think that Isobel and Charlotte were referring to the assessment component of the therapeutic relationship. Isobel was uncomfortable with Charlotte's analysis of her functioning, and Charlotte felt defensive about this aspect of her positioning as clinician. However, one of the intrinsic paradoxes of social work practice is that while workers eschew being judgmental because it hinders the engagement and development of the therapeutic relationship (Rogers, 1942), at the same time, making judgments is a key component of social work. This is the process Charlotte employed when she "presumed" to make interpretations about Isobel and which Charlotte rejected as an illegitimate subject position for herself. She expressed, "I'm really sorry if you felt that I presumed. I didn't mean to." This behaviour was not a preferred subject position for Charlotte.

But what distinguishes social workers from empathic friends, for example, is a sanctioned use of expertise to make judgments about standards that distinguish health from illness and normalcy from deviance. Workers support some ways of being in the world, while others are discouraged. Social workers have been charged in society with the responsibility to distribute limited resources and to protect those who are most vulnerable. These are necessary judgments since we live in communities of more than one person. Koehn (1998, p. 14, italics in the original) says, "the problem is to figure out precisely how simultaneously to honor the concrete otherness of persons *and* rule out behaviors that interfere with our ability to sustain a shared communal life." At times the concrete otherness of a client will not be honoured because behaviours will be censured when the worker perceives them as interfering with societal norms or when they are seen as injuring others. Charlotte was authorized to make analyses and interpretations about the young women in the maternity home, in part to protect their young children. Her discomfort with this positioning was expressed as not wanting to "add more on their [the clients'] plates" at the same time that she recognized, "But I do, when I act more in challenging them."

I believe a just and caring society requires the function of judgment, but it comes at a cost. Koehn elaborates: "when there are competing claims which cannot both be honored, there is a need for a weighing process that culminates in a judgment" (1998, p. 31). The consequence of competing claims is that some will be met while others denied. In that process, harm may occur. No use of self can avoid this potential dilemma. Power adheres to the one who is permitted to make those judgments, resulting in the potential to trespass. What I mean by trespass is "the harmful effects... that inevitably follow not from our intentions and malevolence but from our participation in social processes and identities" (Orlie, 1997, p. 5). Being part of the ruling class that contributes to the construction of the social order, social workers are particularly susceptible to trespass because social workers contribute to and extend patterns of rule through their interventions and determinations of how we should live in society (Orlie, 1997, p. 23). Every action, no matter how laudable or well intentioned, has unexpected and unforeseen consequences that have the possibility of injuring. Therefore, in a discussion about the uses of self, no matter what subject positions are taken up, social workers will trespass. A dominant perspective in social work theory has been that ethical practice will follow from self-reflexivity and subsequent careful decision making (Reamer, 2001; Robinson & Reeser, 2000). However, I believe that regardless of how the self is used in the therapeutic context, ethical trespass is inevitable.

In addition to the concern about judgment interfering with the development of the relational tie and the potential for trespass, I think Charlotte's rejection of making judgments was tied, in part, to issues of gender. Women are associated with affective components in relationships while men are identified with those that are analytical and dispassionate (Jones, 1988). To judge is to evaluate from a detached point of view processes that minimize the relational ties that women value. Charlotte preferred to see herself as a "feminist" practitioner and feminist practitioners value egalitarianism in the therapeutic relationship (Enns, 1997). Furthermore, feminists attempt to equalize the power imbalance in therapeutic relationships and the component of judgment requires a top-down approach to power. Also, a principle in feminist therapy is the debunking of the myth of the expert whose evaluations are more accurate than those of the clients (Greenspan, 1983). Consequently, to judge another's functioning contradicted another of Charlotte's preferred subject positions, namely that of a "feminist," leading to the conflict that Charlotte experienced in this case and to her own sense of trespass.

Institutional Subject Positions

Another contributing factor to Charlotte's conflict about her use of self was that Charlotte felt caught between institutional demands and her preferred subject positions. Charlotte thought that "repairing ... the

relationship [was] just a time element." But she lamented that she did
not "have enough time." The volume and pace of the work are elements
that are consistently raised by workers in the field and lead not only to
a narrowing of practice but to a reduction in the quality of relationships
with clients, even while organizational expectations are on the increase
(Aronson & Sammon, 2000). The uses of the self cannot be examined
outside of the broader dimensions of an era of shrinking resources and
the politics of scarcity (Bakker, 1996). The insufficiency of options fosters
a system that is lacking, at best, and is punitive, at worst. The dilemmas
for workers about which subject positions to take up so as not to be part
of a system that further victimizes the victims are inextricably linked with
these very real limitations of resources.

It was not just workload that impacted on Charlotte's actualization of
institutional subject positions. She felt that the overall program expectations
of Isobel in the residence worked against meeting Isobel's wishes. She
believed Isobel's first choice would have been to live with her boyfriend.
Isobel had "done a lot of her own [emotional] work" and probably would
not have chosen to "go to programs" in the residence. Charlotte's preferred
subject position would have been to "support her [Isobel] in doing that [not
attending]" but the residence was not established as strictly "housing."
One reason a maternity home is not designed as simply accommodation
is that to qualify as a social service agency, it must provide mental health
services. A program that is primarily bricks and mortar could be staffed by
employees without social service qualifications. Consequently, to ensure
the viability of the agency and the positions for its workers necessitates
defining clients as requiring clinical interventions. The maternity home
structure was set up to meet the needs for funding rather than the needs
of clients. Isobel's desire for solely a place to sleep was problematic under
the terms of this institutional requirement.

When practitioners feel a conflict between what they want to do and
what they feel they have to do, those moments signal discomfort with
dominant discourses or practices. They represent a recognition (perhaps
not fully conscious) that a required way of acting may have inherent harms
attached to the implementation. In those instances, I think workers may
sense an ethical trespass. Despite the articulated concept of an "individual
plan of care," Charlotte's perception was that the residence "was moving
to a position of requiring clients to do "everything" [attend all programs].
She argued that Isobel "could be using [the] services in a different way, [but
they were] not set up to do [that]." This stance conflicted with Charlotte's

↗ judgy

"feminist" principles of empowering clients, leaving Charlotte actualizing a subject position that, at times, was not preferred — namely, making Isobel attend more programs than Charlotte believed Isobel needed or wanted.

Despite Charlotte's preferred subject position, for her to fight for Isobel to be exempted from attending programs was "exhausting" and "a slog" because she did not "have the total support from staff." She was not sure she was "willing to go to bat for that" and consequently, at that moment in time, actualized a subject position that was not preferred to protect herself from burnout and from conflict with other staff. Furthermore, Charlotte had responsibilities to other players in the maternity home. This quandary is especially acute in group settings. Charlotte's responsibilities extended to other clients, staff, agency personnel, funders, and her own professional group. Social workers do not work with individuals in isolation and actions that may help one individual may inadvertently injure another. Charlotte felt caught in the middle between the demands of the clients and those of the workers. One of Isobel's major objections was that the staff, including Charlotte, were not responding to client complaints about policies and procedures in the maternity home. Charlotte explained that she "was feeling the pressure of having girls come to [her] ... saying, nothing is getting changed ... as far as [the] rules [of the residence]." At the same time, because she was in a middle management position, staff expected her to manage behavioural issues with residents. Consequently she felt stuck in the middle when she had "staff coming to [her] saying nothing's getting changed with the residents." Charlotte was left "thinking what the *hell* am I supposed to be doing?"

No choice of subject positions can eliminate the potential dilemma that what is good for one individual might not be for another person in the same site. An issue arose where Isobel was "one of the ringleaders" in a "revolt one night." A rule in the residence was that the television was to be turned off and the girls were to go upstairs to bed at 11:00 p.m. Instead, "eight of them just didn't go up," including Isobel. The paradox of social work as both caring and control is apparent in the institutional subject positions available to the worker. Charlotte was caught between, on the one hand, being expected to ensure the smooth running of the house, the implementation of policy expectations, as well as the safeguarding of other clients who might want to sleep and, on the other, the needs of those young women who did not want to turn off the TV and go to bed. The unavoidability of trespass was evident in the dilemma of resolving the competing needs of the various people in this scenario.

Furthermore, the social workers are also expected to enforce rules in part to ensure a hierarchy of authority and a sense of enforceable order. Her discomfort with Isobel's power is implied in the negative designation of her as a "ringleader." At the same time, Charlotte's preferred subject position was to see herself as someone who worked to make the relationship more egalitarian by ensuring that Isobel could make those personal choices. While Charlotte may have wanted to empower Isobel to make her own decision about bedtime, she affirmed, "As much as I don't want to work with that power system, I kind of always know that it's there." She acknowledged:

> Maybe I have this illusion that, you know, I'm doing all this ... empowering ... [Supporting a] power equilibrium between myself and the young women that I work with, but maybe I'm not at all. And maybe this is somebody [Isobel] that knows the difference and is willing to fight until we get to that point [of equality] and it's going to mean that [I have] to examine everything ... I've been doing. Have I been really true to the young women that I've worked with?

Part of Charlotte's discomfort in this case was her recognition that despite her preferred way of working, at times she did not feel she was successful or true to either her clients or herself.

THE RESOLUTION

Charlotte admitted that she was uncomfortable with Isobel's challenges and her reactions to those challenges. She expressed, "I don't ... think I feel comfortable that I feel that way toward [Isobel]." Charlotte felt "a little bit nervous in an encounter with her [Isobel]." Despite her discomfort, she stayed open to this process. Charlotte was prepared to examine her own feelings. She expressed:

> I think what I need to do is go back to it and say okay, she's bucking me, ... she's obviously trying to get her equilibrium back, she wants a different sort of way for me to work with her, and I'm prepared to do that.

Charlotte recognized that Isobel acted as "if she [was her] peer as opposed to her being a client." When I pursued what constituted being a peer rather than a client, she stated that, "they [clients] don't often challenge whatever that relationship is." Charlotte was responsive to Isobel having more say regarding the terms of their relationship and to examining the traditional one-up, one-down form of interaction. Benjamin (1998, pp. 85, 97) postulates that negativity from the other presents significant possibilities in the development of the subject, at the same time that confronting this negativity is a strain that is necessary to recognize and acknowledge. One ethical concern is how respect for difference can be maintained without reducing the other to the same as oneself (Benjamin, 1998, p. 86). The significance of both Charlotte's discomfort and her willingness to stay open to this process and to challenge herself was to accept the monster, the Other within, rather than repudiating those aspects as not part of herself. Only through staying open to this discomfort, and to an awareness of contradiction and ambivalence, can difference be recognized and accepted without turning it into something foreign from the self or the monster without, namely, the "cocky" "ringleader" Isobel. In acceptance of the discomfort, there was also recognition of the impact of the other on the self (Benjamin, 1998, p. 91) for Charlotte.

Charlotte demonstrated self-reflexivity and an awareness of the power differential. She elaborated that she "had a lot more power in [her] own home to decide how [she was] going to live" than her clients. She contrasted this privilege with that of the young women in the maternity home when she questioned, "How do you effectively support young women when you have such a constricting structural box [the maternity home]?" She stated that the residents have "so much that they're up against." She explained, "We [the staff] make decisions for people [the clients]." Part of her anxiety about the subject positions enacted was that she did not want to be a factor in "setting her [Isobel] back in any way." Charlotte did not want to replicate relations of domination in her interventions that resulted in further deterioration for Isobel.

While Charlotte believed that Isobel "deserve[d] to be able to get the best out [of] ... the encounter," Charlotte thought there were two components to how she needed to use herself: "Challenging the structure of what we provide ... and giving her what she needs from me in the relationship." Charlotte chose to use herself differently in her relationship with Isobel, but she chose not to undertake the advocacy of fighting for a different structure in the agency. She said "I don't have power necessarily to change the whole system of [the residence, but] ... I do have control over myself."

Ultimately, her solution around the conflict of preferred subject positions was to be more available to Isobel. Despite organizational pressures around the volume of work, which would interfere with spending more time, Charlotte used instrumental activities to try to repair the relationship. After the incident described at the beginning of the chapter, Charlotte explained that she "took her [Isobel] to a doctor's appointment ... [and] spent the whole day with her at the hospital," which she was "not supposed to do" because spending a "whole day on medical appointments is not ... necessarily an effective use of time." However, she had the support of her supervisor for this deviation. She also attempted to ask herself "Where [do] I feel effective?" and to let go of those things that were not her responsibility. She put fighting to change the "administrative" structures as outside her purview. She expressed to Isobel, "I'm just saying *please* ... forgive me if there is something that I'm doing, but please let me know what that is."

Her perception was that her interventions worked. She asserted, "I'm not walking on eggshells with her.... What I am doing is being respectful and [trying] very hard not to presume...." Furthermore, she declared that they had regained "the original ease that we had when we first start[ed] working together." When I explored how Charlotte felt about the outcome of her interventions, she stated that she felt "wonderful" because "it was something that [she] could do differently." Charlotte also felt proud of herself that she was "able to say, 'I was wrong.'"

WHAT WAS MISSING/OTHER OPTIONS FOR CHARLOTTE

While Charlotte stated that she "did something wrong," she was "not sure exactly what" the problem had been. What was missing in Charlotte's intervention was the opportunity to understand what she had "done wrong" in the relationship. This would have encompassed three components: (1) an exploration of transference and (2) countertransference issues, as well as (3) further examination of some elements of the intersubjective component of the relationship. While exploration of transference would have improved the quality of treatment, the other two aspects are critical in terms of use of self in ethics. Through the recognition of difference, the Other contributes to one's constitution of the self. "Every version of the 'other'... is also a construction of a 'self'" (Clifford & Marcus, 1986, p. 23). Charlotte missed an opportunity to explore those aspects of herself that in some ways constituted the monster, the Other within. Examining countertransferential issues might have provided that opportunity for Charlotte. I believe we throw out the baby with the bath water if we reject the potential of understanding countertransference issues in the use of self. However, in critical practice, focus solely on this dimension of the self is insufficient.

We need to explore the intersubjective elements as well. By apologizing without awareness of what was wrong for Isobel, Charlotte shut down the discussion prematurely. A dialogical relationship is a central tenet of both feminist and critical social work (Brown, 1994; Healy, 2000). Isobel's claims were only partially attended to in Charlotte's interventions with Isobel because Charlotte failed to probe, through active listening, to reach some understanding of Isobel's position. The significance of this is that only through a thorough exploration of Isobel's point of view could Isobel, as an "independent center of self" (Nissim-Sabat, 2003, p. 270), be recognized, understood, and valued.

Furthermore, given the necessity of judgment in the social work relationship, a reasoned judgment must be based on an investigation and understanding by the practitioner of the claims of the client. Isobel's claims were only partially heard and comprehended. This resulted in an apology from Charlotte that was not an apology. One cannot really apologize when there is a lack of understanding about what injury has been wrought.

Furthermore, Charlotte had an opportunity to meet the negative in herself, but to some degree, avoided this by her apology, which shut down the dialogue. While there was some self-reflection by Charlotte, there was also an avoidance of the details about the monster, the Other within. Being open to the monster contributes to an ethical therapeutic alliance.

Racial and Cultural Subject Positions

Another aspect that was missing in Charlotte's efforts in the clinical relationship was Charlotte's exploration of issues of race and ethnicity. I asked if there was a cultural difference between her and Isobel, and she replied, "She's biracial — of a White mom and ... I think he is an Ecuadorian father." However, both she and I failed to examine the implications of the difference with her as a White worker with a client from another cultural background. I replicated the silence of the importance of this aspect of the relationship when I did not pursue what implications (if any) she felt that distinction may have had on her as a worker or on her use of self. The privilege and dominance of whiteness, in part, comes from its taken-for-grantedness without being investigated or troubled. My failure to push this issue contributed to whiteness as the norm and as advantage. It is crucial that White people start to investigate whiteness. Otherwise issues of race and ethnicity are problematized only for those of colour, but not for those who are White. If I had pursued the difference between Charlotte and Isobel in the area of ethnicity, I would have been highlighting the hegemony of whiteness and opening up another potentially hidden dimension of the power differential between Charlotte and Isobel. In a critical perspective on the uses of selves of the clinician, issues of difference such as ability, ethnicity, race, and sexual orientation are significant dimensions. If use of the self as a concept is to be recovered as a tool for critical practice, it must include an examination of marginalities.

Subject Positions of Advocacy

While Charlotte empathized with Isobel's complaints about the way the maternity home was organized, she decided that fighting for a different structure in her agency was beyond her responsibilities. Critical social work is committed to the social transformation of processes and structures that have historically oppressed the marginalized, and perpetuated exploitation and domination (Leonard, 1994). Advocacy and the support of political action are necessary parts of that transformation and crucial to the revitalization of the "use of self."

CONCLUSION

Critical approaches to social work have emphasized the significance of self-reflexivity in practice. But what constitutes "the self" that one is to be reflexive about is much more complicated than it appears on the surface. There are infinite opportunities to take up a range of selves operating in many dimensions: intrapsychic, intersubjective, institutional, cultural, and professional. These registers may conflict, presenting dilemmas for the worker about which subject positions to enact. This complexity is exacerbated by the paradoxical nature of clinical work in which no choice of action is free from the risk of ethical trespass, and by the fact that no intervention can ever completely bridge the unknowability and difference of the other (Levinas, 1993). Despite the unavoidability of trespass, the analytical tools of "preferred" and "actualized" subject positions offer a means to explore those occasions when a worker may be experiencing some sense of trespass. This awareness is a preliminary step in lessening ethical trespass.

I believe it is a worthwhile project to recuperate the term "use of self" because the self is the central vehicle in the therapeutic relationship. One means to restore the utility of the term is to explore the multiple dimensions in a worker's uses of her self. There is a need to incorporate an understanding about how broader systems influence the use of self. Awareness of limitations in resources, agency mandates, and responsibilities to a range of players, as examples, would increase the usefulness of the notion of "use of self." Political action on those structural barriers is another important dimension. Issues of marginality such as culture, race, ethnicity, and sexual orientation also need to be explored to avoid the pitfalls of seeing the therapeutic alliance in a one-person field. Otherwise, the systemic barriers that impact on an individual's functioning may be misinterpreted as individual psychopathology. At the same time, understanding countertransference for the worker at the intrapsychic level is valuable in examining the monster, the Other within, both to avoid the misuse of power and the potential of retaliation in the treatment relationship. It is through finding means to scrutinize the "use of self" that a step can be taken toward more ethical practice for practitioners. While there is the inevitability of some level of failure, workers must keep on keeping on, attempting to find ways to act ethically and to work toward liberatory social transformation.

NOTES

1. I will utilize the feminine form of pronouns as both a corrective to the dominant practice, which privileges men, but also because both the worker and client in this case vignette were females.
2. All proper names are pseudonyms.

REFERENCES

Abess, J.F. (n.d.). Glossary terms in the field of psychiatry and neurology. Retrieved July 8, 2003, from www.abess.com/glossary.html#E.

Aronson, J. & Sammon, S. (2000). Practice and social service cuts and restructuring. Working with the contradictions of "small victories." *Canadian Social Work Review*, 17(2), 167–187.

Bakker, I. (1996). Introduction: The gendered foundations of restructuring in Canada. In I. Bakker (Ed.), *Rethinking restructuring: Gender and change in Canada* (pp. 3–25). Toronto: University of Toronto Press.

Baldwin, D.C., Jr. (2000). Some philosophical and psychological contributions to the use of self in therapy. In M. Baldwin (Ed.), *The use of self in therapy* (2nd ed.) (pp. 39–60). New York: Haworth Press.

Baumeister, R.F. (1986). *Identity: Cultural change and the struggle for self.* New York: Oxford University Press.

Benjamin, J. (1995). *Like subjects, love objects: Essays on recognition and sexual difference.* New Haven: Yale University Press.

Benjamin, J. (1998). *Shadow of the other: Intersubjectivity and gender in psychoanalysis.* New York: Routledge.

Brown, L.S. (1994). *Subversive dialogues: Theory in feminist therapy.* New York: Basic Books.

Clifford, J. & Marcus, G.E. (Eds.). (1986). *Writing culture: The Poetics and Politics of Ethnography.* Berkeley: University of California Press.

Cooper-White, P. (2001). The use of the self in psychotherapy: A comparative study of pastoral counselors and clinical social workers. *The American Journal of Pastoral Counseling, 4*(4), 5–35.

Davies, B. (2000). *A body of writing, 1909–1999.* New York: Alta Mira Press.

Enns, C.Z. (1997). *Feminist theories and feminist psychotherapies: Origins, themes, and variations.* New York: Harrington Park Press of Haworth Press.

Greenspan, M. (1983). *A new approach to women and therapy: How psychotherapy fails women and what they can do about it.* Blue Ridge Summit: Tab Books.

Hanna, E.A. (1993). The implications of shifting perspectives on countertransference on the therapeutic action of clinical social work. Part II: The recent-totalist and intersubjective position. *Journal of Analytic Social Work, 1*(3), 53–79.

Healy, K. (2000). *Social work practices: Contemporary perspectives on change.* London: Sage.

Jones, K.B. (1988). On authority: Or, why women are not entitled to speak. In I. Diamond & L. Quinby (Eds.), *Feminism and Foucault: Reflections on resistance* (pp. 119–133). Boston: Northeastern University Press.

Koehn, D. (1998). *Rethinking feminist ethics: Care, trust, and empathy.* New York: Routledge.

Leonard, P. (1994). Knowledge/power and postmodernism: Implications for the practice of a critical social work education. *Canadian Social Work Review, 11*(1), 11–26.

Levinas, E. (1993). *Outside the subject.* Stanford: Stanford University Press.

Nissim-Sabat, M. (2003). Toward a visionary politics: Phenomenology, psychoanalytic feminism, and transcendence. In R.E. Groenhout & M. Bower (Eds.), *Philosophy, feminism, and faith* (pp. 260–281). Bloomington: Indiana University Press.

Orlie, M.A. (1997). *Living ethically, acting politically.* Ithaca: Cornell University Press.

Reamer, F. (2001). *Ethics education in social work.* Alexandria: Council on Social Work Education.

Robinson, W. & Reeser, L.C. (2000). *Ethical decision making in social work.* Boston: Allyn & Bacon.

Rogers, C.R. (1942). *Counseling and psychotherapy: Newer concepts in practice.* Boston: Houghton Mifflin Co.

Sidran Foundation. (2005). Trauma disorders glossary. Retrieved September 8, 2005 from www.sidran.org/glossary.html#intrapsychic.

Weedon, C. (1997). *Feminist practice and poststructuralist theory* (2nd ed.). Cambridge: Blackwell Publishers.

Wetherell, M. (1998). Positioning and interpretive repertoires: Conversation analysis and post-structuralism in dialogue. *Discourse and Society, 9*(3), 387–412.